Who Is Antiracist?

GEORGE YANCEY AND HAYOUNG DAVID OH

Who Is Antiracist?

Beliefs, Motivations, and Politics

TEMPLE UNIVERSITY PRESS
Philadelphia • *Rome* • *Tokyo*

TEMPLE UNIVERSITY PRESS
Philadelphia, Pennsylvania 19122
tupress.temple.edu

Copyright © 2025 by Temple University—Of the Commonwealth System
 of Higher Education
All rights reserved
Published 2025

Library of Congress Cataloging-in-Publication Data

Names: Yancey, George A., 1962– author. | Oh, Hayoung David, 1998– author.
Title: Who is antiracist? : beliefs, motivations, and politics / George
 Yancey and Hayoung David Oh.
Description: Philadelphia : Temple University Press, 2025. | Includes
 bibliographical references and index. | Summary: "This book proposes an
 index to measure survey respondents' level of agreement with antiracist
 principles, as defined in popular literature. It then observes the
 characteristics and beliefs of those with high levels of agreement and
 concludes that the movement runs the risk of becoming too partisan to
 appeal to new audiences"— Provided by publisher.
Identifiers: LCCN 2024016432 (print) | LCCN 2024016433 (ebook) | ISBN
 9781439925683 (cloth) | ISBN 9781439925690 (paperback) | ISBN
 9781439925706 (pdf)
Subjects: LCSH: Anti-racism—United States—Public opinion. | Scaling
 (Social sciences) | United States—Race relations—21st century—Public
 opinion. | United States—Race relations—21st century—Political
 aspects.
Classification: LCC HT1563 .Y36 2025 (print) | LCC HT1563 (ebook) | DDC
 305.800973—dc23/eng/20240913
LC record available at https://lccn.loc.gov/2024016432
LC ebook record available at https://lccn.loc.gov/2024016433

9 8 7 6 5 4 3 2 1

Contents

	Acknowledgments	vii
1.	Introduction	1
2.	Theoretical Origins of Antiracism	12
3.	Constructing the Antiracism Attitude Scale	28
4.	Who Is an Antiracist?	50
5.	Impact of Modern Antiracism	69
6.	Political Partnership of Antiracism	95
7.	Conclusion	114
	Appendix A: Methodological and Statistical Findings	129
	Appendix B: Antiracism Literature	169
	Appendix C: Selected Questions from Chapman Survey of American Fears	171
	References	175
	Index	197

Acknowledgments

George: I thank the reviewers of the drafts of this book supplied by Temple for their insight and aid in strengthening the book. Other reviewers of earlier papers also helped guide this work. Unfortunately, since I do not know the names of any of the reviewers, I cannot name them here. But I can name a couple of scholars who aided this project. Byron Johnson helped me find the funding for such a project, and Christopher Bader allowed us to test the antiracism attitude scale with his survey. I am deeply grateful to you both. Finally, I thank Andromeda, who is the best supporter a man can hope for, and dedicate the book to my boys, Leo, Mitch, and Lyndon.

Hayoung: For Dad, Mom, Nathan, and Eunice. I love you all so much.

Who Is Antiracist?

1

Introduction

In 2020, while the United States was still in the middle of the health crisis created by COVID-19, the racial divide in our nation grew wider. First, in February, the murder of Ahmaud Arbery at the hands of three white men, while he was jogging, set the country on edge. While, unfortunately, there had been other murders of African American men at the hands of European American men, the delayed arrest of the men guilty of Arbery's murder became national news and created racial tension. Then, the murder of George Floyd set off a series of protests in the United States and around the world. His murder at the hands of a police officer was not another shooting that could be marked as a mistake made in a quick-second decision where the officer's life was at stake. Office Derek Chauvin knelt on Floyd's neck for almost ten minutes, suffocating him as onlookers recorded every second. In March, Breonna Taylor was fatally shot in her apartment during a botched raid. Her story went largely unnoticed by national media until weeks after the murder of George Floyd was televised for all to see in May. Though many more incidents rose to public attention in this period (2020), these three incidents were the primary drivers that set off a nationwide and global movement against injustices such as those that played out in Georgia, Louisiana, and Minnesota. It was within these conditions that the idea of antiracism emerged into the public consciousness of the United States.

In the summer of 2020, several books promoting antiracism (ex. *White Fragility, How to Be an Antiracist, So You Want to Talk about Race*) were highly placed on the bestseller lists as concerned observers committed themselves to seeking guidance on how to aid the movement. Prominent antiracism lecturers were able to command high speaking fees for their services (Carter 2021, Nomani 2021). Being an antiracist shifted from a fringe idea to a commonplace reality. These authors and other thought leaders told this new audience that it was not enough to decline to be racist but rather that social change demanded a more active civic orientation: a commitment to being antiracist. This attention to antiracism coincided with increased general attention to racism. Google searches for racism dramatically jumped after the death of Floyd (Barrie 2020). The increased attention to racism was tied to protests done under the umbrella of antiracism, as seen in media coverage of the sites of those protests (Pressman and Devin 2023). There was a dramatic change in how issues of racism were discussed in that antiracism, which had been a topic among academics in previous years, became, in 2020, a viable and popular way for the general public to express their frustrations at the lingering effects of racism in the United States and the rest of the world.

What do we make of this increasing movement toward antiracism? How do we define the philosophy of antiracism so many have endorsed? What do advocates of antiracism want? How likely are they to succeed in achieving those goals? What are the characteristics of those who support antiracism? Who is most likely to be swayed to this set of commitments, who is not, and how do they understand each other? What is the possible trajectory of this movement? These are questions that we can only begin to answer as we move beyond the 2020 summer of antiracism protests into a season of increased antiracism activity. In a society that consistently throws those with racially progressive attitudes into conflict with those seeking to maintain a racial status quo, it is valuable to understand both sides of this debate. While there are many academic and nonacademic attempts to comprehend the motivations of those adhering to reactionary or even racist attitudes (Bonilla-Silva 2001, Daniels 2009, Feagin and Hernan 2000, Gilmore 2019, Hage 2012, Jones 2021, McRae 2018), there have been few systematic attempts to understand the motivations and intentions of racial progressives. To the best of our knowledge, this book is the first systematic attempt at accomplishing that task.

The Racial Landscape

The events of 2020 did not happen in a vacuum. Those racialized events were simply the latest in a series of racial controversies that continue to trouble the United States. Racial events and tragedies often provoke a reaction from groups concerned about the embedded racism in our society. In 2012, it was the death of Trayvon Martin that set off the events that led to the formation of the Black Lives Matter Global Network Foundation. A couple of decades earlier, the beating of Rodney King also led to nationwide protests. These events are not merely the catalyst for reactions to social groups but also reflect the ongoing racial tension in the United States. Protests are reminders of the racialized society in the U.S., which is tied to a history of racial abuse. And yet, acceptance of overt racism, defined as "observable and whose modus operandum is palpable, operating in unconcealed, unapologetic forms of ethnocentrism and racial discrimination" (Elias 2015), has dwindled to almost nothing in modern society (Schuman et al. 1997).[1] Overt racists still exist, but most Americans see them as immoral (Crandall, Eshleman, and O'Brien 2002, Major, Sawyer, and Kunstman 2013). The modern racial landscape can be characterized as both impacted by the effects of historical racism and stigmatizing explicit racial hostility.

The separate demands posed by these two forces—the legacy of racism in the U.S. and the stigma of explicit racism—create distinct responses to the challenges of a racialized society. For those who strongly believe that explicit racism is the most important and only form of racism, "colorblindness" is a common strategy to combat that stigma, one that attempts to ignore racial identity. The general idea of colorblindness is that we live in a post-racial society whereby we no longer need to pay attention to the racial identity of others. This assertion assumes that we have a society basically free of racism and that "fighting racism" only draws attention to and perpetuates a largely solved problem. The logic goes that acknowledging racial identity invites racism. But critics of the colorblind approach point out that to recognize racism, it would seem to be necessary to recognize racial identity. Proponents of colorblindness sometimes claimed Martin Luther King Jr. was an advocate of this colorblind approach (Myers 2019, Watson 2023, Hughes 2019).[2] It is against the backdrop of claims of colorblindness that we understand an alternate approach to dealing with our contemporary racial landscape. This alternative approach is a racial perspective that attempts to bolster opportunities and resources for racial minorities (Garam and Brooks 2010, Bonilla-Silva 2006, Turner 2012) and restitution for the harms racial minorities have historically suffered (Aiyetoro and Davis 2009). Such advocates envision the source of racialized problems as the actions and values of majority group members as well as the structural advantages they have amassed (Hagerman 2017, Rich 2010). While this approach has had other names (i.e., encounter

---

1. Some may argue that there is a rise of white nationalism, and events such as "Unite the Right" show an increase of overt racism. It is possible that overt racism is on the rise; however, to this date, we have not seen an appreciable rise in quantitative assessments of racial attitudes. It is wise to continue the monitoring of racial attitudes to see if a rise of overt racism will take place in due time.

2. It should be noted that scholars of King often decry such a use of his work to promote colorblindness and envision this as a misappropriation of his teachings (Polletta and Maresca 2021, Turner 1996, Yanco 2014, Dyson and Jagerman 2000).

groups, diversity awareness programs), it is best known as antiracism today. The full definition of antiracism is discussed in Chapters 2 and 3, but for now, we can merely conceptualize it as the attempt to eradicate racism in all its varied manifestations.

Modern discussion of antiracism occurs in the context of a global society largely dominated by European and European American influences. Moreover, the struggle against racism is not limited to a single country's struggle against whiteness, but rather, participants see it as a global struggle against a Europeanized Western tradition. Indeed, any country where individuals of European origins have a contemporary disproportionate impact or have had a disproportional historical impact can be a place where antiracists battle racism. Although the focus of our work will center on the United States, it is important to keep this global impact in mind as we consider our findings.

Why Focus on Antiracism?

Given the racial atmosphere in our society, there is great value in understanding the major players engaged in shaping how our racialized society will deal with the controversies emerging from that racialization. As we pointed out, many attempts have been made to understand those with conservative racial perspectives. We welcome those attempts since racial conservatives play a major role in the shaping of societal racial norms. The political power of racial conservatives has been and will be felt for the foreseeable future. However, merely concentrating on racial conservatives will not provide a complete picture of the racialized reality in the United States and the rest of Western society. A concentration of academic resources on only racially conservative populations is likely to paint a distorted vision of the racial atmosphere.

While racial conservatives are able to influence racial norms in our society, so can racial progressives. For example, it is estimated that $8 billion a year are spent on diversity programs for businesses (Newkirk 2019). Furthermore, the Black Lives Matter (BLM) organization received $90 million in contributions in 2020 (Morava and Andrew 2021), and the Center for Antiracist Research at Boston University received $10 million in a single donation from Jack Dorsey, former CEO of Twitter. Racial progressives do not lack financial resources. They also do not lack cultural support, as education is correlated with support of progressive racial efforts such as affirmative action (Alvarez and Butterfield 1998, Oyinlade 2013). Much of this activity has been driven by the ideals of antiracism. This activism indicates that antiracists are a powerful group that will have an enduring impact on the racial climate in Western society. While antiracists often focus on actions and activism, there are underlying attitudes supporting this activism that we look to comprehend.

Beeman (2022) makes a distinction between liberals and radicals on racial issues. She designates liberals as progressive white people who deny their role in perpetrating racism. They may support certain racial progressive goals but also hold on to racial tropes that allow them to evade notions of responsibility and tend to oppose confrontational activism. On the other hand, radicals not only approve confrontational activism but also promote a racism-centered intersectionality that seeks to decenter the capitalist foundations of society. Radicals seek a more fundamental alteration of society as a solution to racism and are distinguishable from liberals who may have progressive racial beliefs but do not engage in the activism that is embedded in antiracism efforts. Beeman connects practices of antiracism to racial radicals. Our focus is to understand the underlying attitudes of such radicals as they express their ideals through their support of antiracism.

While much of the earlier work has focused on the attitudes driving racial conservatives, our interest is on the other end of the political spectrum. The dearth of work on racial radicals deprives researchers of the ability to understand the full breadth of the racial climate in the United States. For example, while racial identity clearly matters in the shaping of racial attitudes, our data indicates that political ideology plays as big a role, or even bigger, in predicting support of antiracism. Our work disputes simplistic notions that all African Americans support antiracism and reveals the importance of understanding the general political atmosphere that allows antiracism to thrive. To this end, we do not see this book as a stand-alone project by which one may gauge the racial climate of our societies. Rather, we envision this book as a necessary component of a comprehensive effort to understand not only the current racial climate of the U.S. but also how racial conflict may play out in the coming years.

With the emergence of popular books on antiracism during and immediately after the events of 2020, we find "antiracism" to be a useful term that allows us to capture the attitudes of those outside the academic world who are committed to radical racial ideals. While the concept of antiracism originated in academia, it has grown tremendously in popular appeal. We will further dissect the use of this term and what it means, but at the very least, among many individuals, it indicates an assertive effort to seek racial justice. There are other terms in the national consciousness tied to progressive racial ideology, such as "woke" and "critical race theory." These terms, however, are often used as pejoratives by their opponents in an effort to stigmatize them. These terms are controversial and contested, and racial progressives may perceive them as attacks rather than descriptions. "Antiracism" is a term that racial radicals have adopted in large part for themselves, as the titles of many of their popular books indicate. While no term is free of controversy, "antiracism" is at the very least a term that racial radicals themselves have endorsed and supported. To this end, it is a useful term for capturing the sentiments of a given group of individuals who support racially radical perspectives.

Orientation of the Book

We come to this book as curious researchers who want to provide information that enlightens us about the continuing racial conflict in our society. Nonetheless, this research is contextualized by certain factors. First, our research is based on data collected in the United States, and thus, our findings are going to be most relevant to the racial climate in this country. However, many of the trends in the United States undoubtedly impact other nations due to the United States' economic and cultural power, as well as the central role it has historically played in the establishment of white supremacy. We have strong reason to believe that our findings are reflective of antiracism in a global setting to some extent.

Second, we are very interested in who is an antiracist and their motivations for racial justice. We understand that there are obvious reasons why individuals want to work to overturn historical and institutional racism. A desire to address these issues, however, does not automatically lead one to accept the principles antiracists claim as central. Social scientists tend to look beyond the obvious answers to locate possible commonalities between members who share certain beliefs. There is an antiracism community, both in a traditional sense and online, where like-minded individuals socially and intellectually reinforce each other. Our data do not allow us to do a deep ethnography of this subculture, but we can locate systematic patterns among those with beliefs rooted in antiracism. Although this is an incomplete picture, it is an important initial step toward understanding the values underlying popularized antiracism.

Third, we acknowledge that we come into this research as outsiders to antiracism in that we are not seeking to intentionally promote antiracism. Much of the previous work on antiracism is by individuals openly advocating for this approach. They place themselves very much within the community of antiracists and promote the concepts outlined in this book. There is great value in learning about an important social and political philosophy by its adherents. Literature by such advocates of antiracism provides insight into the implications of how antiracism impacts individuals within an antiracist subculture. However, there is also a great benefit to having outsiders look at the antiracist community, as we are not committed to the promotion of that ideology. Both are necessary. We are sociologists, not philosophers. Consequently, we choose to neither critique nor affirm antiracist ideals, enabling us to conceptualize both the strengths and weaknesses of antiracism as a social movement without an attempt to make it seem better or worse than it is in its current form. Of course, this does not mean we are objective, since being unbiased is impossible. However, our biases will differ from those of supporters or critics of antiracism and can lead to new insights likely overlooked by its advocates and detractors.

To that end, our final orientation is that we envision this work as descriptive rather than prescriptive. Our effort is geared toward describing antiracism, not what we want antiracism to become. In the final chapter, we build on our observations to outline potential choices for the future of antiracism. The choices we outline are not attempts to promote a certain direction for this community, as all choices are fraught with potential advantages and disadvantages. However, we contend that our findings do present popularized antiracists with options on whether they desire to maintain their current course or take risks that may increase their overall political and social power. The major question that proponents of the movement must consider is how expansive antiracism should become to embrace political issues that are not explicitly racial. Since we have defined ourselves as outsiders to the antiracism community, we are agnostic about this choice but feel obligated to clearly outline a potential alternate direction for popularized antiracism.

Our Basic Premise

Having set our orientations, we contend that antiracism appeals to followers not merely as a racial identity but also as a political one. Specifically, antiracism is not merely a political identity tied to certain political issues, but it is also tied to goals commonly espoused at the national level by the Democratic Party. This is unsurprising as the U.S. is a politically polarized society where many issues are strongly divided between two political parties. In this book, we provide data indicating the type of symbiotic relationship that popularized antiracism has with Democrats.

Of course, this is not to state that antiracists and Democrats are in perfect agreement. There are many instances of antiracists complaining about the lack of commitment from the Democratic Party and white liberals toward their racial and political goals (Reed 2018, Nichols 2020, Warren 2010, Beeman 2022, Marable 1990, DiAngelo 2021). The radical nature of antiracism ensures that it will be difficult, if not impossible, to be completely compatible with a political party seeking to appeal to the general public. Arguing that antiracism is a partisan identity is not stating that antiracists are satisfied with their political allies. Antiracists want to alter the political party with which they are aligned. However, in a polarized society, a movement with ambitions for political and social change can find it more advantageous to link itself to an imperfect, but perhaps reformable, vessel for promoting its interests than to remain unaffiliated. The strength of such a situation for antiracism is clear since such alignment produces allies who are available to promote the interests of antiracists. However, in a polarized society, this arrangement also produces potential detractors who may work to ensure that the changes desired by antiracists never take place. In our last chapter, we revisit this premise and offer an alternative path for antiracism that brings its own potential problems, as well as possibilities.

Outline of the Book

The rest of the book discusses, in detail, the questions and arguments proposed previously. In Chapter 2, we deal with the theoretical origins of contemporary antiracism. While most individuals know of antiracism through popularizers such as Ibram X. Kendi, Robin DiAngelo, and Reni Eddo-Lodge, the philosophy of antiracism developed out of vital academic frameworks. Early Marxism eventually gave rise to the Frankfurt School, which was the birthplace of critical theory. The ideas of critical race theory developed as a way to focus on the unique challenges faced by ethnic minorities in the U.S. The emergence of Afro-modern and postcolonialism studies was pivotal to antiracism, as antiracism focused scholarly attention on how modern racism, and other social factors, impacted populations of color, with a specific emphasis on African Americans. Although there are several aims, the primary aim of antiracism centers on the betterment of marginalized racial and ethnic groups. Norms and values promoted in academic discussions of antiracism would pave the path for academics such as Kendi (2019), DiAngelo (2018), and Michelle Alexander (2010) to translate antiracism into popular books for laypeople.

Chapter 3 is an investigation of who is an antiracist. Using the writings of contemporary antiracists, we devised a scale using 15 statements to assess the degree to which individuals accept the ideals driving popularized antiracism. From those writings, we developed four foundational themes within popularized antiracism: 1) racism is pervasive in the United States, 2) racism is multifaceted, 3) white and nonwhite people hold differential roles, and 4) society must face massive reform. Utilizing two convenience samples collected at Amazon Mechanical Turk and Survey Monkey, we used factor analysis to identify five core statements and two supportive statements that make up a potential antiracism attitude scale. We sent out an open-ended questionnaire asking respondents why they provided the answers they did for these seven key statements. A qualitative assessment of the answers indicates that the respondents who supported these statements did so within the context of rationales one would expect from antiracists, verifying that the scale measures antiracist attitudes. Finally, confirmatory factor analysis (fully explained in the appendix) provides us with high certainty in the viability of the scale on these convenience samples.

In Chapter 4, we placed the five core statements and one of the supportive statements in a national survey—the Chapman Survey of American Fears (CSAF). The statistical diagnostics that fit well with our convenience sample also fit with the national sample, providing us confidence in the usefulness of this scale on a national level. With a usable scale for antiracism in hand, we assess the factors related to whether a person adopts the values of modern popularized antiracism. First, we look at the relative prevalence of those who support antiracism in comparison to those who oppose it. We do this by not only examining the size of the different extremes of the antiracism attitude scale in the CSAF sample but also comparing the relative percentage of higher scorers of antiracism to a comparable percentage of individual scores in racial resentment and Christian nationalism scales. We find that there is arguably more support for antiracism than either racial resentment or right-wing authoritarianism. Then we use the CSAF to assess the strongest predictors of acceptance of antiracism. It is not surprising that we find political viewpoint and racial identity to be the strongest predictors. But what may be a little surprising is that political viewpoint often has a stronger effect than racial identity. Political progressives have a similar, or even stronger, level of adherence to antiracism than racial minorities, even though people of color are more likely to experience the effects of racism. We explore potential motivations for the level of support offered by political progressives. The results connected to the antiracism attitude scale on a national sample are reflective of the reality that progressive political ideology, perhaps even more so than racial identity, is the source of progressive racial ideals in the United States. This is why we conclude that antiracism is at least as much of a political identity as it is a racial identity.

In Chapter 5, we explore the attitudes that antiracism predicts. Since the antiracism attitude scale has only been used in the CSAF, we are limited to the questions in that survey to assess the attitudes potentially shaped by popularized antiracism. While the focus of the survey is an assessment of fear, meaning our analysis will be largely limited to assessing fears, understanding how the fears of antiracists differ from others is insightful for comprehending why some individuals support antiracism. Fortunately, there are enough attitudinal questions to provide preliminary clues to the type of attitudes associated with antiracism. We find that the antiracism attitude scale is strongly related to attitudes tied to racial concerns (i.e., immigration, legal reform). Indeed, the effect sizes of level of antiracist sentiment exceed those of overall political ideology. However, attitudes toward antiracism are also powerfully associated with issues not explicitly tied to racial concerns, such as January 6 and climate change. Even here, we see that the antiracism attitude scale is at times a better predictor of these political concerns than general political orientation. Antiracism was not a good predictor, however, of one's attitude toward the economy or crime. Using surveys assessing which political party is seen as more favorable on given political issues, we theorize that antiracism matters greatly on issues central to the platforms of political progressives, such as climate change, but does not matter at all on issues central to the platforms of political conservatives. Thus, antiracism is not merely a political identity but also predicts a partisan identity tied to modern progressive political ideology.

Chapter 6 delves further into the question of how political ideology impacts antiracism and vice versa by examining how antiracism is represented when other political issues are discussed online. Using content analysis, we investigated online antiracist articles we linked to issues that tend to be more salient to political progressives (e.g., climate change) or conservatives (e.g., inflation). We found that these articles discuss antiracism as a way to address the dysfunctions in how Americans deal with climate change but not in how they deal with inflation, even though African Americans are disproportionately negatively impacted by both phenomena. These findings indicate that there is a deep relationship between antiracism and partisan political priorities. Antiracism must be seen through the lens of partisan interest to fully understand its attraction and limitations. We do not have the data to confidently assert whether progressives have co-opted the racial concerns that gave rise to antiracism to promote their political causes or if antiracism took advantage of the concerns of political progressives to promote their racial interest. The intertwining of antiracism and progressive political interests, however, needs further interrogation in future empirical work.

We bring the book to a conclusion in Chapter 7 by exploring the implications of our findings. Education is a predictive variable of antiracism, and it should be expected that antiracism has a prominent place in institutions shaped by higher education. The place of antiracism in our society is often overlooked by scholars in those institutions of higher education, perhaps because this ideology is already embedded as the default framework. In a politically polarized society, however, this assumption is subject to challenge. We argue that antiracism has a powerful voice in our society, but its appeal may be restricted due to its partisan political relationships and inability to recruit nonprogressives to its ranks. The power of antiracism to win over political conservatives, and perhaps even moderates, may be limited. The growth of antiracism as a philosophy is evident, especially among political radicals.

Yet, as the research suggests, the level of success from such efforts, paired with resistance from political conservatives, may limit this growth to only Democrats and progressives. To gain a full understanding of racial attitudes in our society, it is not sufficient to explore racial attitudes linked to reactionary concerns. We also must explore the racial attitudes of those seeking reform or even revolution. To this end, this book can be seen as the first major systematic effort to understand those who support notions of antiracism, with future work to build upon this effort.

2

Theoretical Origins of Antiracism

In the fall of 2021, a series of protests occurred at school boards across the United States (Ruwe 2022, Oxford Analytica 2021). One of the major issues at stake was the assertion that school boards were attempting to force a critical race theory (CRT) agenda into the curriculum. CRT is an idea often taught in graduate programs, and it is not likely that high schools would attempt to teach a fully fleshed-out form of it to students not equipped to deal with the complexities of CRT. Indeed, some have asserted that many of the protesters do not understand CRT (Benedetti and Holba 2022, Bayless, Hampton, and Jones 2022). We contend that individuals often use CRT as a proxy for progressive racial efforts. Those who oppose these efforts can express their frustration at school board meetings by labeling what they do not like as CRT and fighting against it. For example, one school board member who opposed antiracism training in Wisconsin illustrates the conflation of CRT and antiracism by commenting, "I don't like the 'programming' word or the 'restorative practices.' It sounds like re-education to me.... As the CRT stuff is being discussed, I would argue that putting a group of kids in the corner and telling them you're the oppressed group—that's programming" (Koran 2022).

Antiracism has an interesting relationship with CRT. As we discuss in this chapter, the antiracism we see today is related to CRT, and these philosophies often work alongside each other, but they are not identical. At the level of the general population, these differences are not well understood, as the "CRT" that protesters decry is, more often than not, based on an antiracist philosophy. If protesters come to understand the role antiracism has played in the measures they oppose, then it is likely that antiracism, as well as CRT, will become their target (Lennard 2021). Thus, the fate of efforts to promote CRT may be tied to the fate of efforts to promote antiracism. While individuals may use these terms interchangeably, academic treatment of antiracism requires greater specification. An exploration of how scholars have developed and expressed the tenets of antiracism ideals in an academic form situates our study of popularized antiracism.

This chapter deals with the theoretical origins of contemporary antiracism. The philosophy of antiracism developed through vital academic frameworks. Although most individuals have not read this academic literature behind antiracism, certain ideas from that scholarly foundation have emerged to shape the popularized form we see today. In this chapter, we start to recognize some of those ideas.

From Critical Race Theory to Antiracism

The relationship between CRT and antiracism emerged in part due to how modern academic antiracism builds off the philosophy of CRT. Early Marxism eventually gave rise to the Frankfurt School, which was the birthplace of critical theory. This set up a framework where, by the later twentieth century in the U.S., critical race theory developed to focus on the unique challenges faced by ethnic minorities. CRT emerged in the mid-1970s with the writings of Derrick Bell (1973, 2018), Kimberlé Crenshaw (2010), and Richard Delgado and Jean Stefancic (2000, 2023). The focus of the early CRT writings is the legal system. The major question these scholars grapple with is the lack of progress for civil rights through that legal system. This led CRT scholars to conclude that racism is a core part of American society embedded in institutions—meaning not reliant on individual animus. Laws that seem to be equitable, such as the First Amendment, were actually used to uphold the racial status quo (Demaske 2009). They contend that since laws cannot be content neutral, there must be a deliberate effort to create them in ways that combat racism. But the creation of such laws will not be easy since European Americans are heavily invested in maintaining their dominance in society. It is within CRT that the concept of interest convergence (Donnor 2005, Milner 2008, Milner, Pear, and McGee 2013) developed. Interest convergence is the idea that majority group members will not allow any change in the legal system unless it works out for their benefit. Racial minorities cannot wait for the goodwill of majority group members to create avenues for racial justice since majority group members will only provide that justice if they can benefit from efforts to produce racial justice. Furthermore, racism is not merely about individuals with hostile attitudes toward people of color. To end racism, racial minorities must overturn systems of racism designed to legitimate the continuing existence of white supremacy. For example, some argue that ideals of fairness and equality not only fail to acknowledge racial differences and contexts but are weaponized to deprive African Americans of justice (Mukherjee 2016, Moschel 2007, Crenshaw 2019, Srivastava 2005).

While CRT started within the legal system, its influences did not stay there. Scholars in the fields of education (Edirmanasinghe et al. 2022, De Lissovoy and Brown 2013, Dixson and Rousseau Anderson 2018, Turner Kelly 2005), health care (Ford and Airhihenbuwa 2010, Graham et al. 2011), criminology (Coyle 2010, Gonzales Rose 2016), and political science (Graham 2007, Hawkesworth 2010, Bracey 2015), to name a few, also incorporate CRT as a lens into their scholarship. CRT has become a way to address racial discrepancies in many institutions and dimensions of our society, and some proponents argue that racism is so prevalent that there are no segments of society that are free of racism (Crenshaw et al. 1995, Patel 2022). It is from the intellectual tradition of CRT that we see the emergence of efforts to understand the implications of modern racism, such as implicit bias, microaggressions, and white supremacy. Thus, CRT has become a vital source of progressive, and even radical, perspectives on racial discourse in the United States.

It is in this context that antiracism developed to focus scholarly attention on how modern racism, and other social factors, impacted populations of color, with a specific emphasis on African Americans. In many ways, antiracism represents the practical application of the theoretical ideals promulgated by CRT. Given the role antiracism has played in promoting racially progressive and radical perspectives, in our society, there is a natural connection between antiracism and CRT. Antiracism shares a similarity with CRT in that neither cognitive construct offers a single underlying statement of definition (Gillborn 2006). However, both conceptualize the United States from a white supremacy framework and concentrate on the best way to eradicate racism, if such eradication is even truly possible. Both philosophies serve each other. For example, CRT's tool of counternarrative has been found to help create an antiracist school identity (Blaisdell 2021). To this end, CRT supplies a praxis by which lived experiences of marginalized groups become relevant (Ford and Airhihenbuwa 2010), providing antiracism proponents with a way to legitimate their proposed reforms. On the other hand, antiracism can be seen as an action-oriented application of CRT (Ford and Airhihenbuwa 2010), as opposed to an intellectual one. It is perhaps here where antiracism and CRT diverge in that CRT focuses on theoretical assertions about eradicating racism while antiracism is an applied application of the ideas formulated under CRT and other frameworks such as racialized organizations theory and decolonization theory.

Origin of Antiracist Thought

Antiracism arises from the assumption that racism is still a real problem for racially marginalized individuals. Unlike proponents of colorblindness, antiracists believe that the depth and breadth of the problem of racism are such that only a powerful and concerted effort can overcome the lasting and contemporary effects of racism. If antiracism can be conceptualized as the struggle against racism, then a philosophy of antiracism can be said to have emerged as early as the efforts for the abolition of slavery. Given that reality, some antiracist scholars talk of an early origin of antiracism that predates the Civil War (De Lissovoy and Brown 2013, Zamalin 2019). Following this theme, then, it is reasonable to argue that other historical movements, such as Reconstruction and the civil rights movement, are also part of a larger movement toward antiracism. While it is reasonable to label any effort against the pernicious racism that troubled the United States as antiracism, doing so does not offer special insight into the scholarly treatment of antiracism. Thus, we look toward specific developments tied to the emergence of modern antiracism to gain insight into how this ideal manifests itself in contemporary society.

Antiracism is tied to the Afro-modern tradition (Zamalin 2019), which is a merging of Western modernism with a centering on the concerns of Africans and African Americans. This intellectual tradition pushes against the notion that modernity is limited to a single line of development. In Afro-modernism, European Enlightenment values are applied in ways to benefit the interests of Africans and African Americans. For example, modernism's emphasis on self-realization can be used by leaders in African American communities to express their spiritual identity (Gooding-Williams 2010). When certain aspects of European modernity fail, however, to serve the interest of Africans and African Americans, those elements of modernity are rejected. For example, when notions of rationality and reason are used to disrupt the use of the counternarrative by antiracists, then it is permissible to prioritize the counternarrative over rationality. In the Afro-modern tradition, modernity does not have the final say. Rather, because the core of philosophical antiracism is to ultimately benefit marginalized individuals, modernity is only a tool that is selectively applied to remove barriers for those marginalized individuals.

Antiracism and postcolonialism have often been linked together (Power 2006, Pacini-Ketchabaw 2014, Cowlishaw 2000, Lawrence and Dua 2005, Grosfoguel 2011). Postcolonialism has been defined as an effort to understand the continuing problems created for marginalized groups due to the imposition of colonization and imperialism by European nations (Hamadi 2014, McEwan

2008, Mishra and Hodge 2005).[1] It naturally comports with arguments in antiracism about the persistence of oppression of racial and ethnic groups, even in a society where overt racism has been stigmatized. Thus, it is not surprising that the two concepts are popularly linked together. Indeed, the focus of postcolonialism on the origin of relations between majority and minority group members allows for an argument about the origin of the racism antiracists seek to promote. Antiracism and postcolonialism can be conceptualized as focusing on distinct elements of a desire to solve the same problem of racial oppression in Western culture (Grosfoguel 2011, Power 2006, Cowlishaw 2000). While antiracism has become a desired orientation in popular culture, postcolonialism offers very similar answers for overcoming the lasting effects of racism. However, one difference between postcolonialism and antiracism, at least as antiracism is discussed in public, is that postcolonialism is not so focused on the plight of African Americans as popularized antiracism.

To this end, antiracism developed as a measure by which political goals could be accomplished. Antiracism naturally developed out of African American political thought (Zamalin 2019) as African Americans' interest in self-determination and freedom from oppression formed the core of this political tradition. While there are varied ways in which African American interests can be defended, it is the focus of defending that interest infused into considerations about combating racism. Even as society moved from overt racism to a reliance on institutional mechanisms to reinforce a racial status quo, innovative strategies such as modern racism (McConahay 1986) and symbolic racism (Sears 1988) emerged to serve the dominant racial group that scholars named and conceptualized. In a similar vein, antiracism adjusts to new demands placed upon the changing nature of racism.

The emergence of antiracism in conjunction with an Afro-modern tradition and African American political thought indicates that antiracism developed primarily to address the racial situation of African Americans. The plight of African Americans has been and still is the primary focus of antiracism today. This is not to say that the concerns of other racial minority groups are unimportant. Antiracism has been used to address issues concerning Indigenous people (Nicholls 2022, Lawrence and Dua 2005), Hispanic Americans (Lugo 2016, Nicholls 2022), Asians and Asian Americans (Nguyen-Truong et al. 2023, Tsong, Chopra, and Cheng 2022), and Middle Easterners (Fourlas 2021, Islam 2018). Principles of intersectionality—combinations of oppression along different aspects of identity—have also led an-

---

1. The concerns of postcolonialists would also extend to the actions of Europeans even if they favor a non-European nation. An obvious example of this is the hostility toward Israel, at least in part because the nation was provided territory by the actions of European nations.

tiracists into discussions about sexism (Rabaka 2006, Ng 1993, Twine and Blee 2001) and homophobia (Srivastava and Francis 2006, Loutzenheiser 2001, Gardiner and Riches 2016). However, the strongest emphasis of antiracism is anti-Black racism perpetuated by Europeans and European Americans who are conceptualized as the main perpetrators of anti-Black racism (Zamalin 2019). Furthermore, in our examination of antiracism scholarship, we found no instances of minority-on-minority racism being deeply addressed. While antiracism may share certain ideals dictating some degree of commonality among proponents of antiracism, it is wise not to overstate the level of agreement between those proponents. In the next section, we explore the varieties of antiracism.

Varieties of Antiracism

The basic goal of antiracism is to challenge and eradicate the enduring racism within our cultures. However, there are many ways to challenge this racism. There are different problems connected to racism and different emphases individuals can place on their activism. Antiracism is multidisciplinary in nature (Van Dijk 2021) and allows for multiple approaches to a similar problem. Thus, it is not surprising that varieties of antiracism exist. We conceptualize the existence of different types of antiracism as distinct ways to address the same concern of eliminating the effects of racism on the lives of people of color. Understanding the distinct forms of antiracism allows for an appreciation of the general nature of antiracism.

An important aspect of the variations of antiracism is the level of analysis conducted by antiracism scholars. There can be a focus on macrolevel structures such as entire societies (Hübinette 2013, Dunn et al. 2009, Kubota 2015), on midlevel structures such as institutions within that society (Ford and Airhihenbuwa 2010, Edirmanasinghe et al. 2022, Blaisdell 2021), or on microlevel structures such as interpersonal communications (Srivastava 2005, Manning 2020). There are vital implications for the antiracism associated with each of these levels. For example, the further one goes from micro level to macro level, the less important the attitudes of the individual racists become and the more central political activism, institutional accountability, and legislation become to the analysis. Historically, antiracism placed more emphasis on a focus of microlevel concern with efforts to alter the attitudes of majority group members. However, over the last few decades, there have been more concerted efforts to operate at the middle and macro levels in attempts to win political victories.[2] If racism has the greatest impact as a structural agent, as

---

2. A related, but alternative, classification of the racism system was developed by Jones (2000) and is widely used in public health spaces. She argues for three different levels of racism: in-

many antiracists contend, then altering political attitudes and voting polls does more to mitigate its effects than eradicating overt racism in racist individuals. Thus, we have seen a switch in the mode of antiracism as concerns about racism result in institutional and structural problems for marginalized racial groups that have gained more attention relative to problems connected to overt individualized racial hatred.

One of the ways antiracism is expressed is by directly confronting racism. However, the aggressiveness of that confrontation can vary. Some antiracists utilize a microlevel approach to pressure individuals in their social circles to adopt antiracist ideals or stop racist actions (O'Brien 2009, Vanderbilt 2023, McKee and Pedersen 2018, Marshburn et al. 2021). Others believe that important social and political changes will not come without public agitation and protests (Dunivin et al. 2022, Smith 2017, Forbes-Erickson). These differing levels of confrontation likely correlate to the level of societal alterations a particular antiracist perceives as necessary (Ellefsen, Banafsheh, and Sandberg 2022). Reform-minded antiracists may believe that society can move away from racism by using the current political and social system. For such activists, persuasion of individuals within said system is sufficient to accomplish desired goals. More revolutionary-minded antiracists insist on protests and social agitation in hopes of sparking the revolution that leads to an overthrow of the current societal system. Those content to write and lobby government officials are likely somewhere in the middle of these groups. A match of methods to goals provides a deeper understanding of the different formats of antiracism.

Over time, the goals and means of the movement have gravitated toward efforts at revolutionary structural alteration and protests to achieve that goal. Efforts to reform society through interpersonal contact have not disappeared, and it is not fair to say that such reformative, individual efforts are not valid examples of antiracism. They are a less revolutionary antiracism, but they still share the same goals of the eradication of racism as their more revolutionary peers. But moving away from a focus on convincing individuals to reject overt hostility toward a desire to alter existing social and political institutions has created a variation of antiracism more revolutionary in nature.

Marxism has provided a theoretical framework for the way many individuals conceive of and push for radical, and even revolutionary, change. A foundational Marxist tenet is the need to completely overhaul society's eco-

---

stitutional, personally mediated, and internalized. Institutional racism is tied to the way social structures and historical reality perpetuate racial inequality. Personally mediated racism is envisioned as individualized prejudice and discrimination, whether the prejudice and discrimination are intentional or not. Internalized racism is when members of stigmatized groups accept negative messages about their own abilities and worth.

nomic framework, profoundly altering the rest of society (Holton 1981, Saran 1963). Marx believed in the necessity and inevitability of an economic revolution and supported revolutionary efforts even if it meant a violent overthrow of society (Schaff 1973, Finlay 2006). One needs not support violence to be a Marxist, but understanding Marx's expectation of societal overthrow indicates the natural inclination within Marxism to support fundamental social and cultural change. It is reasonable to consider the role of Marxism in an antiracism framework. Indeed, Young (1998) contends that postcolonialism arose in the 1960s just as Marxism died down. Antiracism can be envisioned as a replacement for Marxism's revolutionary potential. Others argued that postcolonialism is limited by its powerful focus on racism to the relative exclusion of other types of oppressions (San Juan 2002, Bartolovich 2002). Because of the focus of Marxism on economic-based conflict, these arguments suggest a certain level of incompatibility between antiracism and Marxism.

Nevertheless, other scholars argue for the compatibility of antiracism and Marxism. Marxism has been conceptualized as an important mechanism for theorizing about race and racism (Dua 2014). While Marxism did not originally focus on explaining the impact of racial differences, it has been argued that the framework built by Marx contributed to ideas connected to a "politics of differences" (Bakan 2008) in the centrality of alienation within Marx's work. This allows scholars to better understand the dehumanization connected to whiteness and how a dominant group engages in social control. Furthermore, Marx's challenge of a traditional Western philosophy creates a space by which a postcolonial critique can find its footing (Bogues 2014). It can be argued that, in important ways, Marxism and antiracism share a similar goal of displacing an oppressive class so that an oppressed group can find relief. For some antiracist scholars, this commonality can allow them to perceive Marxism as a potential path toward ending racism (Greene 2011, San Juan 2005).

The influence of Marxism can lead to an antiracism connected to other forms of stratification. Bannerji's (2014) identity as a Marxist antiracist feminist indicates that it is not difficult to develop an epistemology anchored in Marxism but incorporating race and gender concerns. To that end, a flexible understanding of whiteness allows for linkages of it to European American capitalist modernity (Arat-Koç 2014). This expansive definition of whiteness also allows for a connection between whiteness and Zionism (Bakan 2014). An intersectionality element within antiracism scholarship allows for the reimagining of society whereby a variety of distinct oppressions are eliminated. The vision of such a reimagining would lead to a society that looks very different from our current social world. Discussions of activism within antiracism can take many forms, but the idea of revolution is not unknown within antiracism literature (Reed 2017, D. Benson 2016, Middlebrook 2019, Taguieff 2020, Combahee River Collective 2014). Thus, another difference between various conceptions of antiracism is the degree to which nonracial forms of stratification are emphasized.

Variations of antiracism expressed in academic circles can work their way into popularized culture in a variety of ways. O'Brien (2009) argues that there is a promising form of antiracism emerging in non-Black racial minority communities. Individuals in those communities often do not perceive traditional antiracism approaches as meeting their needs and have more diversity in their strategic approaches to combating racial oppression. For them, traditional antiracism can be seen as an exclusionary movement that does not accept hybrid efforts that members of these non-Black racial minority communities tend to endorse. Individuals from such communities may not even identify themselves as antiracists, even if they are pursuing similar goals as antiracists. Another example of a variation of antiracism developing within general society can be seen in the development of self-imposed stigma among white antiracists (Hughey 2012a). European Americans who identify as antiracists do not shun stigma for their racial status and indeed even embrace such stigma. Similarly, Thompson (2001) points to how white antiracism activists helped craft a multiracial antiracism movement even as those white activists struggled with finding their new place in this movement. Thus, variations of the themes are found in that scholarly antiracism is often manifested in various ways among popularized antiracist activists.

Modern Antiracist Philosophy

Understanding the origin and variations of antiracism provides knowledge and context about the nature of this ideology in the present moment. A historical analysis, however, is not enough to replace an examination of how academics discuss and understand the nature of modern antiracism. To understand the nature of modern antiracism among scholars, it is vital to situate the social dynamics in which they operate. Before the murders of Floyd and Arbery, attention to antiracism was largely relegated to activists and scholars, developing in an atmosphere where it received limited attention from the larger society. After the events in the summer of 2020, popularized versions of this philosophy emerged on the national scene. As we see in this chapter and the next, the popularized versions of antiracism fit neatly with the ideals put forth by antiracism academics, although more popular versions emphasize different aspects of antiracism.

One key event shaping modern antiracist thought and the discourse it engages was the election of President Barack Obama in 2008. With his election, individuals began to discuss the possibilities of a post-racial society

(Mukherjee 2016, Tesler 2016, Love and Tosolt 2010), although there was evidence of an increase in racial polarization within the United States at the same time (Tesler and Sears 2010, McDermott and Belcher 2014). Attitudes affirming a post-race sentiment provided a foil for antiracist scholars. Antiracist academics perceived that notions that America was now post-racial imply that criticisms against continuing racism are unwarranted (Lentin 2011). Support of post-racialism can buttress the idea of colorblindness as the path by which a society can escape the problems created by historical and institutional racism. Antiracists argue that colorblindness can be used to resist antiracism efforts as it ignores the reality of the racism embedded in the United States (Mukherjee 2016, Srivastava 2005).

Antiracists link strategies of colorblindness to support of modern racist ideals. Indeed, scholars have identified colorblind racism (Burke 2018, Carr 1997, Bonilla-Silva 2013). Furthermore, antiracists judge intentional efforts to eliminate racism as problematic if they do not go far enough, arguing that these efforts are largely symbolic and fail to achieve structural change. Such is the attitude of antiracists toward efforts of multiculturalism. Multiculturalism has been conceptualized as a way to address diversity by producing tolerance between different racial/ethnic groups (Berman and Paradies 2010, Turner Kelly 2005). However, academic antiracists argue that this type of tolerance does not sufficiently address the powerful ways racism operates through institutions and corrupts the core of our societies (Mukherjee 2016, Gillborn 2006, Berman and Paradies 2010). From an antiracist perspective, the comprehensive nature of racism's impact on society indicates that it is insufficient for individuals to merely learn how to accept other cultural norms. Racism in our societies must be deliberately removed. This requires a wide adaptation of antiracist cultural norms. Efforts of multiculturalism to promote cultural tolerance may even lead to a maintenance of the racial status quo (Case and Ngo 2017, Gillborn 2006). For antiracists, the goal of eradicating racism is far more important than the pluralism of multiculturalism (Gillborn 2006, Turner Kelly 2005, Mukherjee 2016). Unlike multiculturalism, antiracism does not highlight different cultural values in a desire for cultural tolerance. Rather, antiracists promote their principles to eradicate the persistent racism rooted in Western societies.

Antiracist scholars are not interested in grounding an argument against the social forces that offer intellectual resistance to their goals but rather in discovering methods of activism that can be used to further their goals of eliminating racism in all its multifaceted dimensions. They see racism as persistent and adaptable, taking different forms to maintain itself (Paradies 2005, Gillborn 2006, Bakan 2008). Thus, some antiracism scholars have argued that antiracism must also be flexible in responding accordingly (Bonnett 2000, Gillborn 2006, Laughter and Hurst 2022). In this framework, efforts toward colorblindness can be seen as a shield used by social and political conservatives to ignore racism, while multiculturalism can be envisioned as a weak response endorsed by some political progressives to the larger racial dysfunctions in our society.

Accordingly, one antiracist approach is to place the lived experiences of racial and ethnic minorities at the center of analysis (Dei et al. 2005). Turner Kelly (2005) contends that a culturally conservative perspective envisions antiracism to be of lesser value due to its reliance on subjectivity compared to quantifiable data that can be observed and tested. However, a culturally liberal perspective understands that all knowledge is socially constructed and that there is great value in the lived experiences of the marginalized. These lived experiences are valuable for exploring how racism impacts marginalized individuals (Ford and Airhihenbuwa 2010) and legitimating efforts to confront racism in all its varied forms. For example, it was commonplace to hear the phrase "Say Their Name"[3] during BLM protests, which emphasized two things. First, the unjust deaths of nonwhite people have been historically marginalized and silenced. Second, the phrase implies the power of the lived experience of the nonwhite person experiencing the unjust systems of racism. Although saying the names of Arbery, Taylor, and Floyd will not bring them back, it allows protesters to validate the unique lived experience of each victim while unifying the cause against injustice.

The idea of using lived experiences as a source of knowledge is more grounded in antiracism than a Eurocentric Enlightenment approach. In this manner, antiracists use some of the academic arguments championed by CRT scholars on the value of lived experiences, in contrast with Enlightenment modes of evidence gathering (Ford and Airhihenbuwa 2010, Housee 2012, Hylton 2010), to promote the value of lived experiences in antiracist activism. The promotion of lived experiences over politics motivated by a desire for assimilation and a desire to argue that racial differences are unimportant (Lentin 2011) indicates that certain lived experiences, particularly those of marginalized groups, need to be promoted more than others. Lived experiences that legitimize antiracism efforts and illustrate the continuing oppression of marginalized racial and ethnic groups are prioritized over lived experiences that cannot be used in such a manner. The lived experiences of marginalized racial group members and the oppressions they have faced, and continue to face, in a racist society will remain at the center of antiracism efforts.

---

3. Technically, the phrase was "Say Her Name," specifically created to highlight how Black women are also killed by police brutality. Like antiracism, the movement expanded to include men, hence "Say Their Name" (Stanford University 2020).

This leads to a second tool for antiracist activism, which is the use of the counternarrative. The counternarrative is also an idea that emerged from CRT literature (Gillborn 2006, Blaisdell 2021) but has been useful in cementing an antiracist identity. According to Blaisdell (2021), the counternarrative is useful for understanding the effects of power, deconstructing majoritarian narratives that dismiss the impacts of racism, fighting against the silencing of voices of color, and encouraging activism. The counternarrative can provide an atmosphere conducive to the pursuit of racial justice as it seeks to disrupt a white epistemology. Counternarratives can empower the voices of marginalized groups, who so often have their voices silenced in the dominant culture (Lawrence and Dua 2005). The counternarrative becomes an important legitimization tool for antiracists because compelling stories can increase support for the concerns of antiracists, especially in the face of quantitative data that is assumed by some detractors to be more "credible." With the counternarrative, supporters of antiracism emphasize certain messages and resist messages that work against their efforts. Such resistance is applicable regardless of whether the troubling problematic message is based on the notion of colorblindness or multiculturalism.

Antiracists use lived experiences and counternarratives to reorder the current racial hierarchy, taking power from the majority group to the minority group by the values embedded in antiracism. While European Americans enjoy sizable advantages over people of color in society at large, it is the stories of marginalized racial groups that carry great weight within an antiracism community. It is those stories that provide fuel to justify social change by placing a greater emphasis on the plight of racial minorities than the plight of majority group members. Given that antiracism is a mechanism that promotes a given set of values and norms, rather than a philosophy such as multiculturalism that seeks to understand and tolerate different sets of cultural values, it is valuable to recognize the types of moral claims made by supporters of antiracism. One such moral claim is the valuing of the experiences and fate of racial minorities over the fate and experiences of majority group members.

Given this moral claim within antiracism, and despite its focus on institutions and structures, there is substantial focus by antiracists on the alteration of the attitudes and actions of majority group members. The focus of counternarratives is to convince majority group members to aid in the dismantling of social structures that perpetuate the advantages of those majority group members. Majority group members may have to undergo an existential crisis where an identity shaped by white supremacy will be rejected (De Lissovoy and Brown 2013). The difficulty such majority group members have in overcoming their reliance on that identity and the advantages arising out of it and their position in society can be one of the biggest barriers to creating the solidarity needed for overcoming white supremacy. Thus, the focus of much of the work in antiracism is not simply correcting overt expressions of racial bigotry. While some antiracists do discuss this type of racism, overt racism is low-hanging fruit. Antiracist writings also spend a relatively generous amount of space critiquing progressive whites who might otherwise be seen as their allies (De Lissovoy and Brown 2013, Lally 2022, Srivastava 2005, Badenhorst et al. 2022, Osamudia 2022, Comer 2021, Macoun 2016). The challenging nature of these writings, as it concerns majority group members who are most sympathetic to the concerns of antiracists, illustrates the dichotomous way antiracism distinguishes its treatment of whiteness as opposed to ideologies and values found within nonwhite cultures. Indeed, majority group members have been asked to be "race traitors" in that they should work to abolish whiteness (Gillborn 2006, Ignatiev and Garvey 2014), which is clearly a request that antiracists would never make to racial minorities. Whiteness, despite the plethora of ways antiracists have defined it, is consistently seen as the enemy of human flourishing in our society. This distinguishment reinforces the moral value of prioritizing the needs of marginalized racial/ethnic groups over the maintenance of the dominant racial/ethnic groups.

Strengthening this distinction between the comfort of majority and minority group members is the attitude antiracists take toward European American culture. Support of antiracism is not limited to the United States. Antiracism has become an international phenomenon but with a special focus on Western nations with a European heritage. Thus, some authors detail concerns in countries such as Canada (Lawrence and Dua 2005, Kubota 2015, Calliste 1996), Great Britain (Gillborn 2006, Solomos 1995, Huq 2008), and Australia (Berman and Paradies 2010, Dunn et al. 2009, Pedersen, Walker, and Wise 2005). The overall attitude that unites their concerns is that nations situated within the Western world are heavily troubled by racism. Although European nations have moved away from old tribalism, antiracists perceive these nations as societies shaped by the enduring effects of racism, even in their modernized forms (Rabaka 2006). The type of antiracism culture that advocates support can be envisioned as an evolutionary move away from old nation-states troubled by systems of racism and exclusion.

To this end, academic supporters of antiracism envision efforts to promote it to be worth major alterations in their societies and their actions. Some have looked at the overturning of capitalism as an important component of fulfilling the goals of antiracism (Mynott 2002, Casey 2016, Lally 2022, Case and Ngo 2017). Others have critiqued resistance from assumed progressive allies such as white feminists (Comer 2021, Srivastava 2005) and even other antiracists who do not take the effects of colonialization seriously (Lawrence and Dua 2005). Antiracism seeks to overturn the core of society insofar as that core consists of the underpinning of racism. With some exceptions, modern antiracism is generally not reformative (Gillborn 2006, Rabaka 2006). The scope of change desired by different academic proponents of antiracism can vary. However, it is accurate to state that antiracism is a philosophy that does not settle for tinkering with the status quo. It is a venture that has as a goal the alteration of society so that racism, seen as deeply embedded into the core of that society's institutions and structures, is eradicated. To engage in such eradication, one must be aware of the depth of the problem and have the resolve to do whatever is necessary to complete the task of eradication. Antiracists believe the social world they want to create will look significantly different from the social world we have today.

Given the assertion by antiracists about the multifaceted nature of racism, it is not surprising that they desire corrections that may be revolutionary. The alterations that antiracist scholars seek are also multidimensional. They seek multifaceted reform that penetrates all aspects of our society. Although intersectionality is an important value among many antiracists (Müller 2021, Dhamoon 2015, Kubota 2021, West 2020), the focus of antiracists tends to be about the many ways racism continues to deprive people of color. Calls to center racism in other types of oppression, such as sexism or classism, are not likely to gather the support of all antiracists because some antiracists will want to focus exclusively on racial issues. The core of this movement is dealing with racism wherever it is found, and no sector of society is safe from the scrutiny of antiracists.

Power in relationships is a vital idea within antiracism research (Dei et al. 2005). Fear of unchecked power is a key reason why antiracism tends to be antiauthoritarian (Zamalin 2019). The recognition of the different levels of power in relationships is an idea that pulls together many of the other themes within antiracism. It is concerned with the way the powerful can use the concept of a post-racial world to maintain their power that moves antiracists to fight against the notion of a colorblind society (Mukherjee 2016) or a multiculturalism focused on mere tolerance of difference (Dei et al. 2005). Counternarratives and the telling of lived experiences are important for illustrating the misuse of power by the dominant group (Blaisdell 2021). The entrenched power of an oppressive racial/ethnic class makes it important to empower a social movement with enough strength to topple that power (De Lissovoy and Brown 2013). Because of the disproportionate power in our society, minor reforms are not enough. Antiracism demands an overhaul of our society because of the breadth and depth of the misuse of the way power has been distributed within Western cultures. Different ideals espoused in antiracism can be seen as attempts to alter the basic power relationships in our society as they pertain to racial and ethnic status.

From Academic Theorizing to Public Consumption

Probably most scholars in the social sciences and humanities have wondered whether the issues they write about matter outside the walls of academia. Accessibility is low, as the average American is unlikely to pick up an academic journal while waiting in the doctor's office. Even given the advantages of publishing on the Internet, academic writings are not easily found and are often hidden behind expensive paywalls. For the brave souls who venture into those sites, the writing is often difficult and obtuse to those who have not had graduate school training. The style of academic discourse is not accessible to most of the general public. Given these barriers, it is easy to believe that academics are largely merely talking to each other, with little real alterations in the attitudes of the general public.

However, it is a mistake for us to underestimate the power of scholarship to impact the nonacademic world. It is difficult, if not impossible, for social movements to gain sufficient influence to promote and sustain social reforms without the intellectual support provided by scholars. That support can be vital in the establishment of justification for social movements and can connect underclass revolutionaries with elite allies. Even a brief inquiry into popular writings and teachings today reveals the impact of Marxism and the tremendous change it has produced in society. Some may postulate that this change may have occurred only because Marx was an activist as well as a scholar. If this is true, then it bodes well for antiracist scholars, where activism is a vital part of their academic responsibilities. The controversial 1619 Project is a contemporary example of academics contributing to a journalistic endeavor that served as a source of antiracist education in the school system (Bui et al. 2022, Feuerstein 2022) and provided intellectual support for antiracist efforts. The important role of scholars in the promotion of social movements is even more important in a modernist society with a strong legitimization of scientific knowledge and intellectualism.

The emergence of the Internet and the promulgation of information also have increased the importance of scholars in shaping social change. With the ease by which individuals and organizations can publish stories, articles, and blogs online, it has become simpler to highlight the results of a particular study or the arguments by a given scholar.[4] The fruits of an academic's labor may be available in an article as soon as a few days after publication. That academic may be invited to a podcast to discuss the findings of the article. Whereas, in the past, it could have taken months or even years for an aca-

---

4. Of course, not all attention to one's work is desirable, as the lead author found out when his research documenting the greater hesitation of women to interracially date relative to men (Yancey 2009) was used by a white supremacist group to promulgate its racist agenda.

demic's research to be disseminated in a format easily understandable for the public, that delay can now be measured in weeks, if not days.

However, there is no guarantee that any particular scholar's article or book will reach a larger audience. While a certain degree of happenchance plays a role in whether a particular article or book breaks through to the consciences of the larger public, it is also important that the proper social conditions must develop to maximize the chances that the work of the academic will be noticed by the larger public. When the attention of the public is focused on a given issue, then it becomes much more likely that research focusing on that area will gain notoriety. For example, given the role conservative Christians played in the election of President Donald Trump (Ayris 2021, Dick 2017), it is not surprising to see an upsurge of attention surrounding academic work debating the nature and effects of Christian nationalism since 2016. Likewise, social conditions have developed to where it is reasonable to understand the increased attention on the work of antiracism scholars. Given the rise of attention to racial inequities during the events of 2020 as well as the backlash to racially progressive efforts in 2021 (Kamenetz 2021, Osamudia 2022), it is not surprising that many individuals would look toward academic efforts to understand both past and current racial unrest and solutions to move forward. Furthermore, the activist orientation of antiracism research places these efforts in a powerful position to shape social movements that further progressive, and even radical, efforts to alter a racialized society. Attention to altering the power dynamics in our society as it concerns racial/ethnic identity feeds into the larger general polarization in the United States, as the vocabularies of concern and the strategies to address them vary and stratify (Poole and Rosenthal 1984, Iyengar et al. 2019). It is not surprising that antiracism went from a concept largely limited to the vocabulary of scholars and activists to a common buzzword among public policymakers, human resources personnel in businesses, and education administrators.

When the events of 2020 occurred, books and presentations translating antiracism research for the general public already existed. Attention to the events of 2020 made those books and presentations relevant to a wider audience. Those events also spurred the movement of resources to the creation of other efforts to promote antiracism to that larger audience. Antiracism can no longer be seen as mere debates among academics as it has now become a concept discussed among nonscholars. A generous body of nonscholarly literature has developed, promoting the ideals of antiracism to the public. As we see in Chapter 3, that literature reflects well many of the themes found among antiracism scholars. Documenting the ideals of this popularized antiracism and developing an empirical tool to measure the adherence of individuals to the values of that antiracism is the focus of the next chapter.

3

Constructing the Antiracism Attitude Scale

Discussions on racial issues are often impeded by definitions.[1] For example, the literature surrounding and expanding critical race theory is vast and substantive (Valdes, Culp, and Harris 2002, Hatch 2007, Closson 2010, Rashid 2011). Arguments in mainstream settings about the use of critical race theory, however, have been characterized by distorted interpretations of the definitions of critical race theory (Lockhart 2021, Goldberg 2021, K. Benson 2022). In the past few years, some critics of critical race theory have created strawman versions of it, which they then proceed to rhetorically demolish. As critical race theory shifted from a legal theory to a highly politicized and controversial issue in the United States, it quickly became a proxy for whether individuals support or oppose diversity, equity, and inclusion (DEI) programs or other diversity efforts, regardless of the degree to which those efforts are consistent with the ideals within actual critical race theory.[2] As ideas from academia disseminate and interact with the gen-

---

1. A previous version of this chapter appeared as George Yancey and Hayoung Oh, "Finding Antiracists: Construction of an Antiracism Scale," *Sociological Focus* 57, no. 2 (2024), 230–251, https://doi.org/10.1080/00380237.2024.2330470. © 2024 North Central Sociological Association, https://www.ncsanet.org, reprinted by permission of Taylor & Francis Ltd, http://www.tandfonline.com, on behalf of North Central Sociological Association, https://www.ncsanet.org.

2. Some editorialists (Edsall 2021, Iati 2021, Ray 2022) argue that the setting up of critical race theory as a proxy was not an accident but an intentional effort of conservative activists such as Christopher Rufo to demonize critical race theory to gain support in opposing progressive racial reforms.

eral public, we find that these public debates over critical race theory do not necessarily comport with how it was defined in primary texts.

Like critical race theory, the public's understanding, perception, and definition of antiracism may not necessarily reflect scholarly interpretation. Notably, while there are powerful critics of antiracist efforts, the public debate on antiracism has not reached the intensity of the debate on critical race theory. One explanation may be that antiracism is considered a practical application of critical race theory (Ford and Airhihenbuwa 2010, Gillborn 2006). For this reason, critics would rather attack what they perceive as the source of the problem (e.g., critical race theory) than spend their time on antiracism, which they consider to be a second-order issue (Moody 2021, R. Sanchez 2021). Antiracism may be considered by the public or CRT critics as belonging within the umbrella term of critical race theory, and attacks on that overarching umbrella will impact both CRT and antiracism.

Without substantial attention, the relative lack of debate about the definition of antiracism may leave much of the freedom to define antiracism in the hands of its proponents. But having proponents of antiracism fashion a public definition of the concept is no guarantee that this definition will reflect the academic treatment of the term. After all, it is still plausible that proponents shape a definition that aids them in their advocacy for racialized reforms rather than a focus on definitional accuracy. It would be expected that public interpretation of antiracism will be shaped to meet the needs of interest groups, regardless of whether those groups support academic antiracism.

While an academic definition of antiracism is necessary to understand the intellectual context behind the development of the concept, there is no guarantee that this definition is how antiracism is generally understood. If there are discrepancies between an academic and a public definition of antiracism, then understanding the public definition is also an important endeavor to understand how antiracist ideas have developed in the general public's consciousness. It is the popularized concept of antiracism motivating those who use the idea of antiracism to promote social change. When individuals discuss promoting antiracism, they are not usually talking about Du Bois but are more likely to talk about Kendi. To investigate how the concept of antiracism is used to motivate a community to action, we must go beyond academic discussions of the concept and explore how the concept is conceptualized in public. Once we have a solid understanding of a public conception of antiracism, we can create methodological tools that assess who has these attitudes and how these attitudes are connected to other social attitudes.

In this chapter, we present an index to identify the degree to which individuals accept a popularized concept of antiracism. While we introduce the index in this chapter, a more complete description of its development can be seen in an earlier article (Yancey, 2024) and the appendix. The index offers the opportunity for us to determine the demographic and social characteristics of those most likely to accept antiracist ideals and beliefs. We began our understanding of the popularized conception of antiracism and the index with a primary literature review.

What Is Antiracism?

To define popularized antiracism, our literature review consisted of a list of books commonly used by popular antiracist proponents in late 2020 and early 2021, as interest in antiracism was high due to BLM protests and campaigns.[3] Books were selected for their relative popularity and if they clearly articulated a desire to promote some form of antiracism. We used a few online articles (Tomkin 2020, Snyder 2020, Hoffower 2020, McKenzie 2019) to validate if the same themes in the book are supported in the articles. Generally, however, we leaned more heavily on the books than the articles in our full exploration of antiracism since book authors have more space to fully develop their ideas about antiracism.

Several organizations and prominent individuals have offered definitions of antiracism readily accepted in the general culture. According to the Alberta Civil Liberties Research Centre (2020), antiracism has been defined by the Ontario Anti-Racism Secretariat as "the practice of identifying, challenging, and changing the values, structures, and behaviors that perpetuate systemic racism." The same article also states that the NAC International Perspectives: Women and Global Solidarity defines antiracism as "the active process of identifying and eliminating racism by changing systems, organizational structures, policies and practices, and attitude, so that power is redistributed and shared equitably." A prominent supporter, Robert J. Patterson (Hoffower 2020), stated, "Anti-racism is an active and conscious effort to work against multidimensional aspects of racism." Furthermore, Ibram Kendi (2019, 18) argues, "An antiracist policy is any measure that produces or sustains racial equity between racial groups. By policy I mean written and unwritten laws, rules, procedures, processes, regulations, and guidelines that govern people. There is no such thing as a nonracist or race-neutral policy."

From these definitions, we find a few generalizations about antiracism. First, a popularized understanding of antiracism promotes a comprehensive, intentional struggle against entrenched multidimensional racism plaguing the United States. Antiracism requires an intentional individualized and collective effort to combat racism. These definitions indicate that antiracists perceive racism as commonplace in the United States. We further explore

---

3. These books can be found in Appendix B.

these generalizations in four themes of antiracism: 1) pervasiveness of racism, 2) racism is multifaceted, 3) societal change, and 4) differential white/nonwhite responsibilities.

Four Themes of Popularized Antiracism

In our assessment of popularized antiracism, the focus is on shared values and ideas found in a majority of the readings. While there is some subjectivity to the literature selection, we still found common concepts in the writings. Our readings of the primary literature on antiracism deepen and expand on some of the ideas evident in these definitions. While our identification of these themes is not exhaustive, and although it is plausible that there are other common themes in the literature that we do not identify, we are confident that the themes we articulate are present in all the major popularized antiracism texts.

Pervasiveness of Racism

Much of the extant literature discusses the pervasiveness of racism in the United States. Some antiracists contend that we live in a system of white supremacy that continues to work to the advantage of whites (Jewell 2020, Kivel 2017, Oluo 2019, Tomkin 2020). This pervasiveness impacts people of color and negatively affects them in almost every aspect of life: health, education, and socioeconomic status (Oluo 2019, DiAngelo 2018, Kivel 2017). Thus, Kivel (2017) argues that "we have seen how racism is a pervasive part of our culture. Therefore we should always assume that racism is at least part of the picture. In light of this assumption, we should look for the patterns involved rather than treating most events as isolated occurrences" (87). Eddo-Lodge (2020) adds, "In a world where blunt, obvious acts are just the tip of the iceberg of racism, we need to describe the invisible monolith. . . . We need to see racism as structural in order to see its insidiousness. We need to see how it seeps, like a noxious gas, into everything" (222). Jewell (2020) contends, "Racism is so deep within us. It is all around us and we have to be constantly aware of it so we don't get consumed by this smog. It is so easy to rest inside of it, especially if you benefit from the system that has been designed for you" (146). The authors of these books assume that it is difficult, if not impossible, to find an element in our society that is not touched by racism. For antiracists, racism is omnipresent.

For the authors of antiracism books, it is not merely their belief that racism impacts everything or almost everything in our society. This effect is seen as not only pervasive and widespread, but the impact is also deep within the institutions where racism is found; it is seen as having a deep and perversive impact. For example, Fidel (2020) reveals this perspective in his discussion of racism in literature:

> This is literary racism, and it negatively impacts all students in various ways. It creates a literacy disconnect for Black students and other students of color that excludes their life experiences, and an actual engagement divide between these students and White students. Because of the lack of representation in the classroom, we are conditioned to believe that our stories, experiences, cultures, and dialects are seen as having little or no value in academic settings, which can sometimes trickle into everyday lives. Studies show that students are the least engaged in literature when they don't see themselves in it. These students then are judged by their "lack" of performance in the classroom, which is ultimately caused by racial biases. (16)

For antiracists, racism is not merely found in most, or all, institutions in our society, but it is deeply infused in those institutions. For many antiracists, racism is a strong foundation that dominates our society. America is seen as a system of racism that impacts all of us. The notion of America being a system of racism is generally assumed, as seen by this quote from Olou (2019): "Until we have dismantled the system of White Supremacy and racial oppression, we will always need to talk about it" (230). Or in this quote by DiAngelo (2018): "Because racism does not rely solely on individual actors, the racist system is reproduced automatically. To interrupt it, we need to recognize and challenge the norms, structures, and institutions that keep it in place" (135). These comments, among others, indicate belief that racism is a pervasive system deeply embedded in all the dimensions of our society, which is related to the next theme from the antiracism authors.

Racism Is Multifaceted

The second theme is the contention that racism is multifaceted. We define this differently than pervasiveness in that racism can be pervasive but may be one-dimensional. Primary antiracist authors argue that racism is multidimensional and different forms of racism are impactful to our society. Thus, racism is seen as more than overt racial hatred. While there is an acknowledgment that individualized racial hate still exists, proponents of antiracism contend that white people do not have to be overtly hateful to disseminate the effects of racism (Saad 2020, Oluo 2019). Some antiracists argue that majority group members reducing racism down to individualized bigotry helps maintain structural and institutional racism (DiAngelo 2018, Eddo-Lodge

2020, Saad 2020). Antiracists often argue that majority group members attempt to relieve themselves of the responsibility of dealing with racism by emphasizing their racial tolerance (Saad 2020, Eddo-Lodge 2020). These proponents are not impressed with an individual's tolerance as this is often used to dismiss the painful ways racism impacts marginalized racial groups, particularly through structures and systems. Antiracist authors argue that a concentration on an individual's overt racism minimizes the problems of systemic and multifaceted racism.

To illustrate the importance of addressing systemic racism, Oluo (2019) links racial bigotry with systemic racism:

> Tying racism to its systemic causes and effects will help others see the important difference between systemic racism, and anti-white bigotry. In addition, the more practice you have at tying individual racism to the system that gives it power, the more you will be able to see all the ways in which you can make a difference. Yes, you can demand that the teacher shouting racial slurs at Hispanic kids should be fired, but you can also ask what that school's suspension rate for Hispanic kids is, ask how many teachers of color they have on staff, and ask that their policies be reviewed and reformed. Yes, you can definitely report your racist coworker to HR, but you can also ask your company management what processes they have in place to minimize racial bias in their hiring process, you can ask for more diversity in management and cultural sensitivity training for staff, and you can ask what procedures they have in place to handle allegations of racial discrimination. (34)

This propensity to develop concepts of racism beyond an overt expression of racism to include a concern about systemic and institutional issues is fairly common in the work of antiracism. This can be seen in the work of Kendi (2019), who argues that "'Institutional racism' and 'structural racism' and 'systemic racism' are redundant. Racism itself is institutional, structural and systemic:" (18). Furthermore, Jewell (2020) argues, "Together people and our institutions create a solid structure of racism through policies, rules, and opportunities that give more resources to one group over another" (39). Antiracists promote an expansive definition of racism inclusive of individual and institutional concerns, and thus they define racism as multifaceted.

We see similar concerns of institutional factors in the work of DiAngelo, who remarked, "When a racial group's collective prejudice is backed by the power of legal authority and institutional control, it is transformed into racism, a far-reaching system that functions independently from the intentions or self-images of individual actors" (20). She makes it clear that the forces attributable to racism do not necessarily rely upon individual conscious acts of hatred. She followed that comment by arguing, "This authority and control transforms individual prejudices into a far-reaching system that no longer depends on the good intentions of individual actors; it becomes the default of society and is reproduced automatically. Racism is a system" (21). The claim of racism as a system disentangles racism from merely being tied to racial hatred; rather, it has become a self-sustaining process that reproduces itself in the social structures of our society.

This multifaceted definition is useful to antiracists since it allows them to make multiple demands of the majority group members. For some antiracists, the focus of whites on only individualistic overt racism is a part of the problem of racism. Kivel (2017) states, "Racism . . . is barely touched by changes in individual white consciousness. We often find it difficult to see or to know how to challenge institutional racism because we are so used to focusing on individual actions and attitudes" (160). Saad (2020) also expresses this sentiment in arguing, "This idea that white supremacy only applies to the so-called 'bad ones' is both incorrect and dangerous, because it reinforces the idea that white supremacy is an ideology that is only upheld by a fringe group of white people. White supremacy is far from fringe. In white-centered societies and communities, it is the dominant paradigm that forms the foundation from which norms, rules, and laws are created" (13). For antiracists, a focus on overt individualized racism is a distraction from the multifaceted way racism impacts our society. Complaints of the advocation of colorblindness fit into this concern of antiracists, as stated by Eddo-Lodge (2020): "Colour-blindness is a childish, stunted analysis of racism. It starts and ends at 'discriminating against a person because of the colour of their skin is bad,' without any accounting for how structural power manifests in these exchanges" (82). Antiracists include individual acts of racism as part of the overarching antiracist framework but argue that unless institutional structures are addressed, racism will continue to persist.

Societal Change

Third, given the popular antiracists' perception of the pervasiveness of racism and its multifaceted nature, it is not surprising that antiracists desire a push toward major societal reform. Antiracists link white supremacy in our society to centuries of racial abuse and see it as unrealistic to overcome the effects of white supremacy in a short period (Eddo-Lodge 2020, Kendi 2016, Tomkin 2020). Some proponents of antiracism conceptualize racism and white supremacy as institutional systems that must be dismantled (Tomkin 2020, Saad 2020, Oluo 2019). Minor reforms will not suffice to eradicate racism. Thus, Kendi (2019) not only wants to address issues directly connected to racism but also argues that institutions historically linked with white supremacy, such as capitalism, must be combated. He argues that "to love capitalism is to end up loving racism. To love racism is to end up loving capitalism. The conjoined twins are two sides of the same destructive body" (183). In this perspective, racism will not be eliminated by altering a few public policies. Kendi argues that we will not eradicate racism until we alter the basic economic system undergirding our society. Regardless of whether antiracists desire the end of capitalism, they are not afraid of calling for an overhaul of our society, as seen in Jewell's (2020) statement:

> If you are white, light (like me), or a non-Black Person of the Global Majority, use your privilege and your proximity (or closeness) to the center of the dominant culture box to fracture the very foundation of our racist society. If you keep doing this and continue to put more cracks and dents into the structure you'll shake it all up so that it can crumble. (96)

Even beyond alteration of political and economic systems, antiracists advocate that individuals must take on a comprehensibly different mindset, allowing them to more easily recognize the problems created by racism and be ready to consistently fight against racism in the coming years (Kendi 2019, DiAngelo 2018, Oluo 2019, Saad 2020). For example, DiAngelo's (2018) book attempts to address white fragility, which she conceptualizes as "a state in which even a minimum amount of racial stress in the habitus becomes intolerable, triggering a range of defensive moves" (103) Her argument is not merely a seeking out of institutional change but an alteration in how individuals, most notably majority group members, think about race relations and marginalized racial groups. Majority group members have a responsibility to proselytize based on this new mindset, as stated by Saad (2020):

> I invite you to cast your view out to all your friendships and acquaintance circles. Your coworkers. Your peers. Other parents in your community. Other students in your school. Other worshippers in your spiritual community. Other entrepreneurs in your business circles. Other artists in your creative circles. Family friends. Your partner's friends. Friends of friends with whom you have spent time. And so on.

The intention of promoting this attitude change is to lead to systemic alterations that help them combat racism. Kivel (2017) contends, "Although institutional change seems difficult to tackle, we are already involved in several institutions in our daily lives. Our workplace, the schools we or our children attend, the stores we patronize, the places we socialize, the community with which we congregate for religious worship—we have some leverage at each of these institutions" (179). Furthermore, Fidel (2020) states, "I am here to make people aware of the injustices that are rarely covered or encountered in-depth by mainstream media . . . from their root causes to workable solutions. It is past time to work together to give insight into how we all can do better" (xxii). Finally, Oluo (2019) states the following:

> I know that the issue of racism and racial oppression seems huge—and it is huge. But it is not insurmountable. When we look at it in its entirety, it seems like too much, but understand that the system is invested in you seeing it that way. The truth is, we all pull levers of this white supremacist system, every day. The way we vote, where we spend our money, what we do and do not call out—these are all pieces of the system. We cannot talk our way out of a racially oppressive system. We can talk our way into understanding, and we can then use that understanding to act. (234)

Targets for social change by antiracists encompass alterations of both individual attitudes and institutional structures, and efforts at each type of social change complement each other. But antiracists desire to alter the entire system and not merely elements of that system. While some are more revolutionary than others, societal alteration as an intentional effort is a goal consistently found in the writings of antiracists.

Differential White/Nonwhite Responsibilities

Fourth, the differential role of majority group members compared to the minority group is another key belief expressed by proponents of popular antiracism. The literature generally calls upon whites to make the sacrifices necessary to achieve racial justice, and their actions signal whether whites are legitimate allies and antiracists (Hoffower 2020). Antiracism is a philosophy written to challenge whites, and they appear to be the target audience for several popularized antiracism books (DiAngelo 2018, Eddo-Lodge 2020, Oluo 2019, Kivel 2017, Saad 2020). Indeed, even the title of some of the antiracism books—*White Fragility, Why I'm No Longer Talking to White People about Race, Uprooting Racism: How White People Can Work for Racial Justice*—indicate a desire to instruct white people, but not racial minorities, on what they need to do to eliminate racism. Majority group members may be called upon to reject their racial identity (DiAngelo 2018), work to convince other whites about the value of antiracism (DiAngelo 2018, Eddo-Lodge 2020, Kivel 2017, Saad 2020), develop humility in their interactions with people of color (Saad 2020, Oluo 2019, Hoffower 2020), and provide financial resources (Eddo-Lodge 2020, Jewell 2020, Tomkin 2020). In addition to these sacrifices, majority group members should not expect to have a significant leadership role in the antiracist movement (Tomkin 2020, Saad 2020, Eddo-Lodge 2020) or get credit for acting in an antiracist manner (Oluo 2019, Saad 2020). Instead of accepting the benefits of their racial status, whites are admonished to be "race traitors" and work against unfairly obtained benefits (Moon and Flores 2000). While many demands are made of majority group members, relatively few are made of minority group members, revealing the different roles each has in the antiracism movement. People of color can provide insight into the racist nature of society, and whites can benefit from their insight if they allow themselves to be taught by people of color (Saad 2020, DiAngelo 2018). However, antiracism proponents also argue that engagement is taxing for people of color and they should not be expected to engage with whites (DiAngelo 2018, Oluo 2019, Saad 2020).

DiAngelo (2018) strongly illustrates this by criticizing whites who "argue, minimize, explain, play devil's advocate, pout, tune out or withdraw to stop the challenge" (112). When people of color criticize whites, they are expected to "graciously receive it, reflect and work to change the behavior" (113). These comments reveal the disproportionate expectations placed upon whites compared to nonwhites. People of color would never be asked by antiracists to graciously receive the criticisms of whites. That role is only to be played by majority group members. Antiracism is not a philosophy that promotes identical responsibilities for whites and nonwhites. The pain that people of color have suffered does not allow for equal responsibilities. The benefits that whites gained through the larger system of white supremacy shape an expectation about how contrasting effects of our racialized society differently impact whites and nonwhites. Thus Eddo-Lodge (2020) argues, "Discussing racism is about discussing white identity. It is about white anxiety. It's about asking why whiteness has this reflexive need to define itself against immigrant bogey monster in order to feel comfortable, safe, and secure. Why am I saying one thing and white people are hearing something completely different?" (215).

Perhaps the contrast between the differing expectations of whites and nonwhites is most clearly laid out by Oluo (2019). She asserts, "If you are white, remember that White Supremacy is a system you benefit from and that your privilege has helped to uphold. Your efforts to dismantle White Supremacy are expected of decent people who believe in justice. You are not owed gratitude or friendship from people of color for your efforts" (210). She then goes on to discuss the expectations of people of color by stating, "As a person of color, you don't have to call out every microaggression against you, but you have the right to call out each and every one that you choose to. Do not let people convince you that you are being oversensitive, that you are being disruptive or divisive. What is harmful and divisive are these acts of aggression against people of color that are allowed to happen constantly, without consequence" (174). We again see the contrast whereby majority group members have obligations toward bettering race relations but people of color have few direct obligations.

Justifications for these different responsibilities are tied to the contrasting social positions of whites and nonwhites. It is not merely that majority group members have more resources than people of color. It is also argued that historically, the concerns of whites are prioritized over those of people of color. There needs to be an adjustment to our social order that allows racial minorities to have the voice and autonomy that they have not had in the past, even if this means that majority group members cannot bring up their own concerns. Saad (2020) contends, "So when we talk about being called out or called in, a common reaction by people with white privilege is to focus on their intention rather than their impact on BIPOC [Black, Indigenous, and people of color]. This is a form of white centering, which prioritizes how a person of privilege feels about being called out/in versus the actual pain that BIPOC experiences as a result of that person's actions, whether intentional or unintentional" (165). Saad argues that the reason why whites should accept correction by people of color and not offer their critiques of marginalized racial groups, or even defenses of their actions, is the need to decenter the whiteness embedded in our society. The differential responsibilities of whites and nonwhites are conceptualized as the road to racial justice and equity to compensate for the oppression they have suffered at the hands of majority group members.

Commonality of Themes in Popularized Antiracism

These themes denote common assertions of popularized antiracism and offer ideas about the goals of this movement. From these themes, antiracists position themselves to make political demands. The belief of antiracists in those assertions creates a cognitive framework by which they understand racialized elements in American society. We acknowledge that the antiracism movement is diverse in thought and consequently not a monolith, indicated by how some of the literature emphasized certain themes more than others. For example, DiAngelo's (2018) argument of white fragility greatly emphasized notions of the differential role of whites relative to people of color. The bulk of her book is an exhortation to majority group members to confront their fragility generally by having whites listen and meet the concerns of marginalized racial minorities. On the other hand, Kendi (2019), unlike DiAngelo, acknowledges the existence of antiwhite racism. He places far greater priority on antiracism for everyone as a conduit to social change.

Simply because we found these four themes among antiracists does not mean that they all equally show up in primary antiracism texts. It may well be the case that certain antiracism literature focuses on certain themes to meet larger needs in the antiracism community. Our assessment of antiracism primary literature and assertion of these themes is focused on a holistic assessment of several sources with differing emphases of complementary antiracism ideals.

It is a mistake, however, to use the strong emphasis of DiAngelo on differential white/nonwhite responsibilities and Kendi on social change to argue that other themes of antiracism do not appear in their work. While DiAngelo focuses on the perception of whites, she also notes, "We can take action to address our own racism, the racism of other whites, and the racism embedded in our institutions.... We can get involved in organizations working for racial justice" (145). Clearly, DiAngelo is not limiting her antiracism goal to just listening to people of color but has expectations of larger social change as well. Furthermore, while Kendi does acknowledge the existence of antiwhite racism, he does not treat it the same way as anti-Black racism. Antiwhite racism is generally limited to racist ideals, while anti-Black racism includes institutional aspects, such as capitalism, which are not intrinsically tied to anti-Black hatred. Institutional elements that work to the disadvantage of whites are not to be seen as antiwhite racism (Kendi 2019). Kendi does operate out of a differential roles mindset for whites and nonwhites, even if he allows for the existence of antiwhite racism.

The academic framework discussed in the last chapter furthers our assessment of the themes of popularized antiracism. Evidence for all four themes can be found within the academic literature. Academics have written about racism as pervasive (Berman and Paradies 2010, Lentin 2011, Mukherjee 2016, Rabaka 2006), racism as multifaceted (Edirmanasinghe et al. 2022, Berman and Paradies 2010, Ford and Airhihenbuwa 2010), the distinct responsibilities of whites/nonwhites (Dei et al. 2005, De Lissovoy and Brown 2013, Blaisdell 2021, Srivastava 2005) and a desire for drastic social alterations (Zamalin 2019, Gillborn 2006, De Lissovoy and Brown 2013, Edirmanasinghe et al. 2022). The antiracism discussed in academic circles is more global in its outlook than popularized antiracism. Furthermore, postcolonial literature contains more discussion of the plight of non-Black marginalized racial and ethnic groups within academic antiracism than popularized antiracism. This should be expected since the rise in popularized antiracism was brought about by violence against African Americans in the United States. The trajectory of popularized antiracism, as it has moved from initial popularizing work (DiAngelo 2018, Kendi 2019, Saad 2020), has led to attention to some forms of non-Black oppression such as the Stop AAPI (Asian American and Pacific Islander) Hate campaign, but the core of popularized antiracism is more centered on anti-Black racism than the more varied interest expressed in academic antiracism. Differences between academic antiracism and popularized antiracism are more due to the context in which these philosophies have developed rather than qualitatively distinct values between the two expressions of antiracism.

Our analysis of the primary literature on popularized antiracism has resulted in basic definitions of the concept and four themes that, to varying degrees, are reflected by different foundational texts in the literature. However, it is not clear whether this framework is the same as the philosophy of antiracism that has enjoyed a rise in popularity over the past few years. In light of the emerging attention given to the notion of antiracism, and the willingness of individuals to promote notions of antiracism, it is valuable to learn if this framework is an accurate way to measure to what extent individuals in the United States conceptualize racial attitudes. With our identification of these themes, we can conduct empirical tests to discover if an index for antiracism is plausible. We now shift our focus to this empirical effort.

Constructing and Testing an Antiracism Attitude Scale

Measurement scales have commonly been used to measure concepts such as racial resentment (Kam and Burge 2018, Wilson and Davis 2011), right-wing authoritarianism (Altemeyer 1988, Zakrisson 2005, Whitley 1999), and social dominance orientation (Pratto et al. 1994, Ho et al. 2015). While these scales measure attitudes connected to racism, there is a need for instruments assessing those desiring to challenge the racial status quo and seek racial justice. Previous attempts to create an antiracist index include an indicator for states (Larson 2022), an index of generalized antiracism behavior (Pieterse, Utsey, and Miller 2016), a racial fragility scale for teachers (Knowles and Hawkman 2020), and an index of reflexive antiracism addressing the concerns of Indigenous Australians (Paradies 2016). There has also been a focus on creating a localized white fragility scale (Langrehr et al. 2021, Hill, Mannheimer, and Roos 2021). None of these efforts, however, attempt to develop an antiracism attitude scale using the concepts enunciated in popular antiracism literature beyond *White Fragility*, which is a text primarily targeted at a majority white audience. Such a scale would allow a researcher to better comprehend how the attitudes exhibited in a fuller body of that literature manifest themselves among potential antiracists.

Kinder and Sanders (1996) theorized that assessment of attitudes toward contemporary racial issues might be the best way to test for the principles of democracy needed to create a racial resentment scale. Efforts to construct indexes focusing on white fragility have relied on analysis of primary source material (Langrehr et al. 2021, Hill, Mannheimer, and Roos 2021). Likewise, we utilized our primary literature review to build an index on the themes of the pervasiveness of racism, the multifaceted nature of racism, the desire for societal overhaul, and differential roles for white and nonwhite people. We created items to test by using the concepts emerging from popularized antiracism literature. We also sought out items on existing surveys to see if they fit into one of the antiracism themes identified from our examination of primary literature. From this effort emerged 15 statements theoretically connected to antiracism ideals to construct a scale of antiracism attitudes. In 13 of these statements, respondents selected whether they "Strongly disagreed," "Disagreed," "Slightly disagreed," "Neither agreed nor disagreed," "Slightly agreed," "Agreed," or "Strongly agreed." These statements are:

1. It's really a matter of some people just not trying hard enough: if Blacks would only try harder they could be just as well off as whites. (TRY HARD)
2. Overall the group Black Lives Matter has been good for our country. (BLM)
3. America is basically a racist society. (RACIST SOCIETY)
4. A serious barrier to healthy race relations in the United States is that whites become defensive when confronted by information about racial injustice. (WHITE FRAGILITY)
5. An act can be racist even if a person did not intended it to be racist. (RACISM INTENT)
6. Most Blacks who receive money from welfare programs could get along without it if they tried. (WELFARE PROGRAMS)
7. The norms of white supremacy do not have much influence in the United States. (WHITE SUPREMACY)
8. People of color do not have any special insight on racial issues because they have experienced racism. (RACIAL INSIGHT)
9. Generations of slavery and discrimination have created conditions that make it difficult for Blacks to work their way out of the lower class. (SLAVERY)
10. Irish, Italian, Jewish, and many other minorities overcame prejudice and worked their way up. Blacks should do the same without any special favors. (SPECIAL FAVORS)
11. Government officials usually pay less attention to a request or complaint from a Black person than from a white person. (GOVERNMENT REQUEST)
12. Over the past few years, Blacks have gotten less than they deserve (BLACKS DESERVE)
13. A person can be a non-racist without actively fighting against racism. (NO NON-RACISTS)

The survey included another question: What do you think the chances are these days that a white person won't get a job or promotion while an equally or less qualified Black person gets one instead? (UNQUALIFIED BLACK).

> Respondents selected whether they thought that these chances are "Very likely," "Likely," "Slightly likely," "Neither likely nor unlikely," "Slightly unlikely," "Unlikely," or "Very unlikely."

The survey asked one final question: Some people say that because of past discrimination, Blacks should be given preference in hiring and promotion. Others say that such preference in hiring and promotion of Blacks is wrong because it discriminates against whites. What about your opinion—are you for or against preferential hiring and promotion of Blacks? (PREFERENTIAL HIRING).

> Respondents selected whether they "Strongly favor," "Favor," "Slightly favor," "Not favor or unfavor," "Slightly unfavor," "Unfavor," or "Strongly unfavor" such preference.[4]

We cannot, however, be certain that these statements are related to a central concept. Theoretically, the thematic characteristics discussed in the previous paragraph show up in these statements. RACIST SOCIETY, RACISM INTENT, WHITE SUPREMACY, NO NON-RACISTS, SLAVERY, and BLACKS DESERVE can speak to the pervasive nature of racism in the United States. PREFERENTIAL HIRING and GOVERNMENT REQUEST can reflect the potential multifaceted nature of racism. BLM and SPECIAL FAVORS can reflect desires to overhaul society.[5] Differential requirements for white and nonwhite people can be exhibited in TRY HARD, QUALIFIED BLACK, WHITE FRAGILITY, and RACIAL INSIGHT. Some statements likely reflect multiple themes, as the potential linking to multiple characteristics in a cognitive construct is expected if those characteristics are connected to the larger construct. Given our focus on popularized antiracism, a strong index emerging from these statements can preliminarily be defined as an antiracism attitude scale built upon a popularized ideal. This index can in-

---

4. TRY HARD, WELFARE PROGRAMS, WHITE SUPREMACY, RACIAL INSIGHT, SPECIAL FAVORS, NO NON-RACISTS, QUALIFIED BLACK, and PREFERENTIAL HIRING are reversed coded in the analysis.

5. BLM has advocated efforts such as defunding the police (Waldron 2020, Sinanan 2020) and abolishing ICE (U.S. Immigration and Customs Enforcement) (Nishiyama 2022, McKanders 2020). It is not clear how much average individuals know of such revolutionary efforts, but individuals highly committed to antiracism are likely to have such knowledge and use that knowledge in their calculation of whether to accept BLM.

dicate the powerful potential of a common central concept linking the different themes identified in the earlier portion of this chapter.

Since we had 15 statements to assess, it was not viable to fund a national probability sample to test all 15 statements. However, if we identified a fraction of the statements that fit into a larger construct, then we would be able to test a smaller set of statements with a national sample. We used convenience samples for this task. A survey with these statements was administered to two groups of paid respondents. One group was found through Amazon Mechanical Turk and the other through Survey Monkey. Amazon Mechanical Turk has been criticized for not producing diverse samples (Chandler et al. 2019); however, there is evidence that Amazon Mechanical Turk is valid for psychological research on political ideology (Clifford, Jewell, and Waggoner 2015). Nonetheless, it is advisable to include respondents from a second source whenever possible, so a sample was collected through Survey Monkey. Amazon Mechanical Turk differs from Survey Monkey in that Survey Monkey's respondents tend to be slightly older and have higher socioeconomic status (SES) than average. Survey Monkey's respondents are more highly educated than the general public. Bentley, Daskalova, and White (2017) find that surveys using Amazon Mechanical Turk and Survey Money tend to underrepresent females. However, they also found that the error rate of Amazon Mechanical Turk and Survey Monkey panels was under 10%, although it could be higher than 5%.[6] If an index fitting both groups could be created, then we would have more confidence that the statements' relationship to each other is not uniquely tied to a given sample.

Respondents were not asked demographic questions since the goal at this stage was to assess the relationship of the statements to each other, and more questions incurred additional costs. We ignored demographic assessments given the inability of this sample to be used to generalize group differences to the larger population and make assertions about the demographic makeup of supporters of antiracism. The Amazon Mechanical Turk sample began with 207 respondents and produced 200 completed surveys. The Survey Monkey sample began with 206 respondents and produced 197 completed surveys. The statements TRY HARD, WELFARE PROGRAMS, WHITE SUPREMACY, PREFERENTIAL HIRING, RACIAL INSIGHT, SPECIAL FAVORS, and NO NON-RACISTS were reverse coded so that for these statements, higher scores are theoretically correlated to higher levels of antiracism. The

---

6. An error rate between 5% and 10% would be unacceptable for making definite generalizable claims about differences between groups, but for testing the relationships of statements in an index, this error rate is less of an issue. This error rate is notably less problematic if the relations between those statements hold up with both panels, as demographic differences exist between respondents from Amazon Mechanical Turk and Survey Monkey.

means and standard deviation for all 15 statements are in Table 3.1. Higher numbers predict higher theoretical general public support for potential elements of popularized antiracism. RACISM INTENT and RACIAL INSIGHT have the highest mean scores. Among the respondents, there is broad agreement that acts can be racist even if that is not the intent and that people of color have insights into racism that whites do not have. At the other end of the spectrum, NO NON-RACISTS, PREFERENTIAL HIRING, and SPECIAL FAVORS had the lowest means. It is plausible that remedies relying

TABLE 3.1 MEANS AND STANDARD DEVIATIONS OF ANTIRACISM STATEMENTS			
	Amazon Mechanical Turk N = 200	Survey Monkey N = 197	Total N = 397
TRY HARD*	4.245 2.168	5.358 1.7486	4.783 2.05
BLM	4.33 2.246	4.465 2.118	4.395 2.184
RACIST SOCIETY	4.485 1.829	4.69 1.784	4.584 1.808
QUALIFIED BLACK*	4.305 1.769	4.326 1.728	4.315 1.747
WHITE FRAGILITY	4.485 1.934	5.064 1.558	4.765 1.783
RACISM INTENT	5.265 1.637	5.401 1.358	5.331 1.508
WELFARE* PROGRAMS	4.285 1.942	4.77 1.798	4.519 1.887
WHITE SUPREMACY*	4.525 2.0	5.096 1.76	4.801 1.907
PREFERENTIAL HIRING*	3.655 1.966	3.754 1.676	3.703 1.83
RACIAL INSIGHT*	5.015 1.836	5.246 1.577	5.127 1.718
SLAVERY	4.67 2.155	4.738 1.89	4.703 2.029
SPECIAL FAVORS*	3.86 2.201	4.497 1.782	4.168 2.032
GOVERNMENT REQUEST	4.445 2.009	4.813 1.597	4.623 1.829
BLACKS DESERVE	4.645 2.054	5.005 1.818	4.819 1.95
NO NON-RACISTS*	2.44 1.448	3.075 1.494	2.747 1.502
Note: Means are entries; standard deviations in italics; * reverse coded to indicate theoretical higher support for racially progressive attitudes			

on directly targeting people of color for resources have lower overall support than other antiracism measures. Furthermore, there also is low support for the idea that a person who is not actively fighting racism is a racist.

While there are various ways indexes can be created, factor analysis has recently become a common way to construct indexes as it allows for more rigorous statistical inference than other techniques, such as principal component analysis (Stanojević and Benčina 2019). Exploratory factor analysis allows for the identification of critical constructs that connect variables into common sets (Fabrigar and Wegener 2011). Exploratory factor analysis can be used to "reverse engineer" the discovery of variables theorized to represent a given social construct. The technical details of this analysis can be seen in the appendix. Five core statements—BLM, WHITE FRAGILITY, GOVERNMENT REQUEST, SLAVERY, and BLACKS DESERVE—loaded high enough to warrant future consideration. Two other statements warranting further consideration are WHITE SUPREMACY and RACIST SOCIETY. Since they were close to missing the cutoff criteria, it is advisable to continue to examine the usefulness of these variables. However, from this point forward, we drop all consideration of any of the other statements as useful in constructing a popularized antiracism attitude scale. Indeed, further testing of these variables indicated that at this stage of the research, it is possible to construct either a five- or seven-item index. However, for reasons we discuss in the next chapter and the appendix, the five-item scale proves to be the stronger index.

If BLM represents a desire to overhaul society, WHITE FRAGILITY represents differential responsibilities, GOVERNMENT REQUEST represents the multifaceted nature of racism, and SLAVERY/BLACKS DESERVE represent the pervasive nature of racism, then all four themes documented in the exploration of the primary literature are theoretically represented in the final index. It can be argued that this linking to those themes is subjective as these items may be linked to multiple themes. However, it is reasonable to interpret these themes as representing some degree of inclusion of the major themes found in the primary literature, which is expected if these themes are part of a more extensive cognitive framework within an antiracism community. The items that barely missed the criteria for the index (WHITE SUPREMACY and RACIST SOCIETY) are theoretically linked to the notion of the pervasiveness of racism. Combined with the fact that the pervasiveness of racism theme was the only one with multiple items in the index, a belief in the pervasiveness of racism might be a central concept that is more important than other themes within popularized antiracism.

We need to be certain that the construct we have statistically confirmed does measure what we think it measures, which is popularized antiracism. Our construct may measure other types of racialized attitudes or perhaps just certain political ideals that happen to be connected to racial concepts. To get at this question, this index must be assessed qualitatively as respondents must be free to articulate what these statements mean to them. One acceptable method that has been previously used (Jardina 2019) is to ask the respondent why they answered the questions the way they did. We sent out an open-ended questionnaire through Survey Monkey, targeting political progressives who are theoretically more supportive of antiracism. The questionnaire included each question and gave the respondents space to remark on the rationale for their answers. We eliminated respondents who wrote gibberish or were merely repeating the same statement so they could get credit for completing the survey. Concentrating on those who scored high on the scale (at least 40 on a scale of 49)[7] allowed us to see if their reasoning was in line with themes found in the primary literature. Among those individuals, we discovered elements suggesting recognition of the pervasiveness and multifaceted nature of racism, as well as a desire for societal overhaul and a recognition of the responsibilities of majority group members to fight against racism. Each of the four themes showed up in the answers of at least a third of the respondents (n = 31) who provided usable, qualitative answers.

For example, illustrating the notion of the pervasiveness of racism, a female over 60 responded to WHITE SUPREMACY with the comment, "Trump made being a racist seem 'normal.' It is Wrong!" A male aged between 30 and 44 commented, "America is racist underneath it all. It is still there."[8] A female age aged between 45 and 60 remarked, "An environment of oppression has been created." These are representative comments indicating that those who scored high on the scale perceive racism as the normal state of American society. This perception is also tied to how they answered the questions in the survey, particularly the RACIST SOCIETY and SLAVERY questions, although evidence of this perception can be seen in examples of all seven statements that are under consideration. Beliefs about the prevalence of racism can impact how individuals answer the popularized antiracism index.

There is also evidence that concerns how the multifaceted nature of racism can shape answers to the statements in the index as well. In response to the GOVERNMENT REQUEST statement, a female over 60 stated that "Inner City conditions, bad faith financial transactions, 'red lining' housing opportunities—the list grew, and certainly survives." A male aged between 30 and 44 responded to that question by contending, "To me, it's very evident

---

7. We included open-ended answers from WHITE SUPREMACY and RACIST SOCIETY due to the closeness they come to being placed in the final index and to maximize the qualitative data collected for the analysis.

8. Survey Monkey automatically collects information about age and gender for free, allowing us to offer this information for further context on the respondents without using additional questions.

in the prison complex in America. Officials seem to not take at all seriously when black people are imprisoned wrongly, but there will be a whole media circus and to-do if the same thing happens to a white person." Thus, the question about the government allowed respondents opportunities to comment on the different manifestations of institutional racism in society. However, this was not the only statement where institutional racism showed up in respondents' comments. A male over 60 revealed the idea of the multifaceted nature of racism in response to RACIST SOCIETY with the comment, "There is still racism: unfair treatment of black people for the same crimes as whites commit, valuing homes for less, high costs of education, as some examples." In response to the SLAVERY statement, a male over 60 stated, "History of discrimination, fewer opportunities for good education, including elementary school through college, fewer opportunities for home ownership." We see, in response to the BLACKS DESERVE question, a female aged between 30 and 44 reflecting the idea that African Americans continue to suffer in multifaceted ways by stating, "Many, even today, are still denied basic human rights such as access to good healthcare, safe living spaces, etc." The index provides an opportunity to touch on the same issues of institutional racism and concern to deal with the multifaceted nature of racism that is taught in much of the popularized antiracism literature.

Concerning the need for social change, the BLACKS DESERVE statement has proven to be quite useful. In response to that statement, a male aged between 30 and 44 stated, "It will take a lot more action to eliminate the generational wealth gap caused by centuries of oppression." A female over 60 argued that "BLM was finally brought to the limelight, making more aware of the problem, but the actions to remedy have been slow to change." Although the BLM statement did not produce a lot of answers on social change, respondents who commented on social change did at times refer to the BLM movement in ways that indicated their desire for greater social change. For example, a male aged between 18 and 29 commented in response to the BLACK DESERVE statement that "the Black Lives Matter movement a couple of years ago was mostly met with empty gestures and no real change to make black people feel less afraid of their lives." While BLM did not prove to be the best statement to allow respondents to comment on societal change, there is evidence that respondents associate BLM with efforts to alter society. A different group of respondents might have used BLM rather than BLACK DESERVE to express a desire for social change. Nonetheless, BLACK DESERVE is not the only statement where this desire manifests itself, as a female aged 30–44 commented on the SLAVERY question, "Most black people live in inner cities where education is minimal and there are no resources to help them get out of poverty. Capitalism and racism squash down the potential for improvement." Furthermore, a male aged between 45 and 60 made it known in the

WHITE FRAGILITY question that he was dissatisfied with inadequate attempts at social change, arguing that "whites like to point out token gestures as societal norms when they are not." Respondents found the statements in the index useful for allowing them to state their desire for more than superficial social alteration. These answers also suggest that the uncaring attitudes of majority group members are a barrier to the social change that the respondents believe needs to occur.

Finally, WHITE FRAGILITY proved to be useful in allowing the respondents to express the different roles and expectations placed on whites and nonwhites. For example, a female aged 30–44 stated, "White people still find a way to make themselves the center of the conversation that should focus on Black people and their experiences." A male over 60 responded to that statement by arguing that "whites think they are non racist and don't want to deal with inherent biases and prejudices, so they are not open to learning new information about themselves and trying to change." WHITE SUPREMACY also proved to be useful in allowing respondents to focus on the responsibility of whites. In response to that statement, a male aged 45 to 60 commented, "All white people have racist opinions. They were taught to hate when younger." A female aged between 30 and 44 remarked, "Whites control everything. They have the power." Of course, the perception of differential responsibilities did come up in other statements as well. For example, in response to SLAVERY, a male aged between 30 and 44 stated, "Just look at the facts, it affects the mindset of the oppressed and oppressor for generations." Either through WHITE FRAGILITY and WHITE SUPREMACY or other statements, the respondents' ideas about differential responsibilities between whites and nonwhites can impact the responses to the index. The respondents indicate that whites have responsibilities to learn about racism and overcome their own racism. Thus, they mimic the attitudes on the responsibility of whites as stated in the primary antiracism texts.

We note the potential selection bias, as these respondents had financial incentives. Since they were paid for providing an answer but not for providing a long answer, answers may be shorter in general. Yet, even with short, undeveloped answers, the themes of antiracism showed up often in their answers, although often expressed in fragmented and incomplete ways. Further research may utilize a method, such as in-depth interviews, designed to provide more substantive elaborations on the qualitative attitudes of antiracists to the statements in the index. However, these answers do provide us with a quick peek into the minds of the respondents and allow us to see how they connect the ideals of popularized antiracism to the statements laid out in the index. In combination with the face validity of the questions used, there is good reason to believe that this index captures the general ideas promoted in primary popularized antiracism literature.

Conclusion

We have recognized a set of popularized antiracist teachings. The supporters of these teachings use the term "antiracism" to describe them. Based on our interpretation of these ideas, we developed and tested a series of statements that represent antiracism. Our quantitative tests indicate that anywhere from five to seven of these statements are viable to be included in an index. We gathered qualitative information on how individuals with high levels of agreement with antiracism interpret these statements. We found that their interpretation confirms our belief that these statements reflect attitudes toward acceptance of this popularized antiracism. Based on our quantitative and qualitative analysis, we are comfortable arguing that we have a viable index that can measure popularized antiracism in modern society. In Chapter 4, we provide evidence that this index of popularized antiracism is useful for making a global assessment of antiracism and that the findings we documented hold up to analysis when examining a national probability sample.

4

Who Is an Antiracist?

When we fail to have systematic evidence about social groups, it is easy to develop stereotypes about them. Stereotypes are not necessarily false, as there is work indicating that stereotypes can fairly accurately reflect social reality (McCauley, Jussim, and Lee 1995, Jussim 2017). However, stereotypes often lead to distortions about members of those social groups and can be used to justify the mistreatment and dehumanization of social groups (Loughnan et al. 2014, Boysen, Chicosky, and Delmore 2020, Angermeyer and Matschinger 2005, Lee et al. 2015). Perusing social and traditional media can produce a broad range of stereotypes about antiracists: "woke" agitators (Loury 2022, Stepman 2020), Marxist revolutionaries (Rufo 2021, Loyola 2021), those who deeply care about social justice and promoting equality (Sewing 2022, Toombs 2022), and those who are compassionate about the marginalized (Sangillo 2019). It is not possible to fully vet such perspectives in an initial systematic assessment of antiracists; however, we can provide background information about the characteristics of antiracists. In this chapter, we investigate the social and demographic characteristics of antiracists and some of their social attitudes. With this information, we will be in a better position to assess the nature of antiracism and those who hold to such beliefs in the United States, relying on data rather than social stereotypes.

Previous work has attempted to characterize those who identify as antiracists (Perry, Frantz, and Grubbs 2021). However, we are exploring the characteristics of those who believe the contemporary popularized notions of antiracism, even if they do not identify as antiracist. Regardless of whether individuals self-identify as antiracists, if they embody the same philosophy as popularized antiracism, then it is likely that they will use this antiracism philosophy to construct their ideas about society and even their own social identity. Popularized antiracism can play a prominent role in how individuals envision their role in society and the way they attempt to address racism, even if they reject the term "antiracism" to describe themselves.

There are theoretical reasons why certain individuals are more likely to accept antiracist ideals compared to others. Given that antiracism is a philosophy intended to advocate for people of color, it is reasonable to assert that people of color would be comparatively supportive of antiracism. Previous research indicates that political conservatives tend to emphasize individualistic attributions and downplay the role of structural issues regarding racial realities (Kantack and Paschall 2022, Kluegel 1990, Toosi, Layous, and Reevy 2021). Given that antiracists perceive racism as multifaceted, including both individualistic and structural components, political ideology is highly likely to reflect who supports antiracism. Racial ideology and political orientation are likely the two strongest predictors of antiracism.

There is evidence indicating that education is associated with more progressive racial attitudes (Jardina 2019, Hainmueller and Hiscox 2010, Forman and Lewis 2015, Taylor and Crews 2021). Yet this evidence has generally focused upon assessment of expressions of racial animosity or colorblindness rather than support of progressive racial attitudes. Bonilla-Silva (2006) suggests that working-class whites, rather than highly educated whites, are more likely to be racially progressive. Sikkink and Emerson (2008) show that, among whites, education is linked to claims of racial acceptance but not actions of racial acceptance. It is plausible that the more highly educated are more vulnerable to social desirability effects when asked about racial issues. Education may be linked to lower levels of racial conservatism if the highly educated define racial conservatism as a form of racism, but that does not mean that the highly educated have higher levels of racial radicalism or antiracist attitudes.

While it is reasonable to envision people of color, political progressives, and the highly educated as supporters of antiracism, we cannot have confidence in such assertions without data. Now that we have an established mechanism to assess who supports antiracism, we can assess common social and demographic characteristics of an antiracist and which attitudes are linked to antiracist beliefs. The placement of the antiracism attitude scale in a survey with a national probability sample provides information on those social and demographic factors. To the degree that the survey also provides questions on the social and political attitudes of the respondents, we gain an opportunity to learn about the type of attitudes antiracists possess beyond the assertions directly assessed in the antiracism attitude scale.

We worked with the Chapman Survey of American Fears, an annual survey conducted by Christopher Bader (Chapman University Earl Babbie Research Center 2022), that assesses the fears of Americans. We placed the five core statements of the antiracism attitude scale and one of the supplemental statements in this survey. Given that the survey inquires about basic social and demographic factors, we can now assert the typical characteristics of an antiracist. The survey also asks questions about the fears of the respondents and the respondents' attitudes toward certain social and political issues. While these questions are not exhaustive, they will provide a preliminary assessment of the type of social attitudes antiracists tend to possess. This is an initial opportunity to gain systematic information that allows researchers to understand who is an antiracist and how they may tend to consider racial and other social/political issues.

Use of the Chapman Survey of American Fears to Study Antiracists

In 2014, Chapman University conducted wave 1 of the American Fears Survey. The official goal of the study is "to collect annual data on the fears, worries, and concerns of Americans, the personal, behavioral and attitudinal characteristics related to those fears, and how those fears are associated with other attitudes and behaviors" (Chapman University Earl Babbie Research Center 2022). The data was collected by SQL Server Reporting Services (SSRS), a full-service survey and market research firm. The data was collected with online-based probability panels. SSRS Opinion Panel members are recruited randomly based on nationally representative ABS (address-based sampling) design (including Hawaii and Alaska). Additionally, the SSRS Opinion Panel has recruited some hard-to-reach demographic groups via random-digit dialing telephone sample. Wave 8 was conducted between April 5 and 15, 2022, totaling 1,020 surveyed respondents.

Working with Chapman University, we were able to include six questions based on the antiracism attitude scale in wave 8 of the survey. We included the five core statements found in the last chapter that loaded the highest on the antiracism attitude scale when we tested it with the purchased samples and WHITE SUPREMACY. Because there was a potential problem with agreement bias, BLM was reconstructed to read, "Overall, the Black Lives Matter (BLM) movement has been bad for the United States." WHITE SUPREMACY is already written to counter agreement bias. Thus, it is possible to test

TABLE 4.1 FACTOR LOADINGS OF CHAPMAN SURVEY OF AMERICAN FEARS

	1	2
BLM	.652	.679
WHITE FRAGILITY	.772	.769
WHITE SUPREMACY	–	.602
SLAVERY	.863	.858
GOVERNMENT REQUEST	.829	.823
BLACKS DESERVE	.856	.845
Contribution	3.185	3.543
Total variation	63.99	59.042
Cronbach's alpha	.894	.893

Source: Chapman Survey of American Fears
Notes: N = 1,018
Principal axis factoring after varimax rotation

the viability of WHITE SUPREMACY as a potential inclusion to the antiracism attitude scale and gain further information about whether the scale may be troubled by agreement bias. Whether the five- or six-item scale measures antiracism more accurately can determine which scale should be used for the remainder of the book. The varimax loadings of these variables can be seen in Table 4.1.[1]

In the five-item model, all items loaded at 0.6 or higher. The general requirements for including the variables in an index are met as the variance explained is 63.99 and Cronbach's alpha is 0.894. In the six-item model, WHITE SUPREMACY loads at 0.602, which is lower than the other variables but still a high loading of the latent construct. Furthermore, the general requirements for including the variables in the six-item index are again met as the variance explained is 59.042 and Cronbach's alpha is 0.893. It is reasonable to consider the variables in either the five- or six-item models as suitable for an index. It is worth noting that the inclusion of two reversed-coded statements does not ruin the reliability of the antiracism attitude scale. While the original five-item core used in the convenience samples can be criticized for having a potential pro-agreement bias, that is not a concern for the scales moving forward. However, since the five-item scale explains slightly more variance than the six-item model, we use the five-item scale for the remainder of the book. Future research may continue to test a six- or even seven-item scale to assess if there are situations where they offer advantages over the five-item scale.

---

1. Promax rotation resulted in the same coefficients as the varimax rotation, and thus there is no need to report the results of that test.

The responses to the statements in the CSAF were truncated in comparison to the statements in the two purchase samples discussed in Chapter 3 so that respondents could only answer "Strongly agree," "Agree," "Disagree," or "Strongly disagree." This produced a scale of five questions with four ordinal answers for an antiracism attitude scale that ran from 5 to 20. To assess the relative popularity of antiracism, we calculated the frequencies of the response to the different scores in the antiracism attitude scale. That calculation can be seen in Table 4.2. On a scale of 5 to 20, we found that the average score was 12.83, with a standard deviation of 4.054.[2] Since a midpoint on a scale of 5 to 20 is 12.5, it is fair to say that the popularity of antiracism is roughly the same level as the unpopularity of this ideology given that 46.5% of the respondents scored below the midpoint score. A score of 10 or below indicates that an individual scored no more than an average of 2 for each item on the scale. It is fair to envision such individuals as hostile to antiracism ideals, amounting to 30.0% of the survey respondents. A score of at least 15 indicated that a respondent averaged at least a 3 on a four-point scale. It is fair to envision such individuals as being particularly warm to antiracism ideals, and 37.7% of the respondents fit this category.

It is informative to compare the scores of the antiracism attitude scale to scales used to assess conservative social attitudes. For example, data from the Cooperative Election Study (Schaffner, Ansolavehere, and Luks 2021) allowed us to construct a racial resentment scale. The scale ranged from 5 to 25, with a midpoint of 15 and an average of 11.512. We found that 52.0% of the respondents scored below a score of 10, which represented an average of 2 for each item, 71.2% scored below the midpoint of 15, and only 11.1% scored above a score of 20, which represented averaging a 4 on a five-point scale.[3] We found that antiracism is more supported than racial resentment in the United States. Another example can be seen in the recent attention given to Christian nationalism (Seidel 2019, Whitehead and Perry 2020, Grace and Heins 2021). The 2022 Baylor Religion Study contains a Christian nationalism scale that

---

2. All data from the CSAF, whether in bivariate or multivariate analysis, are weighted using a sample selected from the SSRS Opinion Panel to provide nationally representative and projectable estimates of the U.S. noninstitutionalized civilian adult population 18 years of age and older. The first stage of the weighting was the application of a base weight to account for different probabilities of recruitment to the SSRS Opinion Panel. Next, a non-Internet propensity score adjustment, which models non-Internet households that are excluded from an online panel, was applied. In the final stage of weighting, sample demographics were post-stratified to match population parameters.

3. To make a clear comparison, a score of 20 on the 25-point racial resentment scale is comparable to a score of 16 on the 20-point antiracism attitude scale. The 21.6% of respondents who scored above 16 on the antiracism attitude scale is almost twice the 11.1% who scored above 20 on the racial resentment scale.

TABLE 4.2 FREQUENCY BREAKDOWN OF ANTIRACISM ATTITUDE SCALE

Scale score	Respondent number	Percent
5	41	4.0
6	40	3.9
7	43	4.2
8	42	4.1
9	54	5.4
10	86	8.4
11	91	8.9
12	77	7.6
13	79	7.8
14	82	8.1
15	107	10.5
16	66	6.5
17	63	6.2
18	43	4.2
19	58	5.7
20	46	4.5

Source: Chapman Survey of American Fears
Note: N = 1,018, mean = 12.83, standard deviation = 4.054

ranges from 6 to 30, with a midpoint of 18 and an average of 16.76. We found that 29.9% of the respondents scored below a score of 12, which represented an average of 2 for each item, 50.5% scored below the midpoint of 18, and only 12.0% scored above a score of 24, which represented averaging a 4 on a five-point scale.[4] While the percentage of individuals scoring low on the Christian nationalism scale is comparable to the percentage of individuals scoring low on the antiracism attitude scale, there is clearly a higher percentage of individuals in the upper ranges on the antiracism attitude scale than the Christian nationalism scale. Comparison of the scores from these scales to the antiracism attitude scale suggests that antiracism is more popular than racial resentment or Christian nationalism. Higher scores on the antiracism attitude scale speak to the relative popularity of antiracism in the United States currently.

The basic score of this particular sample suggests that there may be slightly more supporters of antiracism than detractors, but that is an assertion that should be made with care. First, while this is a carefully constructed panel

---

4. It is again reasonable to compare this percentage to the 21.6% who score above 16 on the antiracism attitude scale, which is almost twice the 12.0% on the Christian nationalism scale.

sample, it still has a margin of error of about 4% (Rapoport and Kline 2022). The difference between the percentage of those scoring high on the scale (15 or above) and those scoring lower on the scale (10 or below) is within that margin of error. Second, for reasons we go into in subsequent chapters, there is reason to believe that there is a natural limit on how high the support of antiracism can grow, as well as a floor below which it is unlikely to go. Third, it is possible that our finding is tied to the unique dynamics of this particular sample. We would have more confidence that antiracism supporters outnumber the detractors if additional national samples using the antiracism attitude scale make similar discoveries. Finally, these differences may be due to social desirability influences. It may simply be easier in modern society, especially after the racial unrest in 2020, to admit support for racially progressive attitudes than racially conservative attitudes, regardless of an individual's actual racial beliefs. Given these possibilities, our general assessment is that there is currently a basic parity between supporters and detractors of antiracism but that if one side has a numerical advantage, it is those who align themselves with antiracism.

Since the antiracism attitude scale is viable, we can use it to examine the basic characteristics of antiracists. The data for this examination can be found in Table 4.3. Upon initial examination, we find that those who hold antiracist beliefs fall along racial, political, and educational lines. For example, white respondents score lower on the antiracism attitude scale than Black respondents (11.765 v. 16.482: $p < .001$), Hispanic respondents (11.765 v. 13.87: $p < .001$), and those of other races (11.765 v. 13.473: $p < .001$). Political liberals (defined as those who are either extremely liberal or liberal) score higher than political moderates (defined as those who are slightly liberal, moderate, or slightly conservative) (16.183 v. 13.045: $p < .001$) and political conservatives (defined as those who are either extremely conservative or conservative) (16.183 v. 9.753: $p < .001$). Education matters, as those with a four-year degree score higher than those with only a high school diploma or lower (13.69 v. 12.348: $p < .05$), although not quite significantly higher than those with only some college (13.69 v. 12.476: $p < .1$). Our predictions about race, political ideology, and education hold up in bivariate measures.

Other characteristics also are related to support of antiracism. Females score higher than males (13.266 v. 12.305: $p < .001$). Age matters if we compare those 35 and under to the rest of the sample (14.386 v. 12.149: $p < .001$), but it does not matter much after we look at the youngest cohort. Those with higher incomes score lower on the antiracism attitude scale, as those in households making over $100,000 a year score lower than those in households making less than $50,000 a year, but the difference was not significant. Religion may have an impact given that self-identified Christians score significantly

TABLE 4.3 MEAN SCORE OF ANTIRACISM ATTITUDE SCALE BY SOCIAL AND DEMOGRAPHIC CATEGORIES

	Antiracists
Female	13.266 (509) *3.847*
Male	12.305 (493) *4.197*
White	11.765 (633) *3.999*
Black	16.482 (119) *2.903*
Hispanic	13.87 (174) *3.385*
Other race	13.473 (93) *3.481*
Age: 35 and under	14.386 (298) *3.717*
Age: 36–50	12.892 (220) *4.234*
Age: 51–70	11.695 (346) *3.963*
Age: 70 and over	12.094 (107) *3.564*
High school or less	12.348 (408) *3.799*
Some college but not bachelor's	12.476 (251) *4.201*
Bachelor's	13.169 (177) *4.198*
At least attended graduate school	14.075 (181) *4.001*
Household income: 50K or less	13.018 (541) *3.914*

(continued)

TABLE 4.3 MEAN SCORE OF ANTIRACISM ATTITUDE SCALE BY SOCIAL AND DEMOGRAPHIC CATEGORIES (continued)

	Antiracists
Household income: 50K–100K	12.701 (286) *4.06*
Household income: over 100K	12.48 (190) *4.407*
Political liberal	16.183 (188) *3.095*
Moderate or only leaning liberal or conservative	13.045 (584) *3.574*
Political conservative	9.753 (246) *3.503*
Christian	12.07 (525) *4.062*
Atheist/agnostic	14.664 (68) *4.095*
Non-Christian religion	14.744 (60) *3.676*
None (religion)	13.839 (242) *3.833*
Other (religion)	12.44 (81) *3.814*

Source: Chapman Survey of American Fears
Notes: Numerical estimates are unstandardized betas, standardized betas are in italics, standard errors in parentheses
N = 1,018

lower than atheists/agnostics (12.07 v. 14.664: $p < .001$), those of non-Christian faiths (12.07 v. 14.744: $p < .001$), and those who are considered the nones (12.07 v. 13.889: $p < .001$).[5]

It is valuable to ask if certain characteristics matter more than others. This cannot be determined simply by examination of frequencies since these char-

---

5. Religious nones are those who do not identify with any of the religious or even secular categories on the religious affiliation question. They are a growing group in the United States (Lipka 2015) but may not be easily categorized due to the heterogeneity within this group (Lim, MacGregor, and Putnam 2010).

acteristics are related to each other. For example, it is well known that atheists are more politically progressive than Christians (Schulzke 2013, Simmons 2019, Williamson and Yancey 2013). Thus, are the religious findings due to political differences? Or is it the case that religion has unique effects on acceptance of antiracism and thus it is these religious effects driving the political findings? With regression analysis, we controlled for certain variables to eliminate the impact of the relationship of other variables on acceptance of antiracist philosophy. While we cannot eliminate concerns about the directionality of how the variables interact with each other, we can determine which characteristics are most powerfully associated with antiracism attitudes.

We controlled for gender, age, racial identity, political viewpoint (whether liberal or conservative), education, income, religious identity, religious service attendance, and whether respondents believed the Bible to be the word of God. A full description of the methodology of the model, as well as the estimates, can be seen in the appendix. When we applied regression analysis, we found that the religious factors are no longer relevant, suggesting that the findings of religious effects in Table 3.1 are tied to other variables. A similar finding occurred with age, with its association with the antiracism attitude scale becoming insignificant in the regression model. Gender, racial identity, political viewpoint, education, and income are still significant.

While several variables were still significant, that does not mean that they had the same impact. When we examined which variables were most impactful, two clearly stood out—whether the respondent is an African American and whether the respondent is politically progressive. Intuitively, this may be seen even in the means of the different subgroups in Table 3.1. Note that the subgroups with the highest scores are Blacks (16.482) and political liberals (16.183).[6] The two groups with the lowest scores are whites (11.765) and political conservatives (9.753). It should not be a surprise that being an African American is a strong driver of acceptance of antiracism since much of the concerns that led to the recent interest in antiracism were situated with the murder of Black men. Indeed, it is tempting to argue that racial concerns should be the more powerful predictor of antiracism, and these results are evidence of that power. But is it truly the case that race is the best predictor given the power of political ideology?

---

6. Notably close are atheists (14.664) and those of non-Christian religions (14.744); however, dummy variables of these groups were not found to be significantly different in regression models. This nonsignificance may be tied to the relatively low number of respondents who fell into these categories, but we cannot completely eliminate the possibility that the high score of these groups is driven by the characteristics of those groups, especially their political propensities. This concern is heightened by the fact that the standardized betas of atheists are very low (0.02), suggesting that atheism may not have a uniquely powerful effect on antiracist attitudes.

We gain some clues to the relative power of political ideology and race from the means in Table 4.3. The difference between whites and Blacks on the antiracism attitude scale is 4.717 (16.482–11.765), while the difference between political conservatives and political liberals is 6.43 (16.183–9.753), and thus there is more variability based on political ideology than on race. Since the political categories were created by merging two categories (i.e., extreme liberal and liberal) instead of the most extreme category, even this spread of range does not capture the full variability of the political viewpoint variable. Indeed, looking only at those who identify as extremely liberal and those who identify as extremely conservative indicates a difference of 7.165 (16.59–9.425). The group most supportive of antiracism is not African Americans but those who identify as extreme liberals, although the difference is not statistically significant (16.59 v. 16.482: ns), and the group most likely to oppose antiracism is not whites but political conservatives (9.425 v. 11.765: $p < .001$).

Political viewpoint remains significant even after we fully adjust for other variables. The regression models indicate that political viewpoint has a larger effect size than identity as an African American,[7] and the t-score indicates that we have more assurance that the political viewpoint effect is present in the general population than the African American effect.[8] To be clear, the race effect is a strong predictor but comes second to political viewpoint. The information in bivariate and multivariate analysis suggests that the political ideology effect is simply a little more powerful than a very strong race effect. If we want a targeted prediction of the strongest supporters of antiracism, it would be African American political progressives. Consequently, white political conservatives would be the strongest opposers of antiracism.

There is a correlation between African American identity and political viewpoint that is significant but relatively weak ($r = 0.103$). This suggests that while race and political ideology do impact each other, there are distinct ways they impact support for antiracism. In theory, this is sensible. Given that modern popularized antiracism developed in light of the concerns of African Americans, they are likely the greatest beneficiaries of the values espoused in antiracism. There are likely direct material, cultural, and social benefits for African Americans if the ideals of antiracism are implemented. For example, efforts that antiracists make to address structural racism should make it easier for African Americans to overcome racialized barriers and should enable them to obtain and hold middle- and upper-class jobs. Group interest theory (Oh et al. 2010, Katz and Taylor 2013) suggests that even if a particular African American does not perceive an individual benefit from the application of antiracism ideology, this individual will still support antiracism

---

7. The standardized beta for political progressive is larger than for Black (0.479 v. 0.276).
8. The t-score for political viewpoint is larger than for Black identity (17.462 v. 10.562).

since his or her race as a group will benefit. There is nearly universal acceptance of the tenets of antiracism among Blacks in the CSAF sample. Of the 119 African Americans in the weighted sample, only 16, or 5.1%, scored below the midpoint of 12.5 on the scale.

However, there is also nearly universal acceptance of antiracism among extreme liberals. Of the 45 respondents who identified as extreme liberals in the weighted sample, only 4, or 8.0%, scored below the midpoint of 12.5 on the scale. Clearly, they do not have the same racialized material or social motivations as African Americans, as only 3 of the 45 respondents are Black.[9] If political progressives are not supporting antiracism due to material benefit, and yet they are at least as supportive of antiracism as African Americans, then it is worth considering why this is the case. Since the answer is not as straightforward as it is for African Americans, we spend a little time in the next section speculating on why political progressives are such powerful supporters of antiracism.

Why Political Progressives May Support Antiracism

It is noteworthy that political identity is such a powerful predictor of acceptance of antiracism, given that antiracism is a radical philosophy that may not be fully accepted by moderate political liberals. It is unlikely that political progressives, particularly those who are non-Hispanic white, seek to gain economically from antiracism. However, there may be ways they obtain a cultural, identity, or political benefit from their support of antiracism. Theories about the culture war indicate a potential cultural benefit that political progressives may enjoy. Identity benefits suggest that political progressives may have incentives to create a social identity that separates them from social groups they reject. Finally, a desire to defeat political enemies and advance their political interests may provide political benefits for political progressives. This section looks at these potential benefits one at a time. At this point, we do not make an assertion about which set of benefits is more likely to be relevant in explaining the support of antiracism by political progressives, in part because it is likely that all three sets of benefits may work together to produce support for antiracism among political progressives. Nonetheless, there is value in this speculation as it allows us to consider factors beyond economic or materialistic gain to explain support for antiracism. However,

---

9. To be certain, whites are underrepresented among those identifying as extremely liberal relative to the rest of the sample, as only 26 of the 45 respondents, or 57.78%, are white. However, there is not a significant difference between the white and nonwhite individuals identifying as extreme liberals in the antiracism attitude scale (16.933 v. 16.339: ns), although we lack the statistical power to detect a moderate or small effect since the prior power of this assessment is only .5869.

we end this section by also looking at the possible economic benefits that some political progressives may receive from supporting antiracism.

Hunter (1992) argued for the existence of a culture war that generally pits a traditional view of family, sexuality, and reproductive choice against a modern view. Cultural progressives generally support more access to abortion and alternative family structures, such as same-sex families. Cultural traditionalists, generally seen as conservative Christians, often oppose these social innovations. Generally, this culture war has been fought on issues of sexuality and reproduction; issues that are used in the cultural battle may have expanded to include racial concerns (Hunter 2018). This may be possible due to the association of conservative Christianity with notions of whiteness, which has been observed in both academic (E. Miller 2020, Migliori 2022, Pindi and De La Garza 2018, Razack 2021) and public writings (Luo 2020, Jones 2020, Wallace 2021). If the opponents to the modernist positions in a culture war can be tied to accusations of racism, they become easier to defeat. This possibility may motivate political progressives to be highly supportive of antiracism in contrast with what can be interpreted as racist reactions by their cultural opponents.

A second, but related, possible answer to what political progressives gain from their support of antiracism is found in theories of identity construction. Humans form social identities to meet important socio-psychological needs (Postmes et al. 2013, Duveen and Lloyd 1986, Encheva 2017). A key way such identities are constructed is by the formation of the outgroup (Ting-Toomey 2005, Voci 2006). Outgroups provide examples perceived as dysfunctional behaviors and values to the ingroup. Outgroups allow individuals to define themselves by stating qualities they reject, and thus they identify as being the opposite of those qualities. In establishing an outgroup, a social identity is strengthened, and members of a social group gain more confidence in the values they espouse. The culture war clearly shows one way in which political progressives separate themselves from their outgroups. They define themselves as supportive of women and sexual minorities while envisioning their opponents as bigots. In the framework of meeting the needs of social identity, this definition is not necessarily to win a culture war but provides confidence for political progressives that they have a valued social identity.

In defining their opponents as bigots, political progressives can perceive themselves as the opposite of bigots in qualities such as tolerance. There are reasons to believe that political progressives strongly value tolerance as part of their social identity (Yancey and Quosigk 2021, Ford 2005, Miller, Brewer, and Arbuckle 2009, Fagelson 2002). The place of tolerance within the social identity of political progressives does not have to be limited to issues of gender and sexuality. Such tolerance would also reflect how they approach racial issues. In popular culture, the notion of antiracism is generally set against notions of racism or insensitivity toward racial minorities. Antiracism can be seen as an example of racial tolerance. If this social interpretation of antiracism is correct, antiracism would become a philosophy that naturally attracts political progressives since it appeals to their desire to identify as socially tolerant.

Third, the simple reality of political competition may drive the desire of political progressives to accept antiracism. Political groups have an incentive to seek out allies to promote their political causes (Hojnacki 1997, Cigler, Loomis, and Nownes 2015). To this extent, it is plausible that political progressives are eager to recruit African Americans and other people of color to support their political efforts. Additional allies will come at minimal costs for political progressives if the demands made by their new allies do not conflict with their general political goals. Indeed, the focus of antiracism on equality and proactive government response to social problems may fit well with the general philosophies of political progressives (Flanagan 2016, Feigenbaum and Henig 1997, Henderson 2009, Kelman 1999, Verba and Orren 1985). African Americans were supporting political progressives before the advent of antiracism, and thus the tying together of concerns for African Americans and progressive political identity did not develop with the emergence of antiracism. The acceptance of antiracism as it emerged into the political and social environment has simply become the price political progressives are willing to pay to keep the support of African Americans. In this sense, the political competition explanation is simply a continuation of the long-standing political arrangement that African Americans and political progressives have worked out over the past several decades.

Finally, although the benefits of antiracism philosophy are theoretically very tangible for marginalized racial groups, there may be practical benefits for certain segments of political progressives. McGhee (2022) contends that many of the mechanisms that disproportionately harm people of color, such as lending practices, health care delivery systems, and hiring norms, work against non-elite whites. If political progressives speak for non-elite whites, then they may support antiracism not only for racial minorities but also for those disempowered whites. Antiracism may represent an overarching ideology that transcends racial concerns and is linked to concerns for the general marginalized. Theories of intersectionality (Clarke and McCall 2013, Brah and Phoenix 2004) indicate that social disadvantages are not limited to a single dimension. It is possible that an awareness of, and concern about, racism can make it more likely for individuals to develop concern about the effects of other forms of stratification. The desire to confront prejudice and societal discrimination in all its forms may be a key attraction for political progressives, especially if they perceive themselves to be the victims of such discrimination. Since antiracism may reflect the general efforts to combat the ways our social hierarchy impacts marginalized racial groups, there may be benefits gained by other marginalized social groups. Political progressive subcultures may be the social location for those who will gain from an overhaul of a current social system supporting the vested interest of the powerful.

These possible rationales are not mutually exclusive. Rather, we think of them as supportive of each other. Combatants of a specific culture war can often become opponents in our larger political struggles. Those political struggles can pit beneficiaries of our current stratified society against those victimized on issues of race as well as other categories. The need for a social identity of tolerance can provide an incentive for individuals to engage in cultural and political battles. We currently lack the resources to thoroughly disentangle the different ways these rationales overlap and relate to each other, but we suspect that such overlapping is a feature of the reasons political progressives are supportive of popularized antiracism.

What about Political Conservatives?

Our focus has been on political progressives as the major supporters of antiracism. However, it is also notable to examine the role of political conservatives. Rather than ambivalence, we find that political conservatives are generally opposed to notions of antiracism, such as racism being pervasive and multifaceted, social change, and differential roles for white and nonwhites. It is not lost on us that the scores in Table 4.3 indicate a greater distance between political conservatives and whites in general at the bottom end of the antiracism attitude scale than between Blacks and political progressives at the upper end of the antiracism attitude scale. Political viewpoint may be more explanatory of why people reject antiracism than why individuals support this philosophy.

Support for antiracism has been associated with activism, but this can also be the case for those who oppose antiracism. The recent social and political hostilities surrounding critical race theory are an example of the passion of political conservatives. Antiracism can be seen as a derivative of critical race theory, but it is not synonymous with critical race theory. However, what is true in the academic realm may not be true in the public arena. For example, a primary document from a conservative think tank reveals the use of accusations of promoting critical race theory to oppose the implementation of popularized antiracism works such as those by DiAngelo and Kendi (Manhattan Institute 2021). In the minds of many Americans, critical race theory and antiracism are seen as identical. Much of the agitation in school board meetings (Oxford Analytica 2021, Kamenetz 2021) and resistance to diversity training in other contexts (D. Hamilton 2022) can be seen as politically conservative activism against antiracism. Just as one can argue that support for antiracism drives the passions and social identities of some political progressives, opposition to antiracism drives the passions and identities of some political conservatives.

Despite the important role political conservatives play in shaping the place of antiracism in the United States, we focus on political progressives for a key reason. Our purpose is to understand the nature of support for antiracism. While there are abundant empirical efforts to examine racial conservatives or even racists (Jardina 2019, Fields 2001, Garner 2007, Bonilla-Silva 2013, Jensen 2005, Picca and Feagin 2020, O'Brien et al. 2013, Hage 2012, Jones 2021, J. Sanchez 2018), there is a dearth of literature examining the perspectives of race among progressives. The development and implementation of the antiracism attitude scale provide us with a unique opportunity to partially fill that research niche. Ideally, in the future, there will be other efforts to use the antiracism attitude scale to better understand those who oppose antiracism; however, that is not the focus of this current research effort.

Does Education Matter?

We speculated that education might increase support for antiracism based on previous research indicating that those who are highly educated are less likely to adopt a racially conservative perspective. As we observed in Table 4.3, higher levels of education are correlated with higher support of antiracism. Regression models in the appendix provide two more useful noteworthy findings. First, the relationship between education and support of antiracism remains even after the application of social and demographic controls, meaning the link between education and support of antiracism is not due to a spurious third factor. Second, the standardized beta of education ($\beta = 0.236$) is quite a bit smaller than the standardized betas of political progressive ($\beta = 1.251$) or racial variables such as Black identity ($\beta = 3.493$). This suggests that the effect sizes of educational attainment are probably smaller compared to political orientation and racial identity. Our focus on political viewpoint and race as the strongest predictors of acceptance of antiracism is well founded.

It is worth noting that income has an inverse relationship with acceptance of antiracism both in Table 4.3 and in the appendix. Whites from less advantaged subcultures might perceive antiracism as a way to challenge a social order that has placed them at that disadvantage. If the effects of income hold up among white political progressives, then we may gain insight into why certain types of white political progressives are supportive of antiracism. Looking at just white respondents who indicated that they were either leaning liberal, liberal, or extremely liberal, we found that there was a powerful significant correlation between educational attainment ($r = 0.433$) and SES ($r = 0.27$) with the antiracism attitude scale. Among African American progressives, the relationships with educational attainment (r = −0.249) and SES (r = −0.3) and the antiracism attitude scale were reversed,[10] although only the relationship with SES, but not educational attainment, was significant due to a lack of statistical power tied to the low number of respondents in the sample (N = 36).[11] Thus, among white progressives, being disenfranchised economically and educationally is negatively correlated to accepting antiracism, but among African American progressives, it is those who are disenfranchised who are most likely to support antiracism. It is possible that our scale is tuned to a particular type of antiracism that is more hostile to capitalism and especially concerned with the intersectional oppression of race and class. This would be in keeping with the type of racial radicals discussed in Beeman's (2022) work. But given that we collected our information from a national sample and constructed our scale from books popular on the national level, we are more inclined to think of this dynamic as a natural part of what popularized antiracism is, rather than a subset of antiracism in general, until we find empirical evidence that offers evidence of the subset possibilities.

This interaction of racial identity and education among political progressives speaks to the complicated nature of education as a predictor of support for popularized antiracism. The effects of education may be contextualized depending on the subgroup being studied. The work of Sikkink and Emerson (2008) indicates that education may act to increase social desirability effects among respondents, and thus education under the right contexts, such as among African Americans progressives who may not face the pressure of social desirability, is not linked to higher levels of antiracism support. However, there may be other reasons why African Americans progressive with higher levels of educational attainment do not support antiracism more than those with lower levels of educational attainment. Answering this question is beyond the scope of this book, but discovering why these racial differences impact the relationship between education and support for antiracism can provide information about how, and under what conditions, education operates to support antiracism.

Antiracism as a Political Identity

Regardless of the reasons why political progressives heavily support antiracism, the evidence from the data is clear. Political ideology is at least as pow-

---

10. These findings did not vary when we reduced the group of progressives in the sample to only those who are liberal or extremely liberal and when we reduced the sample to only those who are extremely liberal. However, we decided to use all three categories of liberalism to increase the number in our sample and increase our statistical power.

11. Given that r = 0.249 and with an N of 36, the power one can hope to detect is 0.7, which indicates that powerful effects can be detected but not medium and small effects.

erful as racial status in describing who supports antiracism. Given the innate nature of antiracism, it is expected that there is a racial dimension to the nature of antiracism support. It is theoretically possible that such support would be apolitical. For example, it seems likely that if popularized ideals of antiracism were focused on the elimination of racist terrorist groups such as the Nazis, there would likely be little difference between political progressives and conservatives in supporting efforts to eliminate racial violence. This is not to state that political progressives and political conservatives have similar levels of support for the concerns of people of color, as previous work indicates that this is not the case (Kantack and Paschall 2022, Kousser 2000, Marable 2010, Beyer 2022). However, rejection of racially based violence is so high that there is unlikely to be a great deal of difference by political viewpoint in the propensity of Americans to reject such violence. If the only thing antiracism focused on was racially based violence, then political viewpoint is likely to be of relatively little value in explaining support of antiracism.

However, as established in the last chapter, antiracism is more than mere opposition to individualized racism, much less mere opposition to racial violence. Components of dealing with the multifaceted nature of racism, with attention to structural racism as well as individualized racism and differential roles for whites and nonwhites, have powerful political implications. Political conservatives are less willing to address structural racism (Kantack and Paschall 2022, Toosi, Layous, and Reevy 2021) and more likely to make colorblindness claims (Mayer 2015, Mazzocco 2017, Kousser 2000) that challenge the viability of different responsibilities for whites and nonwhites. It is not surprising that there is a significant political difference between supporters and detractors of antiracism. However, the strength of the difference is more than one may normally expect since the political effect at least rivals, and may surpass, racial identity effects. In other words, support of antiracism is politically driven at least as much as it is racially driven.

If antiracism is a racialized identity, then it is also a politicized identity. We contend it is both, although attention to the racialized elements of antiracism is easier to envision given the overt racialized nature of this philosophy. It is vital to understand not only the racial elements of antiracism but also the political dynamics of antiracism. These political dynamics help indicate how antiracism shapes the social identity of some of its proponents and perhaps most of its more fervent supporters. This political identity is especially relevant given the political polarization in the United States (Jiang et al. 2020, Boxell 2020, Arbatli and Rosenberg 2021, Prior 2013). This polarization can strengthen the cultural and political motivations of political progressives and thus increase support of motivations based on their identity. It is plausible that the intensity of the polarization feeds into the strength of the politicized nature of antiracist identity and that without this polarization, the political effects, which still would be likely to exist, would not rival or possibly exceed the potential racial effects. Antiracism in the United States as a political identity may be exceptional in comparison to antiracism in other nations due to the political polarization in this nation.

To better understand the politized nature of antiracism, it is viable to go beyond looking at general political attitudes to see how support of antiracism factors into support of specific political issues. It is expected that support of antiracism is linked to support of racialized issues, such as immigration or criminal justice. However, since antiracism is a politicized social identity as well as a racialized identity, then it is plausible that antiracism is also associated with other political issues. Indeed, one would expect that there is a link between antiracism and a variety of political issues that are not overtly racial. In the next chapter, we explore this possibility.

5

Impact of Modern Antiracism

As seen in the previous chapter, we found that political ideology is the strongest predictor of an individual adopting antiracist attitudes. That is not surprising given the strength of the correlation (r = 0.572) between the antiracism attitude scale and political viewpoint. This statistical relationship is so strong that we argue that an antiracist identity is also a political identity. However, that degree of strength leads to a question about the role of political ideology in the construction of an antiracism philosophy. Are the supporters of antiracism simply political progressives or radicals? Is it possible that measurements of antiracism are merely proxies for adherence to a radical political ideology? Or are there key ways by which antiracism separates itself from general political progressiveness? Political ideology is the strongest predictor of popularized antiracism, and if we are going to better understand those who adhere to antiracism, we must investigate the relationship between antiracism and political progressiveness.

It is reasonable to assume antiracists are politically progressive because their ideas and policies have found a better home in the platform of the Democratic Party compared to the Republican Party. Given this, one possibility is that antiracists may focus most of their policy attention on racial issues whereas political progressives could spread their priorities to nonracial issues. If antiracists are politically progressive because it is simply a "lesser of two evils" situation, then it is plausible that they are not as politically progressive as other Democrats on nonracial issues, but this lack of attachment to a general progressive political philosophy is compensated by a radical adherence to their progressive stance on racial political issues. Antiracists who are not strongly politically progressive on nonracial issues may still strongly identify as politically progressive if their passion for racial justice is more salient than their relatively nonprogressive stances on nonracial issues.[1]

In this chapter, we investigate this possibility. Using the Chapman Survey of American Fears, we look for issues where proponents of antiracism have similar attitudes as political progressives and issues where their attitudes may differ from political progressives. Antiracists may have powerful political desires only on racial issues. In that case, the strength of the desire of antiracists to support progressive ideals on racial issues is sufficient for creating a powerful correlation between antiracism and political progressiveness. It is also plausible that antiracists do not greatly differ from political progressives on both racial and nonracial issues. To the degree that this holds, it signifies the extent to which antiracism is fused with progressive political ideology.

Chapman Survey of American Fears

Because of the placement of questions in the CSAF, we have an opportunity to explore systematic similarities between strong supporters of antiracism and strong supporters of generally progressive political attitudes. There is a good deal of overlap between the two groups. Those who score at least 16 on the 5–20 antiracism attitude scale and thus average more than 3 on the four-point scale for each of the five questions are identified as highly antiracist. We found that 27.1% of the weighted population was highly antiracist. Those who score at least 6 on the seven-point political progressiveness scale are identified as strongly politically progressive. We found that 18.4% of the weighted population was strongly politically progressive. Furthermore, 123 individuals were both highly antiracist and strongly politically progressive. This means that 44.7% (123/276) of the high antiracists and 65.6% (123/188) of the strong political progressives can be said to be both highly antiracist and strong political progressives. That large block of individuals who are both highly antiracist and strongly politically progressive ensures that there will be significant overlap between the attitudes of antiracists and political progressives. If that overlap is only centered on racial issues, then we may see much weaker statistical relationships between antiracists and political progressives on nonracial issues. Given the role of political progressiveness in the formation of antiracism, we endeavor to learn if and how antiracists differ from political progressives in general. Is antiracist political progressivism

---

1. We do not mean to imply that antiracism is completely accepted by all Democrats, as there is debate within that party as to the level of influence antiracists like Kendi should have in the party (Levitz 2022).

due almost exclusively to the support of political progressives on racial political issues? Or is there a deeper commitment between popularized antiracism and progressive political beliefs that links these two ideas together?

We are fortunate that the antiracism attitude scale has been placed in a probability sample with the CSAF. However, given that we are the original developers of the index and it is placed only in this survey, we are limited to the questions on that particular survey to fully investigate the relationships between political ideology and antiracism. The main purpose of the CSAF is to investigate the fears of Americans. Most of the questions in the survey inquired about the fears individuals have and whether each fear is based on a financial, political, medical, social, or other dimension. Using questions about fears can help us understand political attitudes, even if it is not as efficient as directly asking respondents about those political attitudes. Previous research has identified contrasting fears for political progressives and conservatives (Lippold et al. 2020, Bader et al. 2020, Hatemi et al. 2013, Yang, Chu, and Kahlor 2019). Exploring to see if antiracists share the same fears as political progressives may produce insight into common bonds that exist between these two groups. The CSAF does contain a few questions on political attitudes as well as some questions on attitudes toward Covid. These are all areas ripe with possibilities.

While the CSAF is useful for this initial examination, there are limitations. The first is a methodological concern. The questions are formatted in a four-category scale.[2] This limits the degree of variability for each given question. This is not a problem concerning assessment of the index since it has a range of 5–20, but it would be desirable to have a greater range when assessing individual questions. There is the possibility that we do not capture the full effects of antiracism attitudes due to the limited variability of the four-category questions. On the other hand, as it concerns the development of the antiracist index, it is advantageous to have all questions share the same number of categories. In this manner, no single question is more impactful in establishing a given level of acceptance of antiracism due to contributing a higher number of categories to the final index score.[3]

However, the biggest issue is simply the fact that we are limited to this single survey to conduct our analysis of the antiracism attitude scale. No single survey is going to assess all the necessary categories. The limited time respondents are willing to spend on a survey will prohibit a complete exami-

---

2. Thus, questions dealing with the fears of the respondents have the responses of 1—"Very afraid," 2—"Afraid," 3—"Slightly afraid," and 4—"Not afraid." Those inquiring about the opinion of the respondent to certain statements have the categories of 1—"Strongly disagree," 2—"Disagree," 3—"Agree," and 4—"Strongly agree."

3. The questions used from the CSAF can be seen in Appendix C.

nation of all the relevant questions that we would hope to be answered in this quantitative assessment. For example, the CSAF did not provide any questions assessing attitudes toward women or sexual minorities. Some of the popularized antiracists have identified intersectionality as an important part of antiracism (Kendi 2019, Jewell 2020, Eddo-Lodge 2020). It would be useful to see if those who support popularized antiracism are more open to confronting issues of sexism and homophobia than political progressives in general. Without questions on gender attitudes and attitudes toward sexual minorities, such an examination is not possible. Of course, there are other theoretical questions worth investigating that cannot be touched on with this current survey. Ideally, in the future, questions from the antiracism attitude scale will be included in other surveys, making a more comprehensive examination of the relationship between popularized antiracism and political progressives possible.

Do Antiracists Distinguish Themselves from Political Progressives?

We conducted an initial bivariate comparison of high antiracists to strong political progressives using the criteria discussed in the last section. A comparison of the two groups can be seen in Table 5.1. Since a generous percentage of both high antiracists (N = 276) and strong political progressives (N = 188) fit into both categories, we decided to eliminate those who were both highly antiracist and strongly politically progressive for this table. This increased the chances of us perceiving systematic differences between the two groups. The results from Table 5.1 indicate few demographic differences between antiracists who are not strongly politically progressive and political progressives who are not highly antiracist. At the bivariate level, they do not differ by gender, educational level, SES, region of country, or religiously. The only significant differences concern issues of race and age. Those who are highly antiracist are more likely to be Black, less likely to be white,[4] and younger by nine years, compared to those who are strongly politically progressive. These differences remain significant in regression analysis (available in the appendix), indicating that the major demographic differences between antiracists and political progressives are tied to race and age. Given the approach of antiracism to address the issues of African Americans, it is not surprising that they are more likely to adhere to antiracism when they are not strongly politically progressive. The age difference may be reflective of the attraction

---

4. Those who are high antiracists did not differ from those who are strong political progressive among Hispanics.

TABLE 5.1 COMPARISON OF RESPONDENTS WITH HIGH ANTIRACISM WITH THOSE WITH STRONG POLITICAL PROGRESSIVENESS ON SELECTED DEMOGRAPHIC AND SOCIAL CATEGORIES		
	High antiracism (N = 276)	Strong political progressiveness (N = 188)
Female	53.8% (149) 50.0	57.8% (65) 49.8
White	28.9%*** (153) 45.5	62.4% (65) 48.8
Black	39.9%*** (153) 49.1	6.6% (65) 25.1
Hispanic	20.7% (153) 40.7	18.2% (65) 38.9
Age	40.701*** (144) 16.371	49.95 (64) 18.702
Education (1–8 scale)	4.98 (153) 1.96	4.56 (65) 2.089
Income (1–9 scale)	5.099 (153) 2.629	5.028 (65) 2.585
Northcentral	16.4% (65) 37.3	17.2% (153) 37.8
South	40.7% (65) 49.5	39.9% (153) 49.1
West	22.3% (65) 42.0	25.0% (153) 43.4
Christian	45.5% (65) 50.2	48.0% (153) 50.1
Atheist/agnostic	12.6% (65) 33.4	5.7% (153) 23.4
Non-Christian religion	4.6% (65) 21.6	10.4% (153) 30.6
None (religion)	34.6% (65) 47.9	29.3% (153) 45.7

Source: Chapman Survey of American Fears
Notes: * p < .05, ** p < .01, *** p < .001.
Means/Proportions are entries; number of respondents in parentheses; standard deviations in italics.
Male, other race, Northeast, and other religion are reference groups.

of a seemingly newer idea of antiracism as opposed to earlier efforts, such as multiculturalism, which may be more attractive to older political progressives. Further empirical analysis is needed to assess this possibility or look at other possible sources of this age difference.

These racial and age differences may create discrepancies in how those with high levels of antiracism perceive social issues compared to those with high levels of political progressiveness. We chose to compare the two groups in eight areas that comport well with the questions being asked in the CSAF. The eight areas are 1) overt racial issues, 2) partisan political attitudes, 3) political issues—January 6, 4) political issues—environmentalism, 5) attitudes toward Covid, 6) political issues—economy, 7) foreign policy concerns, and 8) criminal justice concerns. The diversity of these issues should indicate which issues are, or are not, tied to antiracism perspectives, which will help us identify the major mechanisms linking modern antiracism and progressive political ideology. If a focus on racial issues is the major source of such linking, then we predict that there is great similarity between supporters of antiracism and strong political progressives on racial issues, and perhaps even criminal justice, since there is recent evidence that criminal justice issues have become an important part of our current racial dialogue (Hadden et al. 2016, B. Alexander 2016, Martin 2021, Rucker and Richeson 2021). However, the association would be much weaker and possibly nonexistent between the two groups on other social and political issues. Strong agreement between antiracists and political progressives in other areas would provide evidence that the linking between antiracists and political progressives goes beyond explicitly racial issues. Those who are neither highly antiracist nor strongly politically progressive are the control group in the third column.

In Table 5.2, we compare those three groups (highly antiracist, strongly politically progressive, and control group) within those eight areas. Since we are more concerned with mapping the overall effect of antiracism and political progressiveness on these attitudes, to increase our statistical power, we did not exclude respondents who fit into both categories, even though including those respondents may overestimate the degree of commonality of high antiracists and strong political progressives. As expected, both high antiracists and strong political progressives are significantly more progressive on racial issues than the control group. This difference is evident in all overt racial issues in the table. It would be shocking if either of those groups were not more racially progressive than other respondents. Between the antiracists and political progressives, there were only two variables with a significant difference in the overt racial questions. The high antiracists are less fearful of a world without a white majority than strong political progressives are, but strong political progressives are less fearful of being the victim of a racial hate crime than those who are highly antiracist. These differences may be tied to

TABLE 5.2 COMPARISON OF ANTIRACISTS, POLITICAL PROGRESSIVES, AND GENERAL POPULATION ON VARIOUS SOCIAL AND POLITICAL ATTITUDES			
	Antiracists	Strong political progressives	Neither antiracists nor strong political progressives
Overt racial issues			
Afraid of BLM	1.201 (275) 0.643	1.218 (187) 0.695	1.765***/*** (655) 1.041
Support of BLM	3.431 (276) 0.682	3.461 (188) 0.641	2.878***/*** (677) 0.959
Afraid of illegal immigration	1.416 (276) 0.814	1.395 (188) 0.831	2.256***/*** (674) 1.124
Afraid of immigrants	1.111 (275) 0.493	1.097 (187) 0.437	1.405***/*** (667) 0.73
Afraid of world without white majority	1.1 (276) 0.476	1.219* (188) 0.737	1.454***/*** (674) 0.829
Afraid of white supremacy	2.831 (272) 1.134	2.899 (188) 1.082	1.918***/*** (628) 1.06
Afraid of being a victim of hate crime	2.356 (276) 1.233	2.078* (188) 1.186	1.834***/** (677) 0.98
Afraid of Muslims	1.15 (275) 0.568	1.185 (187) 0.563	1.395***/*** (654) 0.715
Partisan political attitudes			
Voted Trump	3.4% (276) 18.1	5.2% (188) 22.2	44.8%***/*** (677) 49.8
Voted Biden	70.3 (276) 45.8	77.9% (188) 41.6	27.0%***/*** (677) 44.5
Afraid of right-wing extremists	2.831 (233) 1.132	2.827 (175) 1.065	1.902***/*** (547) 1.036
Afraid of left-wing extremists	1.784 (228) 1.014	1.569* (169) 0.86	2.238***/*** (554) 1.128
Political issue—Jan 6			
Trump to blame for Jan 6 violence	3.609 (276) 0.688	3.594 (188) 0.762	2.34***/*** (677) 1.117

(continued)

TABLE 5.2 COMPARISON OF ANTIRACISTS, POLITICAL PROGRESSIVES, AND GENERAL POPULATION ON VARIOUS SOCIAL AND POLITICAL ATTITUDES (continued)

	Antiracists	Strong political progressives	Neither antiracists nor strong political progressives
Biden legitimate winner of 2020 election	3.656 (276) 0.658	3.678 (188) 0.748	2.563***/*** (677) 1.11
Can not know who won 2020 election because of election fraud	1.57 (276) 0.942	1.418 (188) 0.831	2.406***/*** (677) 1.077
Jan 6 protestors are patriots	1.479 (276) 0.895	1.313* (188) 0.688	1.922***/*** (677) 0.828
Need new laws to protect against voter fraud	2.01 (276) 1.067	1,782* (188) 0.951	2.805***/*** (677) 0.953
Afraid of widespread voter fraud	1.844 (276) 1.098	1.581* (188) 0.981	2.323***/*** (674) 1.128
Political issue—environmentalism			
Afraid of air pollution	2.934 (276) 0.93	3.005 (188) 0.801	2.224***/*** (677) 0.927
Afraid of water pollution	3.044 (276) 0.96	3.058 (188) 0.912	2.464***/*** (676) 1.009
Afraid of animal and plant extinction	2.843 (276) 1.027	3.035* (188) 0.864	2.209***/*** (676) 1.016
Afraid of climate change	3.134 (276) 0.971	3.294 (188) 0.835	2.081***/*** (677) 1.022
Afraid of climate change affecting where I live	2.835 (276) 0.996	2.826 (188) 0.925	1.948***/*** (674) 0.992
Climate Change Index (4–16 range)	13.823 (276) 2.343	13.987 (188) 2.254	10.398***/*** (677) 3.24
Attitudes toward Covid			
Afraid of pandemic	2.809 (276) 1.003	2.752 (188) 0.994	2.243***/*** (674) 2.757
Afraid of catching Covid	2.301 (276) 1.02	2.26 (188) 0.995	1.776***/*** (677) 0.816
Lost friend because of Covid	2.251 (276) 0.93	2.251 (188) 0.863	1.949***/*** (677) 0.782

TABLE 5.2 COMPARISON OF ANTIRACISTS, POLITICAL PROGRESSIVES, AND GENERAL POPULATION ON VARIOUS SOCIAL AND POLITICAL ATTITUDES *(continued)*

	Antiracists	Strong political progressives	Neither antiracists nor strong political progressives
Spent more time alone because of Covid	3.11 (276) 0.876	3.128 (188) 0.75	2.665***/*** (677) 0.863
Got into arguments more because of Covid	2.452 (276) 1.042	2.606 (188) 0.933	2.314***/*** (677) 0.874
Prepared household more because of Covid	2.548 (276) 0.817	2.441 (188) 0.729	2.228***/*** (677) 0.743
Economic fears			
Afraid of economic collapse	2.729 (276) 1.012	2.574 (188) 1.008	2.629 (674) 0.971
Afraid of not having enough money in the future	2.994 (275) 1.111	2.989 (187) 1,122	2.48***/*** (677) 1.077
Afraid of being unemployed	2.63 (218) 1.193	2.398 (135) 1.133	2.251*** (401) 1.11
Afraid of not being able to pay rent or mortgage	2.635 (252) 1.239	2.563 (165) 1.234	2.232***/** (519) 1.136
Afraid of not being able to pay college debt	2.603 (165) 1.212	2.396 (98) 1.183	2.142*** (255) 1.061
Afraid of not being able to pay medical bill	2.664 (276) 1.143	2.508 (188) 1.138	2.315***/* (677) 1.076
Foreign policy fears			
Afraid of U.S. becoming involved in another world war	2.784 (276) 0.997	2.677 (188) 0.927	2.693 (674) 0.993
Afraid of biological warfare	2.715 (276) 1.05	2.56 (188) 1.039	2.585 (674) 1.016
Afraid of terrorist attack	2.556 (276) 1.042	2.459 (188) 1.042	2.563 (672) 0.985
Afraid of North Korea using nuclear weapons	2.568 (276) 1.094	2.477 (188) 1.071	2.572 (673) 1.024
Afraid of Iran using nuclear weapons	2.393 (276) 1.111	2.175* (188) 1.075	2.523 /*** (673) 1.051

(continued)

TABLE 5.2 COMPARISON OF ANTIRACISTS, POLITICAL PROGRESSIVES, AND GENERAL POPULATION ON VARIOUS SOCIAL AND POLITICAL ATTITUDES (continued)

	Antiracists	Strong political progressives	Neither antiracists nor strong political progressives
Afraid of Russia using nuclear weapons	2.909 (276) 1.059	2.832 (188) 1.006	2.756* (674) 1.000
Criminal justice concerns			
Afraid of gun legislation	1.617 (276) 1.029	1.438 (188) 0.9	2.36***/*** (677) 1.182
Local gov should use curfews during protests	2.512 (276) 0.915	2.33* (188) 0.799	2.747***/*** (677) 0.837
National Guard should be used during protests	2.44 (276) 0.902	2.347 (188) 0.842	2.954***/*** (677) 0.779
We need national law enforcement reform	3.363 (276) 0.774	3.281 (188) 0.782	2.405***/*** (677) 0.84
We need to defund the police	2.289 (276) 0.963	2.326 (188) 0.965	1.443***/*** (677) 0.675
Afraid of police brutality	2.472 (276) 1.202	2.358 (188) 1.168	1.72***/*** (677) 0.99
Afraid of murder by stranger	2.235 (276) 1.175	2.213 (188) 1.123	2.03**/* (677) 1.045
Afraid of being mugged	2.185 (276) 1.012	2.05 (188) 0.942	2.057 (677) 0.956
Afraid of suffer from random shooting	2.63 (276) 1.086	2.568 (188) 1.061	2.265***/** (677) 1.057
Afraid of being a victim of breaking and entering	2.338 (276) 1.056	2.236 (188) 0.956	2.274 (677) 0.952
Afraid of being a victim of property theft	2.394 (276) 1.053	2.252 (188) 0.958	2.231 (677) 0.803
Afraid of being a victim of gang violence	2.051 (276) 1.182	1.901 (188) 1.076	2.056 (677) 1.042

Source: Chapman Survey of American Fears
Note: Means are entries; number of respondents in parentheses; standard deviations in italics.

the higher likelihood of antiracists being nonwhite. Nonwhites could have less fear of a white majority but may feel more targeted for a racial hate crime. But overall, the overt racial attitudes of high antiracists and strong political progressives are similar to each other and distinctive from the control group.

The partisan political attitudes questions deal less with overall political perspective and more with the salience and prominence of issues that reflect partisan political desires. We created a section that was more heavily tied to testing partisan loyalties than attitudes toward specific political issues, even as we recognize that the support of specific issues is often heavily influenced by partisan loyalties. Fears of right- or left-wing extremists are not connected to particular political principles but are linked to outgrouping a given set of political partisans. Furthermore, the respondents were directly asked whether they voted for either Biden or Trump. One can envision a person with politically progressive leanings who does not vote for Biden since Biden is not progressive enough for that individual. In that case, the partisan support for Democrats is not enough to persuade the respondent to support the Democratic candidate. In all partisan political attitude issues, both high antiracists and strong political progressives are more progressive than the control group. However, one might expect that strong political progressives have a higher propensity to take a strong stance on such partisan questions. As it concerns voting for Trump or Biden, there is not a significant difference between high antiracists and strong political progressives. There is a slight difference in fear of extremists in that strong political progressives are slightly but significantly less fearful of left-wing extremists than high antiracists.

We now look toward issues connected to January 6. While both antiracists and political progressives significantly differed from the control group on all issues, partisan loyalty may matter more for January 6 issues than it does for other political issues. For example, a major aspect of the concerns of January 6 are issues of vote count and voting access. Concerns about voting access and voting rights can be tied to partisan efforts to gain an advantage in upcoming elections (Caron 2022, Bateman 2016). Assessment of January 6 may be an indirect assessment of partisan interest but also an issue not intrinsically racial in nature. Results on the issue of January 6 are mixed. There is no significant difference between high antiracists and strong political progressives in assessing blame to Trump, seeing Biden as the legitimate winner, or determining whether election fraud distorted our knowledge of who won the election. Compared to high antiracists, strong political progressives are more likely to not envision the January 6 protesters as patriots, to see a need for new laws against voter fraud, and to be afraid of widespread voter fraud than high antiracists.

Although strong political progressives are slightly more progressive on issues connected to January 6, the difference is not so great that we would not see high antiracists as strongly progressive on January 6. Is this due to the January 6 controversy being a racial event? Innately, the controversy of January 6 is about the interference of a peaceful transfer of power. It is about claims of voter fraud and deception from a former president on the truthfulness of election results. It is not inherently racialized.[5] However, some have discussed the presence of white supremacists at the January 6 protests (Hawkman and Diem 2022, Johnson 2021). The presence of white supremacists may have racialized this event more than other issues of election integrity. On the other hand, events like January 6 often become racialized because of the changing social definition of what occurred during those events. With this current quantitative data, it cannot be determined whether the conception of white supremacy during January 6 is tied to knowledge of a strong presence of white racists during the riots or if the respondents have generated a racial interpretation that emphasizes the presence of white nationalists beyond their actual impact on January 6.

This makes it valuable to explore an issue such as environmentalism. While scholars and activists have argued about "environmental racism" (Henderson and Wells 2021, J. Hamilton 1995, Cole and Foster 2001, Mohai and Bryant 2019), generally, these arguments are focused on local and specific concerns. The environmental questions in the CSAF deal with generalized concerns of air pollution, water pollution, animal and plant extinction, and climate change. While respondents may be influenced by their local environmental concerns when answering these issues, there is not a prompt for localized concerns in the survey on these issues, and one would expect more influence from national or global concerns than local ones. Both high antiracists and strong political progressives significantly distinguish themselves from the control group on all environmental issues. Furthermore, there is less of an ambiguous situation here as the only significant difference between high antiracists and strong political progressives concerns the issue of potential animal and plant extinction, where strong political progressives have more fear. Otherwise, in a political dimension that is not explicitly racial, high antiracists and strong political progressives are nearly identical in their social attitudes.

Respondents' attitudes toward Covid were similar. Covid is an issue that is theoretically tied to the safety of everyone and is not intrinsically racialized. Marginalized racial groups are more likely to die from Covid (Mude et al.

---

5. Racialization is the process by which an issue is attributed with racial characterizations that may be tangential or indirect to the issue at hand. For instance, one can fairly envision the events of January 6 as a riot, uprising, insurrection, protest, or any number of ways that do not explicitly concern racial issues. However, some have focused on racial elements within those events and, in doing so, have racialized January 6. We take no ethical stance on whether any issue should be racialized but only note that racialization seems to be selectively utilized depending on the issue at hand among antiracists.

2021, Alcendor 2020), but death from Covid impacts European Americans too. Thus, there are incentives for individuals across racial lines to find ways of combating it. High antiracists and strong political progressives significantly distinguish themselves from the control group in every single measure. However, there is no significant difference between high antiracists and strong political progressives in their attitudes toward any of the Covid measures. On an issue where there may be a lower expectation of racialization, there is no statistical distinction between antiracists and political progressives.

Moving toward issues of economic fears, high antiracists and strong political progressives do not significantly differ from the control group in whether they fear economic collapse. However, compared to the control, both groups are significantly more fearful of not having enough money in the future, not being able to pay the rent or mortgage, not being able to pay off college debt, and not being able to pay off medical bills. High antiracists, but not strong political progressives, also are significantly more fearful of being unemployed. Given, as seen in Table 4.3, that individuals are less antiracist when they have more income, these results are not surprising.[6] High antiracists and strong political progressives do not significantly differ from each other on any of the economic fear measures. Unfortunately, the CSAF does not ask questions directly about economic policy, so we are left to speculate about economic fears that the respondents may possess. We contend that economic fears between high antiracists and strong political progressives are at such a similar level that such fears would not substantiate a distinct attitude on economic policies between the two groups.

Likewise, the CSAF does not directly inquire about foreign policy but does include questions dealing with fears connected to foreign policy, which provides possible data to speculate on foreign policy priorities. This is the section with the least amount of differentiation between the three groups. There are no differences between the highly antiracist, strongly politically progressive, and control groups on fear of the United States becoming involved in another world war, biological warfare, or a terrorist attack or with North Korea using nuclear weapons. Both the control group and the high antiracists are more fearful of Iran using nuclear weapons than strong political progressives, but the control group is less fearful than the high antiracists of the use of nuclear weapons by Russia. Foreign policy fears is an area where distinctions driven by antiracism are less likely to be relevant.

Finally, we assess the issue of criminal justice. While criminal justice concerns comprise a single section of the assessment, there are two components in that section. First, we assess attitudes toward efforts at criminal justice and

---

6. However, this is not the case for political ideology, as political progressiveness was insignificantly correlated with income (r = −0.02).

maintaining social order. Then we look at the personal fears that respondents have toward certain criminal activities. Concerning criminal justice policies, we see a similar pattern of high antiracists and strong political progressives significantly differentiating themselves from the control group. High antiracists and strong political progressives are less afraid of gun legislation, less willing to use the local government or National Guard to curb protests, more likely to support national law enforcement reform, and more willing to support defunding the police than the control group. Between those two groups, the only significant difference is that high antiracists are more willing to use the local government to curb protests than strong political progressives. As concerns the policy issues of criminal justice, there is little difference between high antiracists and strong political progressives. This may be in part due to the attention criminal justice issues have received from civil rights activists in the last few years.

However, it is worth asking about the role that fears about crime may play in shaping attitudes toward criminal justice. Is the control group less progressive on criminal justice issues due to greater fear of being a victim of crime? The evidence suggests that this is not the case. It is not surprising that high antiracists and strong political progressives have more fear of police brutality than the control group. However, both groups are also significantly more fearful of being murdered by a stranger and dying due to a random shooting than the control group. Fears of crimes traditionally linked to street crime, such as mugging and being a victim of a gang, were not found to be significantly different between the three groups. It is not an overall lack of fear of crime that motivates the attitudes of high antiracists and strong political progressives toward criminal justice policies.

Overall, there is not a great deal of difference between high antiracists and strong political progressives on a wide variety of issues, racial or otherwise. In most cases, when one group significantly differs from the control group, the other group does as well. Furthermore, there are 54 issues addressed in Table 5.2, with antiracists and strong political progressives only significantly different from each other in 9 of those issues. The evidence at this bivariate level of analysis suggests that the similarities between antiracists and political progressives are not limited to racial issues. However, this assessment is incomplete. We are only comparing a certain range of antiracists and political progressives to each other. Only those who score higher than an arbitrary standard are labeled an antiracist or political progressive at this point of the assessment. To gain a better understanding of the relationship between antiracism and political progressiveness on these issues, it is vital to compare the full range of the antiracism and political viewpoint scales in models that control for other demographic and social factors. In the next section, we discuss our results from that assessment.

Impact of Antiracism and Political Progressiveness on Social Issues and Fears

It is not clear if the findings from the last section would hold up after the application of social and demographic controls. This is especially of interest since we already know that high antiracists are younger and less white than strong political progressives. The few differences between those who are highly antiracist and those who are strongly politically progressive may be tied to these racial and age differences. Furthermore, other factors may differentiate high antiracists and strong political progressives from the rest of the population, and those factors may shape the results seen in the table. We constructed a series of regression models that allow us to investigate the effects of political ideology and the acceptance of popularized antiracism on these varieties of issues. To keep it simple, we placed the results of only the coefficients relative to political viewpoint and antiracism in Table 5.3. The full models can be found in the appendix.

First, looking at overt racial issues, it is not a surprise that higher scores on both the antiracism attitude scale and political progressiveness are significantly related to being less afraid of BLM, more supportive of BLM, less afraid of illegal immigration, less afraid of immigrants, more afraid of white supremacy, and less afraid of Muslims. Surprisingly, high scores on the antiracism attitude scale were not significant in the assessment of being afraid of being a victim of a racial hate crime. In a model where the measurement for African Americans was eliminated, we did find the antiracism index to be significant (standardized $\beta = -0.139$; $T = -3.66$; $p < .001$). The relatively high percentage of antiracists who are African American and the higher fear African Americans have of being victimized in a hate crime account for the nonsignificant finding in Table 5.3. It is also noteworthy that although strong political progressives were less fearful of a white majority in comparison to the control group at the bivariate measure, political progressiveness is not significantly connected to a lower fear in the regression models. Finally, we note that except for measurements of being afraid of immigrants and being a victim of a hate crime, the standardized betas of the antiracism index are higher than the measurements of political progressiveness.[7] Although both

---

7. It should also be noted that the t-score of the antiracism attitude scale measure was higher than the t-score of political progressiveness on afraid of BLM (–10.464 v. –2.871), support of BLM (22.091 v. 10.464), afraid of illegal immigration (–10.628 v. –4.976), afraid of world without white majority (–6.318 v. 0.863), afraid of white supremacy (6.757 v. 5.189), and afraid of Muslims (–5.056 v. –2.517). Although the t-score of the antiracism attitude scale was not higher than political progressiveness in the afraid of immigrants (–4.623 v. –5.429) and afraid of being a victim of hate crime (0.729 v. 2.581) models, there is still evidence that the antiracism attitude scale is consistently more powerful in explaining racial issues than general political ideology.

TABLE 5.3 REGRESSION COEFFICIENTS OF ANTIRACISM ATTITUDE SCALE AND POLITICAL PROGRESSIVENESS ON A VARIETY OF SOCIAL ATTITUDES

	Antiracism attitude scale	Political progressiveness
Overt racial issues		
Afraid of BLM	0.407*** (.009) 10.464	0.108** (.023) 2.871
Support of BLM	0.581*** (.007) 22.091	0.27*** (.017) 10.997
Afraid of illegal immigration	0.385*** (.01) 10.628	0.175*** (.025) 4.976
Afraid of immigrants	0.187*** (.007) 4.623	0.212*** (017) 5.429
Afraid of world without white majority	0.257*** (.008) 6.318	0.034 (.02) 0.863
Afraid of white supremacy	0.266*** (.011) −6.757	0.197*** (.028) −5.189
Afraid of being a victim of hate crime	0.028 (.01) −0.729	0.097** (.026) −2.581
Afraid of Muslims	0.213*** (.007) 5.056	0.102* (.017) 2.375
Partisan political attitudes		
Voted Trump	0.39*** (.039) .677ª	0.674*** (.091) .51ª
Voted Biden	0.281*** (.031) 1.324ª	0.658*** (.079) 1.93ª
Afraid of right-wing extremists	0.311*** (.012) 7.202	0.192*** (.03) 4.57
Afraid of left-wing extremists	0.21*** (.013) −4.382	0.154*** (.032) −3.301
Political Issue—Jan 6		
Trump to blame for Jan 6 violence	0.597*** (.008) 20.762	0.18*** (.021) 6.467
Biden legitimate winner of 2020 election	0.489*** (.008) 16.053	0.238*** (.021) 8.055

TABLE 5.3 REGRESSION COEFFICIENTS OF ANTIRACISM ATTITUDE SCALE AND POLITICAL PROGRESSIVENESS ON A VARIETY OF SOCIAL ATTITUDES *(continued)*

	Antiracism attitude scale	Political progressiveness
Can not know who won 2020 election because of election fraud	−0.388*** (.009) −11.317	−0.263*** (.024) −7.918
Jan 6 protestors are patriots	0.188*** (.008) −4.805	0.272*** (.021) −7.189
Need new laws to protect against voter fraud	0.324*** (.009) −9.495	0.3*** (.023) −9.064
Afraid of widespread voter fraud	0.288*** (.011) 7.51	0.217*** (.027) 5.826
Political issue—environmentalism		
Afraid of air pollution	0.229*** (.009) −6.042	0.261*** (.023) −7.105
Afraid of water pollution	0.187*** (.01) −4.722	0.191*** (.025) −4.993
Afraid of animal and plant extinction	0.189*** (.01) −4.922	−2.66*** (.025) −7.145
Afraid of climate change	0.363*** (.009) −10.556	0.323*** (.024) −9.704
Afraid of climate change affecting where I live	0.321*** (.01) −8.744	0.209*** (.025) −5.873
Climate Change Index (4–16 range)	0.466*** (.027) 14.418	0.257*** (.068) 8.223
Attitudes toward Covid		
Afraid of pandemic	−0.262*** (.01) −6.745	−0.149*** (.025) −3.96
Afraid of catching Covid	0.312*** (.009) −8.023	0.087* (.022) −2.312
Lost friend because of Covid	0.121** (.009) 2.844	0.006 (.022) 0.146
Spent more time alone because of Covid	0.187*** (.009) 4.54	0.051 (.023) 1.274

(continued)

TABLE 5.3 REGRESSION COEFFICIENTS OF ANTIRACISM ATTITUDE SCALE AND POLITICAL PROGRESSIVENESS ON A VARIETY OF SOCIAL ATTITUDES (*continued*)

	Antiracism attitude scale	Political progressiveness
Got into arguments more because of Covid	0.054 (.01) 1.283	0.036 (.025) 0.882
Prepared household more because of Covid	.194*** (.008) 4.647	0.03 (.02) 0.736
Economic fears		
Afraid of economic collapse	−0.031 (.011) −0.738	0.014 (.027) 0.348
Afraid of not having enough money in the future	−0.089* (.01) −2.39	−0.074* (.026) −2.39
Afraid of being unemployed	−0.205*** (.014) −4.08	0.054 (.036) 1.163
Afraid of not being able to pay rent or mortgage	−0.062 (.013) −1.653	−0.089* (.033) −2.454
Afraid of not being able to pay college debt	−0.121*** (.013) −3.117	0.034 (.033) 0.91
Afraid of not being able to pay medical bill	−0.141*** (.011) −3.446	−0.061 (.028) −1.549
Foreign policy fears		
Afraid of U.S. becoming involved in another world war	−0.046 (.01) −1.094	−0.004 (.026) −0.095
Afraid of biological warfare	−0.004 (.011) −0.087	−0.029 (.027) −0.711
Afraid of terrorist attack	−0.017 (.011) −0.416	−0.006 (.027) −0.151
Afraid of North Korea using nuclear weapons	0.058 (.011) −1.425	0.006 (.027) 0.147
Afraid of Iran using nuclear weapons	0.007 (.011) 0.179	0.105** (.028) 2.626
Afraid of Russia using nuclear weapons	−0.103 (.011) −2.441	−0.038 (.027) −0.934

(*continued*)

TABLE 5.3 REGRESSION COEFFICIENTS OF ANTIRACISM ATTITUDE SCALE AND POLITICAL PROGRESSIVENESS ON A VARIETY OF SOCIAL ATTITUDES (continued)

	Antiracism attitude scale	Political progressiveness
Criminal justice concerns		
Afraid of gun legislation	0.296 (.011) *8.045*	0.228 (.027) *−6.378*
Local gov should use curfews during protests	0.014 (.009) *0.352*	−0.139*** (.022) *−3.536*
National Guard should be used during protests	−0.128*** (.008) *−3.208*	−0.18*** (.021) *−4.665*
We need national law enforcement reform	0.305*** (.008) *8.578*	0.209*** (.02) *6.059*
We need to defund the police	0.351*** (.007) *10.08*	0.142*** (.018) *4.209*
Afraid of police brutality	−0.124*** (.01) *−3.348*	−0.112*** (.026) *−3.137*
Afraid of murder by stranger	−0.04 (.01) *−1.033*	−0.063 (.026) *−1.691*
Afraid of being mugged	−0.054 (.01) *−1.337*	0.009 (.025) *0.283*
Afraid of suffering from random shooting	−0.09* (.01) *−2.338*	−0.064 (.026) *−1.715*
Afraid of being a victim of breaking and entering	−0.063 (.01) *−1.541*	−0.027 (.025) *0.673*
Afraid of being a victim of property theft	0.012 (01) *0.285*	−0.089* (.024) *2.218*
Afraid of being a victim of gang violence	0.026 (.011) *0.635*	0.022 (.027) *0.545*

Source: Chapman Survey of American Fears
Notes: Means are standardized betas; number in parentheses are standard error; t-scores are in italics; # = odds ratio
Results after applications of controls for gender, age, racial identity, education, household SES, region of country, religiosity, and religious identity

measures are highly significant in most of the overt racial variables, adherence to antiracism can have a larger effect size. Given the central nature of racial issues in the construction of antiracism, such a finding is not surprising.

The findings of the partisan attitudes are as expected, with high scores in both the antiracism attitude scale and political progressiveness significant after controls. The standardized beta scores suggest that political progressiveness has larger effect sizes concerning voting for either Trump or Biden. This should be expected since political ideology is at least an indirect measure of a respondent's voting decisions. What is surprising is that the standardized betas for the antiracism attitude scale are higher than the political progressiveness measure on fear of right- or left-wing extremists. The differences are not great, and it is difficult to argue that the antiracism attitude scale is stronger in predicting attitudes toward left- and right-wing extremists than overall political orientation. However, if such fears are driven mostly by partisan interest, it would be expected that a respondent's political ideology would have much larger effect sizes than adherence to popularized antiracism. Perhaps engagement in antiracism provides more comfort from left-wing extremists and more fear of right-wing extremists than mere assent to progressive political policies. Nonetheless, in all four measures, the antiracism index measure is significant even with the inclusion of measurements of political viewpoints. The failure of political ideology to mediate the antiracism attitude scale indicates that popularized antiracism is not merely a proxy for political progressiveness but also generates a level of partisan loyalty beyond its relationships to the measurement of political progressiveness.

The results of the issue of January 6 are fairly similar to the results of the overt racial issues. Scoring high on the antiracism index and political progressive measurement is significant in all regression models with January 6 measurements as dependent variables. It is plausible to argue that antiracism is at least as consistent a predictor of attitudes toward January 6 as it is toward overt racial attitudes. Furthermore, the standardized betas for the antiracism index are higher than the measurement of political progressiveness on all the January 6 measurements except for asking if the January 6 protesters are patriots. While there may be a racialized element in the January 6 protest, with the consideration of possible white supremacists among the protesters, this event is deeply linked to the partisan struggle over electoral results in the 2020 presidential election. Yet, at the very least, attitudes toward antiracism are as explanatory of the attitudes toward January 6 as political ideology.

Political issues connected to the environment are an area that is not intrinsically racialized. Yet the antiracism attitude scale exhibits the same amount of predictive power as progressive political attitudes in this assessment of environmental and political issues. Both the antiracism index and measurements of political progressiveness are significant to $p < .001$ on all six issues.[8] The antiracism index generates a higher standardized beta than measurements of political progressiveness on half of these questions. Antiracism appears to have an effect on environmental attitudes that rivals that of political progressiveness. Given the political controls in the regression models, there is a pathway by which antiracism impacts environmental attitudes separate from adherence to politically progressive ideals.

One can argue about the degree to which Covid became politicized in the United States. However, there is adequate evidence that Covid did feed into the larger political polarization in our society (Jiang et al. 2020, Kerr, Panagopoulos, and van der Linden 2021, Pennycook et al. 2022). However, the antiracism attitude scale is more predictive of attitudes toward Covid than measurements of political progressiveness. Antiracism attitudes and political progressiveness are significantly correlated to being afraid of the pandemic and of catching Covid. However, higher acceptance of popularized antiracism is also significantly related to losing a friendship over Covid safety, spending more time alone because of Covid, and preparing a household more because of Covid, while political progressiveness is not. Furthermore, the standardized betas for the antiracism index are larger than measurements for political progressiveness in all six variables.[9] Concerns about Covid may be politized and tied to the political polarization in our society. However, the scale of attitudes toward antiracism may be a better predictor of attitudes toward Covid and how Covid impacted the life of a respondent. These findings are in keeping with arguments about the racialization of Covid in how it has worsened the conditions marginalized people of color suffer from (Siu and Chun 2020, Ezell et al. 2021, Kimura 2021) and revealed the racial disparities in our society (Hooijer and King 2022, Allen et al. 2021, Denney and Valdez 2021).

As stated earlier, it is difficult, if not impossible, for us to adequately assess the attitudes of respondents toward economic policy issues; we can, however, assess their economic fears. Given the different economic realities for whites and nonwhites (Oliver and Shapiro 2006, DeNavas-Walt 2010), there are theoretical implications that racial issues can drive some of these fears. This

---

8. Among the variables was a climate change index that consisted of the four variables in Table 5.2 and asked the respondents whether climate change is causing more frequent and severe floods, wildfires, droughts, and hurricanes. Given that these four variables had such a high correlation with each other that the Cronbach's alpha between them is 0.964, it was more efficient to put them in an index than to test them separately.

9. Furthermore, the t-scores of the antiracism attitude scale are higher than political progressiveness on afraid of pandemic (6.745 v. 3.96), afraid of catching Covid (8.023 v. 2.312), lost friend because of Covid (2.844 v. 0.146), spent more time along because of Covid (4.54 v. 1.274), got into arguments more because of Covid (1.283 v. 0.882), and prepared household more because of Covid (4.647 v. 0.736), indicating further the high power of the antiracism attitude scale in explaining attitudes toward Covid than general political ideology.

section has the clearest distinction between antiracists and political progressives. Those scoring higher on the antiracism attitude scale have more economic fears than those scoring highly in political progressiveness.[10] While both antiracism and political progressiveness are not significant in fear of an economic collapse, both are significant in predicting who is more afraid of not having enough money in the future. However, only antiracism is significantly linked to fears of unemployment, not being able to pay college debt, and not being able to pay medical bills. Political progressiveness, but not antiracism, is significantly tied to the fear of not being able to pay rent or mortgage. Since both antiracism and political progressiveness do not show a significantly higher fear of economic collapse after the application of controls, it seems unlikely that either group would rely on fear of economic collapse in making decisions about which economic policies to support. However, antiracists may feel a greater personal economic insecurity than those who are politically progressive, and this insecurity may impact their ideas for economic reforms in the United States. However, it is noteworthy that while antiracists have higher levels of fear concerning their own economic situation (i.e., college debt, unemployment, paying mortgage), their concern for the economy in general collapsing is not significantly higher than the control group.

Fears generated by foreign policy issues likely do not impact the attitudes of those subscribing to antiracism and/or political progressiveness either. While foreign policy fears are not obviously racialized, it has been noted that the consequences of our foreign policies, especially as they pertain to wars, can disproportionately impact marginalized racial minorities (Binkin 2011, Gooden and Crawford 2016, Williams and Slusser 2014). After the application of controls, only fear of Iran using nuclear weapons was significantly related to political progressiveness. But political progressives are less fearful than the general population, so even here foreign policy fears are not instructive to their general political attitudes. None of the measures of foreign policy fears showed significant correlation with popularized antiracism. Popularized antiracism not only does not distinguish itself from political progressiveness in its ability to predict foreign policy fears but also fails to distinguish itself from the rest of the population.

Finally, we examine criminal justice concerns. On the policy issues, we find that neither antiracism nor political progressiveness is significantly tied to fear of gun legislation, nor is antiracism significantly tied to the fear of the

---

10. It is possible that some of this difference is due to the younger ages of the antiracists since controls for age mediates the significant difference between the antiracist and political progressives on fears about paying college debt; however, it does not mediate the significant difference on fears of being unemployed.

local government implementing curfews during protests. Political progressiveness, however, is significantly related to not supporting the curfews of local governments. Both antiracism and political progressiveness are significantly linked to opposing the use of the National Guard during protests, support for law enforcement reform, and support for defunding of the police. Except for whether to use local curfews, there is little difference in criminal justice attitudes between antiracists and political progressives. This is not surprising, given how the discussion on criminal justice reform has been racialized in the United States. It is curious why antiracism does not inhibit the desire for local curfews in the same manner as political progressiveness. Future work that explores this difference may be useful in understanding distinct ideological constructs within antiracism and general political progressiveness.

However, there is little evidence that the attitudes of antiracists and political progressives are driven by fear of crime. Both are significantly more fearful of political brutality than the general population. Antiracism is significantly linked to fear of random shooting, and political progressiveness is significantly linked to fear of being a victim of property theft. None of the other measures of fear of crime are significant for either group. Both groups are not especially fearful of being a victim of criminals, which may partially account for their relative willingness to defund the police and seek law enforcement reform.

Results from this analysis indicate that antiracism is not merely a racial dimension within progressive political ideology. Popularized antiracism reflects elements of political philosophy on issues other than race. Given the limitations of a single survey, we are unable to do a comprehensive exploration of all the political issues. However, from the CSAF, we do find that antiracism is in deep agreement with political progressives on issues concerning January 6 and environmentalism. While it can be conceived that each of these issues has racialized concerns, they are not primarily driven by racial concerns. Some distinctions were detected in our assessment of Covid. Concerning economic and foreign policy concerns, antiracists did not generally differ from political progressives, but neither did either group generally differ from the general population. Finally, with minor distinctions, antiracists share a similar outlook with political progressives on criminal justice concerns. Why do antiracists differ from the general population on some nonracial issues (i.e., environmentalism) but not others (foreign policy fears)? In the next section, we speculate why this may be the case.

Beyond Race and into Partisanship

As we look at where antiracists differ from the general population, we better understand that antiracism is not merely a racialized perspective. It is easy to see that antiracism has a political component. But which issues that do not have an overt racial focus are the ones antiracists care more about than others? From our current analysis, we see that January 6, environmentalism, and Covid fit that criterion, whereas economic and foreign policy fears do not.[11] It is possible that distinctions between antiracists and the general public would have shown up for issues tied to the economy or foreign policy if the respondents were asked policy questions and not merely to discuss their fears on these subjects. However, differences between antiracists and the rest of the population were just as powerful on the questions of fears as they were on policy questions concerning overt racial issues, partisan political attitudes, and January 6 issues. The section on environmental issues consists of questions about the respondents' fears, and yet it is reasonable to argue that these different levels of fears are different levels of concerns antiracists have on environmental policy issues in contrast to the general public. We conclude that the fears exhibited in the CSAF are related, even if imperfectly, to the policy preferences of the respondents. Consequently, it is plausible that the lack of differences in their fears on economic and foreign policy issues reflects a level of agreement between antiracists and the rest of the population on those issues. Future work using the antiracism attitude scale to assess economic and foreign policy preferences can either confirm or refute this assertion.

If this assertion is correct, then it is viable to ask the question of why those supporting antiracism have a distinctive concern for environmental issues but not the economy. Why focus on January 6 and not on foreign policy? An initial response may be that racial minorities are impacted by environmental threats or threats to democracy. Yet are they not also impacted by economic threats or foreign policy decisions that can lead to wars? These priorities are not solely dictated by how a given dimension of issues impacts marginalized racial and ethnic groups. Somehow, environmental and January 6 issues have become racialized in ways that escape issues of economy and foreign policy. Speculations based on this data can provide insight into why this is the case and can supply us with more information about priorities that motivate antiracists.

We start with an obvious observation—that, with minor exceptions, antiracists tend to differ from the general population in basically the same ways as political progressives. They not only share similar perspectives with political progressives on distinctly racial issues but also on issues that are not obvious in their racialization to the general public. What is of particular importance are the particular issues where antiracists and political progressives

---

11. We did not put criminal justice into this assessment, given the degree to which racial issues have been tied to criminal justice concerns, especially since 2020.

differ from the general population. Why do both groups make such distinctions on environmentalism and January 6 but not on issues tied to the economy and foreign policy? We gain some insight into what might be happening by examining a couple of public polls taken before the 2022 midterms. This Pew Research Center poll (Pew Research Center 2022) indicates that the general public prefers Republican platforms on issues of the economy and foreign policy but Democratic platforms on issues of protecting democracy. An NPR survey (Montanaro 2022) indicates that the public favors the Republicans on issues of the economy, controlling inflation, and national security, which can be a proxy for foreign policy. But the public prefers Democrats on issues of climate change, coronavirus, and election security, which are often tied to January 6 issues. Antiracists and political progressives appear to distinguish themselves on issues where they have a partisan ability to appeal to the public. This is particularly the case when the issues are not overtly racialized. The general public may have a preference for Republican platforms on immigration issues (Pew Research Center 2022), but since that issue has overt racial implications, it will continue to be an issue that antiracists care about. But when the racial element is in doubt, antiracists tend to gravitate toward issues where political progressives have a potential advantage.

There is a dynamic of selectivity when exploring why some issues are racialized while others are not. Environmental dysfunctions indeed impact racial minorities more than majority group members (Henderson and Wells 2021, Mohai and Bryant 2019). However, unemployment is consistently higher for people of color than it is for majority group members (Han 2018, Dias 2021, Emeka 2018). Yet this preliminary exploration suggests that economic concerns are not racialized in the same manner as environmental issues. We suggest that this can be due to an ingroup partisan advantage for antiracists to focus on differential environmental impacts by race instead of economic impacts. If the public perceives Republicans as having better answers for inflation than Democrats, then for antiracists to tie the problems of inflation to the problems of African Americans may have an unintended effect of boosting electoral opportunities for Republicans. This suggests that there is more than just a radical political element to antiracism. There is a partisan element as well. We are not merely envisioning antiracism as a political identity. We now envision it as a partisan one. Antiracists are not merely concerned with promoting certain political interests but those interests reveal a partisan strategy.

Such assertions need further evidence than what can be found in the gleanings of survey results. They demand that we explore how antiracists themselves describe their concerns on a range of issues. To this end, we want to see qualitatively how antiracists publicly argue about January 6, environmentalism, or even the economy, to the degree that they do argue about the economy. In the next chapter, we present our endeavor to find and analyze online articles and blogs tying antiracism to these and other political and social issues. This analysis allows us to better understand how those who take up popularized antiracism make sense of issues not innately racial and how they present themselves to the larger society on such issues and will further our insight into the priorities and perspectives of popularized antiracism.

6

Political Partnership of Antiracism

Introduction

In Chapter 5, there was a significant association between identifying as politically progressive and holding antiracist beliefs, even after accounting for confounding variables. A statistical association alone, however, does not fully capture the intricacies of how antiracism is integrated into public discourse on specific political issues. While quantitative analysis helps us understand the systematic patterns of antiracism, it is crucial to explore the thoughts, language, and narratives shaping public understanding of antiracism. Qualitative methods enable us to delve into the underlying motivations and factors that connect progressive politics and antiracism. Both are needed.

This chapter continues our investigation of the association between antiracism and political affiliation through a qualitative examination of antiracist approaches to five political issues in the U.S.: climate change, abortion, January 6, street crime, and inflation. Since surveys have indicated that Democrats have an electoral advantage on issues of climate change, abortion, and preserving democracy while Republicans have an advantage on issues of crime and the economy (Pew Research Center 2022, Montanaro 2022), including these five issues allows us to see primarily how antiracists represent themselves on issues with distinct partisan-based appeals. Furthermore, we are curious if and how partisanship interacts with their concern for racial inequalities.

Consequently, we conducted a content analysis of various websites to find evidence for various directions of the relationship between antiracism and specific political issues. By categorizing and describing website content based on organization, article type, political affiliation, and publishing date, we aimed to identify patterns that may provide nuance to our quantitative analysis. We conclude this chapter with a discussion on the role of antiracist thought and speculate on its future implications in politics.

Content Analysis: Antiracism on the Web

We utilize website content analysis for several reasons. Content analysis capitalizes on the Internet's significant role in identity making, particularly in queer, disabled, and racialized communities (R. Miller 2017, Chan 2017). Online users create and reinforce identities through forums to discuss shared experiences, create community through online friends and allies, and share resources that educate about cultural heritage and history. We find this space all the more important with the emergence of popularized antiracism intersecting with the rapid increase of time spent online during the pandemic (Atske 2021), creating the right conditions for formative racial and political identity making.

An important aspect of identity is the different ways individuals create and maintain how others perceive them. Individuals engage in impression management, the process of using social techniques to present a certain image of oneself or one's community for specific goals that individuals desire (Goffman 1959). For instance, there have been discussions surrounding the performative nature of social justice in digital spaces, such as the act of posting a black square on Instagram as credibility maintenance (Wellman 2022) or partaking in microactivism by retweeting articles relevant to political discourse (Marichal 2013). Depending on what action is taken in these digital spaces, people are either labeled as performative or righteously resisting the current institutions. Antiracism is no exception to the need to engage in impression management. Content analysis can investigate how people who hold popularized antiracist ideals (un)intentionally shape their content to appeal to or reject certain audiences.[1]

Undoubtedly, the Internet will continue to be a vital force in shaping progressive social movements (Jackson 2018), but our research specifically aims to examine how mainstream antiracism permeates into and operates within the general population. While we do include articles with interviews

---

1. The Internet has further complicated impression management, as individuals can choose to remain anonymous or recreate their digital selves over and over again (Chester and Bretherton 2009).

with antiracist leaders (i.e., Ibram X. Kendi) in our analysis, our primary focus is to understand how their work shapes and influences the broader public, rather than solely concentrating on the individual contributions of specific figures. Understanding these differences and nuances serves as a valuable starting point for future research, assessing the extent to which antiracist beliefs intersect with political issues on a racialized level.

Justification of Five Political Issues as Sites of Examination

For the qualitative analysis, we chose political issues that have the potential to be championed by antiracists. The issues we selected—abortion, climate change, January 6, inflation, and street crime—all garnered significant national attention, sparked intense public debate, and strongly divided Republicans and Democrats. The five selected issues are not exhaustive, but they do make an important list to consider how antiracism is or is not utilized in a broad range of topics, particularly given the political division of each issue.

Furthermore, the issues we selected were not explicitly about race, yet antiracists could mobilize over the racial inequalities these issues raise, should they so desire. This latent potential throws into sharper contrast the choices antiracists make about what directions to take their coalitions. Abortion is overtly tied to female autonomy, climate change is about the health and utilization of the earth's resources, January 6 is linked to protest of election results, street crime is seen as an issue of law and order, and inflation represents concerns about the U.S. economy. Each issue, however, has the capacity to be "racialized" through an antiracist and intersectional framework. Thus, antiracists can choose to racialize these issues, but the issues are not so overtly centered on racial concerns that they must racialize these issues. We are keen to explore if and how this racialization process occurs for each issue, if it occurs through an antiracist framework, and where issues with a partisan political appeal may be treated differently than other issues.

Website Inclusion Criteria and Finalizing Search Terms

Three inclusion criteria were used before the formal website analysis. First, using Google search tools, we only included websites that were published or updated from 2016 to 2023. We chose this date range after searching the term "antiracism" in Google Trends, which evaluates the popularity of a term by giving it a value of 100 (the peak popularity for a term), 50 (the term is half as popular), or 0 (not enough data for this term).[2] While we considered lim-

---

2. The scoring system for Google Trends is a relative one, meaning that a score of 100 indicates that the term is the peak popularity of a term relative to other words or phrases at that point in time.

iting our results to 2020 because "antiracism" had a score of 100 in that year, we extended the date to 2016 to capture antiracist rhetoric that may have been present but not mainstream during the Trump presidency, when political polarization and national discourse on race were very high. Although Google shows the dates when websites are uploaded or published in the byline, there were a few websites where the dates were not shown, and they were thus excluded from the study.

Our second criterion was that the website must contain the exact words "antiracism" and the term for one of five issues we examined. In Google, even though parentheses are used in the search, results are based not on exact words but instead on algorithmic relevance.[3] Google tools does have a function where one can search with exact search terms, but it cannot be used at the same time as the date restriction function. We chose the date function because we valued our date exclusion criteria as important, and furthermore, results with parentheses gave similar results compared to the exact search terms function. In addition, we did not use hyphens for other spellings of "antiracism" (e.g., "anti-racism") because Google understands hyphens as the removal of such words from a search. We also did not use other variations of the word "antiracism," such as "antiracist," because, after a few preliminary searches, Google results were filled with primary texts such as Kendi's book on antiracism rather than the secondary sources necessary for our qualitative analysis.

Our third and final inclusion was relevance. Each website was read carefully for relevance, as some articles had nothing to do with either the political issue at hand or antiracism. For instance, some articles had the words "antiracism" and "abortion" on the same website, but only "abortion" was present in the main content while "antiracism" was part of another headline. Websites not relevant were excluded. Repeated articles and articles that could not be accessed due to a faulty URL were also excluded.

With these considerations, we used these search terms on April 20, 2023: "antiracism" AND "climate change," "antiracism" AND "abortion," "antiracism" AND "January 6," "antiracism" AND "inflation," and "antiracism" AND "street crime."[4] We then collected the first 50 unique websites as some were duplicates. After assessing for inclusion/exclusion criteria, the final analytic sample was the following: climate change (n = 41), abortion (n = 31), January 6 (n = 18), inflation (n = 8), and street crime (n = 10).

---

3. Google's decision to choose its algorithmic search for relevance rather than allowing users to search for results with specific key words is a rather recent development of Google that has frustrated many online users. We acknowledge these limitations of using Google for our content analysis, but given that antiracism is a relatively new movement, Google allows us to capture important broad data points.

4. To ensure consistency, we collected all the websites on a single day as opposed to a longer period of time as Internet Search Engine Optimization (SEO) is constantly changing.

Evaluating the Relationship between Antiracism and Political Issues

After finalizing our analytic sample, we assessed if there was a link between antiracism and the political issue, which we defined in two ways. The first definition was when antiracism and the political issue were contained in the same sentence or paragraph. One example could be, "Climate change is antiracism; antiracism is climate change." The second way to define the link between antiracism and the political issue was determined when antiracism and the political issue were not explicitly in the same sentence or paragraph but implied. For instance, several websites were published via the Boston University Center for Antiracist Research, but the article itself never mentioned words such as "antiracist" or "antiracism." If the content included some statement on one of the main tenets of antiracism in presented Chapter 3—1) racism is pervasive in the United States, 2) racism is multifaceted, 3) differential roles for white and nonwhite people, and 4) society must face massive reform—then we recorded "Yes" to question 1. We consider this a permeation of popularized antiracism into the public consciousness where people are talking about it without consciously realizing it.

We then established four potential pathways that may occur between antiracism and the political issue (Table 6.1).[5] Each pathway corresponds to a specific linear relationship between antiracism with potential positive and/or negative associations. Pathways 1 and 2 delved into the impact of antiracism on the political issue, while Pathways 3 and 4 explored the reverse relationship. Specifically, Pathway 1 assessed if antiracism was seen as a solution to the political issue. Conversely, Pathway 2 focused on evaluating the detrimental consequences of a lack of antiracism (presence of racism) on the political issue. Pathway 3 involved an assessment of how the political issue served as a potential solution to racism. Finally, Pathway 4 involved an examination of whether the political issue resulted in negative outcomes related to racism. After our content analysis, we provided a short description, as seen in Table 6.1.

Other Assessments

We organized each website into three types of articles: analysis, activist, and other. Analytic articles described and evaluated historical and contemporary events with no call to action. These analytic articles were often academic and news related. Activist articles were required to have a call to action.

---

5. There are many more pathways to consider. For instance, we chose a linear pathway, but future research should consider multidirectional pathways. Pathways could also cross one another as well.

TABLE 6.1 ASSESSING THE RELATIONSHIP BETWEEN ANTIRACISM AND POLITICAL ISSUE

	Question	Linear relationship	Description
Pathway 1	Does combating racism combat the political issue?	Antiracism → Political issue	Antiracist rhetoric, resources, and calls to action where antiracism was seen as a solution to the political issue.
Pathway 2	Does racism worsen the political issue?	Racism → Political issue	Nearly all of the evidence was a historical analysis of the ways racism made the given political issue worse.
Pathway 3	Does combating the political issue combat racism?	Political issue → Antiracism	Antiracist rhetoric, resources, and calls to action. The political issue was seen as a necessary solution to racism.
Pathway 4	Does the political issue worsen racism?	Political issue → Racism	Most observed pathway in content analysis. We found that statistics that found disproportionate effects by race were cited as a justification for how a given issue worsened racism.

Usually, the rhetoric encourages readers to take personal action to center antiracism in their lifestyle or thought process. A call to action was found in a diverse selection of publication mediums, but most were found in interviews of activists, antiracism resource lists, and statements after a major political event. Events that were neither analytic nor activist were labeled as "other." These included, for example, websites that announced faculty updates (whose work focused on antiracism) or highlighted events about how to utilize data.

Organization type was coded by six items. Academic organizations included any university, academic journal, university website, student organization, or university-related organization. Industries included policy centers, think tanks, and corporations. Governmental agencies were any government report or website with a ".gov." Media was defined as any news and media outlets, local and national. Community-centered organizations included non-student community-centered organizations (nonprofit), activist organizations, churches, and social media posts. All websites that did not meet the first five labels were coded as "other." Some organizations could have been one or more of these categories, but we chose a single category that best fit the description presented in the "About Us" section of the website.

We defined political affiliation as either liberal or conservative. Political affiliation was determined by the following protocol. First, we checked on media bias by using AllSides or InfluenceWatch to label the organization as either liberal or conservative. If there was no information there, we then checked the "About Us" page to see if the website supported a conservative or liberal political agenda, which we defined as explicit endorsements of political candidates or an affirmation/critique of a political party. If we could not establish strong partisan support after these steps, we labeled the organization as "can't tell." Although there were a few organizations that were moderate or center, the sample size was too small and was consequently labeled "can't tell" as well.

Results

Climate Change

There is a major partisan gap in the support for action on climate change in the U.S. In 2020, 84% of Democrats saw "protecting the environment" as a top concern for the president and Congress compared to 39% of Republicans (Kennedy and Johnson 2020). Our qualitative analysis supports the idea that antiracism is strongly aligned with partisan progressive interests. Pathway 1 was the most popular from our climate change content analysis, as we found that a majority (61%) of climate change articles championed antiracism as a necessary component to combat climate change. With titles such as "Climate Change Battle Must Include Environmental Justice" and "Want to Be an Environmentalist? Start with Antiracism," these perspectives make it immediately clear that solving climate change would require antiracism.

Furthermore, having the right antiracist ideas is not enough. Rather, those concerned about the climate must become actively antiracist. The word "active" generally refers to a few different ways to implement antiracism into climate change. For instance, six articles emphasized the need for white people to listen to people of color and amplify their voices because the "climate movement is still overwhelmingly white and middle."[6] Besides providing a seat for nonwhite people in climate change conversations, there are also explicit calls to implement antiracist curriculum and training in schools in three articles, government/legislation in two articles, and medicine in one article.

The language became less activist and more historical when we examined how racism impacted climate change in Pathway 2. Authors and organizations did not view climate change as a universal man-made phenomenon but one that has been specifically caused by white people exploiting non-

---

6. Friends of the Earth, "Climate Justice and Anti-racism | Friends of the Earth," September 30, 2020, https://friendsoftheearth.uk/about/climate-justice-and-antiracism.

white people. An excerpt from an article by Families for Climate effectively captures this interpretation: "Racism is killing the planet: the ideology of white supremacy leads the way toward disposable people and a disposable natural world.... You can't have climate change without sacrifice zones, and you can't have sacrifice zones without disposable people, and you can't have disposable people without racism."[7] In such perspectives, the primary culprit for environmental neglect is not a lack of awareness or corporate greed that is killing the planet but racism. Specifically, it is a racist ideology (white supremacy) that creates sacrifice zones of disposable people, and disposable people are created through racism. Similarly, several articles cited racist histories and practices such as the construction of oil pipelines concentrated near Indigenous communities, the "colorblind" urban planning leading to the Flint water crisis, colonialism, and redlining within the U.S. These examples all showed how racism led to a worsened climate crisis.

In Pathway 3, we only found claims in two articles that fighting climate change would also fight racism. From these two articles, one was titled "Climate Justice Is the Weapon against Racism We Need Now" from an antiracism resource guide. The other was a quote from antiracist leader Ibram X. Kendi: "You can't be an antiracist, you can't even understand what it means to be antiracist, if you are not also fighting against climate change."[8] Like the call to action in Pathway 1 for climate change activists to become actively antiracist, Pathway 3 required antiracists to fight against climate change. Although there is not much more to extrapolate beyond what is presented here, we observe that popularized antiracism is used here to fight for other movements such as climate change.

Last, in Pathway 4, 73.2% of articles highlighted the negative effects of climate change on racism. The primary method of justifying this rhetoric was through the phrase "racial disparity," which was used interchangeably with "inequity" and "inequality." Here is an example from Climate Generation: "Current impact: Climate change is an intersectional issue that disproportionately impacts BIPOC and lower income communities."[9] Indeed, we find in our analysis that popularized antiracist content mentions that nonwhite populations have worse outcomes on morbidity, mortality, and environmental dangers such as flooding and worse pollution compared to their white counterparts. While it is theoretically plausible that the decisions of

---

7. Families for Climate, "Racial Justice and Raising Antiracist Kids," accessed April 20, 2023, https://www.familiesforclimate.org/antiracism-resources.

8. Joel Brown and Ziyu (Julian) Zhu, "Climate Change Battle Must Include Environmental Justice," Boston University, October 3, 2022, https://www.bu.edu/articles/2022/climate-change-battle-must-include-environmental-justice/.

9. Climate Generation, "Centering Antiracism through Partnership," *Climate Generation* (blog), March 10, 2022, https://climategen.org/blog/centering-antiracism-through-partnership/.

nonwhite populations contributed to the disparity, antiracist discourse in two articles made certain to highlight how nonwhite people have experienced the most damage from climate change despite having contributed to it the least. The antiracists focus on power and institutions that typically work to absolve nonwhite populations of complicity in climate change. A disparity in complicity ties into the antiracist tenet of differential responsibilities between white and nonwhite people.

Beyond our pathways framework, we find that exhaustion is a notable theme emerging from our analysis of climate change discourse. Interestingly, this exhaustion did not stem from dealing with those interlocutors outside climate change activist spaces but from within. For instance, a blog discussed how the inability of some climate change activists to understand the political and racial nature of climate change led to the author's exhaustion.[10] A post from Columbia University reiterates the same sentiment well: "To white people who care about maintaining a habitable planet . . . I need you to understand that our racial inequality crisis is intertwined with our climate crisis. . . . I need you to step up. Please. Because I am exhausted."[11] We observe that antiracist authors have to educate not only those outside climate change circles but also those within it on how climate change is intertwined with race.

From the strong rhetoric that affirms the ubiquitous nature of racism, the differential role of white and nonwhite people, and calls to action, climate change as conceived as a progressive issue is affirmed and reinforced by antiracist thought and language. Although most articles were sourced from academic institutions, the content was not peer-reviewed academic articles but presented in blog format, providing access to the general public.[12] Thus, the writings of antiracism and climate change serve an important purpose of popularizing an antiracism perspective on climate change. Future research should consider the potential divisions that may occur with the rise of antiracism within the climate change discourse. We now turn to examine another issue in which surveys have shown a progressive partisan prioritization—abortion.

---

10. Elias Yassin, "Black Lives Matter and the Struggle to Centre Racial Justice in the Climate Movement," King's College London, August 27, 2020, https://www.kcl.ac.uk/blm-and-the-struggle-to-centre-racial-justice-in-the-climate-movement.

11. Victoria Bortfeld, "This 'Green' Space Shouldn't Be So White—State of the Planet," August 21, 2020, https://news.climate.columbia.edu/2020/08/21/environmental-sciences-anti-racism/.

12. There is a robust, long-standing tradition of academic researchers who have analyzed climate change through the lens of race. While we acknowledge that there have been several grassroots activist movements within climate change, antiracism seems to be a new movement that has made climate change activism mainstream.

Abortion

Abortion is another issue where Democrats and Republicans are strongly split along ideological lines. In 2022, 81% of Democrats believed that abortion should be considered legal in most cases compared to a 14% minority of Republicans (Lipka 2022). Again, strong Democratic support (and Republican opposition) predicted the high level of antiracist language in the abortion articles we found in our content analysis.

In Pathway 1, there is evidence that authors see antiracism as a necessary solution to the issue of abortion,[13] but it was mentioned in fewer than half the articles (32.5%). Like the issue of climate change, the antiracist solutions for abortion focused on making space for nonwhite voices in institutional and national discourse and the amplification of the work, products, and activism done by people of color. We found that antiracist solutions for abortion are centered on Black women. One solution highlighted the need to make space for Black women to use their voices to share their stories and lived experiences, which is a crucial component of popularized antiracism. Another solution is about amplification, as "black and brown people already lead the most powerful abortion fund network in the country."[14]

The centering of Black women in Pathway 1 is significant, as authors considered Black women to be one of the most vulnerable populations via intersectionality. Content analysis revealed that the intersection—to be a woman and Black—is a double oppression, as a Black woman is oppressed by both patriarchy and racism. According to the blog *She Seeks Nonfiction*, the liberation of the Black woman is the key to true reproductive justice for everyone: "When we liberate Black women, we liberate Black men, white women, Black and white nonbinary people, and yes, even white men. We liberate LGBTQ+ folks, disabled people, and poor people. True justice and true feminism mean equity for all, and the ability of everyone to make choices for themselves. We will not have reproductive justice and gender justice while we still have abusive police and an abusive prison system, or poverty and hunger, or a number of other injustices that racist policymakers have brought onto Black communities."[15] For the antiracist, to include and amplify the voices and work of Black women is not only the most inclusive act an antiracist can make but also the most profound for society's liberation.

---

13. We decided to include "reproductive health" and "maternal health" as synonyms with "abortion," as some articles included "abortion" in the title but used these phrases in the rest of the article.

14. The Peggy and Jack Baskin Foundation, "Abortion Activism and Access Resources," accessed April 20, 2023, https://baskinfoundation.org/resources/abortion-activism-and-access-resources/.

15. Rebekah Kohlhepp, "Abortion Rights Archives," *She Seeks Nonfiction* (blog), May 21, 2023, https://sheseeksnonfiction.blog/tag/abortion-rights/.

In Pathway 2, several articles discussed how racism has driven abortion through a narrative known as the Great Replacement theory (also known as white extinction). The Great Replacement theory is characterized in our content analysis of antiracists' writings as "the most diabolical of all racist ideas operating today"[16] and "the fear of genetic dominance of Black and Brown people."[17] They envision it as an ideology used by a white population, afraid of the growing minority population, to attempt to control the minority population through reproductive means, such as anti-abortion legislation in the past. Authors from websites argued that because the reversal of *Roe v. Wade* decreased the proportion of white people in the U.S., the Great Replacement theory has become relevant to present opponents of abortion. Although the pragmatic validity of the Great Replacement theory is contested,[18] we note that authors readily utilized the popularity of the Great Replacement theory as a primary reason driving opposition to legalized abortion rather than the religious or ethical considerations voiced by conservatives to support the reversal of *Roe v. Wade* and the larger pro-life movement. The decision to evoke the Great Replacement theory over other traditional arguments made by conservatives is an important example of the racialization of the abortion issue in popularized antiracist contexts.

Only one article in Pathway 3 argued that supporting abortion would combat racism in the context of the Dobbs case, which is a landmark U.S. Supreme Court case that decided that abortion is not a right. According to an article in the *New England Journal of Medicine* (NEJM), "The Dobbs decision rolls back fundamental rights for many people, and it is a direct assault on efforts to improve racial equity in health care. Clinicians can help by providing abortion care, supporting others who do so, and advocating for safe, dignified, humane reproductive health care services to be provided in their health care systems, to the extent allowed by state law. The Dobbs decision raises the stakes for clinicians, health care administrators, and policymakers who value racial justice in health."[19] NEJM, one of the most prestigious med-

---

16. Jessic McKnight, "Five Things You Should Know about Abortion in America," Center for Antiracist Research, accessed April 20, 2023, https://www.bu.edu/antiracism-center/2022/06/20/five-things-you-should-know-about-abortion-in-america/.

17. Carla Bell, "How White Fear of Genetic Annihilation Fuels Abortion Bans," *YES! Magazine*, July 4, 2019, https://www.yesmagazine.org/social-justice/2019/07/04/abortion-ban-fear-white-extinction-babies.

18. The Great Replacement theory does not hold up well against statistics, particularly with the most recent abortion data. It is well documented that African American women are five times more likely to abort than white women, and white women (34%) and Black women (37%) make up a similar proportion of all abortions. With these numbers in mind, anti-abortion legislation would likely reduce the percentage of white people in the United States.

19. Katy Backes Kozhimannil, Asha Hassan, and Rachel R. Hardeman, "Abortion Access as a Racial Justice Issue." *New England Journal of Medicine* 387, no. 17 (2022): 1537–1539, https://doi.org/10.1056/NEJMp2209737.

ical journals in the world, argues that if you value racial justice, then providing abortion access is a way to do so.

Pathway 4 has the highest frequency of all pathways in our abortion content analysis. In this pathway, we find arguments that the effects of racism on abortion are similar to each other, focusing on how an abortion ban or restriction will lead to unequal, unfavorable outcomes for nonwhite populations compared to their white counterparts. The inequitable increase in deaths due to pregnancy (lack of safe abortion) in nonwhite populations compared to their white counterparts is a key metric often mentioned in seven articles. For instance, NEJM writes about how a national abortion ban could "increase maternal mortality by 21% overall and by 33% among Black Americans."[20] Because *Roe v. Wade* was a court decision that gave power back to the states, articles also highlighted how nonwhite women in more conservative parts of the U.S., such as Texas and the Midwest, could experience even greater negative health outcomes.

Unlike climate change, which is framed as a looming, existential threat, the abortion and antiracist discussion seems to be motivated by specific events in the U.S. that threaten the ability to have a legal abortion. While authors highlighted how women, particularly women of color, have long fought for their bodily autonomy and right to have an abortion, the women in those historical examples would not have called themselves antiracists. We find that despite antiracism being a rather recent phenomenon, the willingness of authors to claim historical examples as "antiracist" is a pedagogical tactic to establish the importance of antiracism to abortion. To claim that "we have always been antiracist, and here are the examples to prove it" adds great credibility to the strategic partnership between the issues of antiracism and abortion. We now turn our attention to another issue that is not a phenomenon but an event—the riots of January 6.

January 6

There is a deep partisan divide regarding who is to blame for the January 6 riots. Democrats tended to place a lot of blame on Donald Trump, with 89% of them attributing responsibility to him compared to 15% of Republicans (PRRI 2021). Another survey revealed that 85% of Democrats considered the attackers to be criminals. Only 17% of Republicans held the same view (Milligan 2022). Despite this stark partisan gap, we found that our content analysis revealed less antiracist attention to the January 6 riots compared to the other two progressive issues.

---

20. Koshimannil, Hassan, and Hardeman.

In Pathway 1, we found two ways websites considered antiracism as a solution to January 6. With calls to listen to and amplify Black voices, support nonwhite organizations, and provide an antiracist curriculum, this first solution is similar to what we have seen in the previous issues. Pathway 2, however, assesses why the riots happened and how antiracist implementation could have drastically changed the outcome of January 6. For instance, one author from a website writes, "Failing to address the effects of systemic racism and white supremacy is a security vulnerability, as demonstrated during the January 6 insurrection in 2021. These effects would be much more difficult to exploit if antiracism was at the core of U.S. foreign policy."[21] According to this author, the effect of systemic racism and white supremacy is not confined to a domestic division between people in the U.S. Rather, the larger threat of a security vulnerability is present because foreign disinformation campaigns can exploit the divisions in worldview caused by racism, leading to the differences in understandings that sparked January 6. What could have prevented this? The answer is antiracism. The last sentence, particularly the use of the word "core," is telling of how antiracists perceive the importance of antiracism. If antiracism was at the core of U.S. foreign policy, then the insurrection could have been avoided altogether.

There is plenty of discourse on how racism led to the January 6 Capitol riots, although articles varied on pinpointing when the racism began. For five articles, the racism that led to the riots had been building for some time, mentioning key instances of racial division such as the election of President Obama, the election of President Biden, and antiracist victories. Two articles argued that the riots were yet another example of the racism that has been present since the beginning of democracy. An article says, "But January 6 is not a lapse in democracy. It's a product of a long history of white supremacy that coexists alongside democracy."[22] For some antiracists, the United States has always been racist and discriminatory. Antiracists also argued that there was a disparity in how BLM protests and January 6 were treated by law enforcement, showcasing the racial bias in U.S. institutions. This discourse focused on the differing narratives between how BLM protests were treated compared to January 6.[23] An article states, "The greatest domestic terrorist threat of our

---

21. Sneha Nair, "Equity and Racial Justice: Where Do They Fit in a National Security Strategy?" New America, accessed April 20, 2023, http://newamerica.org/political-reform/reports/equity-and-racial-justice-where-do-they-fit-in-a-national-security-strategy/.

22. Alex Zamalin, "The Democracy Aaron Sorkin Has in Mind Is Missing Antiracism," Beacon Broadside, March 9, 2021, https://www.beaconbroadside.com/broadside/2021/03/the-democracy-aaron-sorkin-has-in-mind-is-missing-antiracism.html.

23. This may be because January 6 was a one-time event and quantitative analysis was difficult due to lack of data. Outside of our content analysis, there have been attempts to quantitatively determine the difference between the January 6 riots and BLM protests.

time is white supremacists. From my understanding, the local Capitol Police assumed that this demonstration wouldn't turn into an insurrection and wouldn't turn violent. To me, it just flies in the face of all evidence. Those demonstrations that were almost uniformly peaceful last year, that were antiracist, there was typically a massive police presence. But for those who are part of a group that is the greatest domestic terrorist threat of our time, it was assumed that those demonstrations would be peaceful, so there wasn't a police force of the same scale."[24] Another author further reinforces the idea that the disproportionate treatment of January 6 was used as a way deny Black Americans human rights to "undermine democracy while upholding systems of oppression such as racism."[25] Notably, we found no evidence for Pathways 3 or 4.

Content analysis shows how authors positively spoke of antiracism as an important framework to consider these three progressive issues—climate change, abortion, and the January 6 riots. However, the relative lack of articles about January 6 compared to the other progressive issues elucidates how other theories, such as election dissatisfaction, misinformation, and economic downturn, may compete with antiracism in progressive politics for the cause of the January 6 riots. Indeed, in our excluded articles, we found that many Americans saw January 6 in light of the prior reasons. The lack of articles may also be due to how January 6 was a one-time and unprecedented historical event whereas the other progressive issues have a long, storied literature. Of course, the continuing coverage of congressional hearings on January 6 may generate further data. Nevertheless, even with limited attention, antiracists still indicated similar patterns of calls for more voices of marginalized racial groups and the need for attention to the lingering effects of racism in their comments about January 6. To begin our examination of issues not tied to a progressive partisan advantage, we now turn to inflation to explore if and how antiracism has permeated within that space.

Inflation

Inflation is the number one concern in the U.S., as 70% of Americans view inflation as a "very big problem" (Doherty and Gomez 2022). Within political parties, Republicans are more concerned about inflation (84%) compared to Democrats (57%), and the lack of antiracist thought in our inflation content analysis is consistent with this partisan discrepancy. None of the authors

---

24. Fabiola Cineas, "Ibram X. Kendi on Why White America Is Still Shocked by White Supremacy," Vox, January 12, 2021, https://www.vox.com/22227102/anti-racism-ibram-kendi.
25. Eagle Rock School, "Social Justice and Anti-racism," accessed April 20, 2023, https://www.eaglerockschool.org/about/social-justice-anti-racism.

argued that combating racism combats inflation (Pathway 1), racism makes inflation worse (Pathway 2), or inflation makes racism worse (Pathway 4). Given the paucity of relevant articles and the lack of discussion of antiracism alongside inflation, we conclude that antiracism is not seen as a solution to inflation in popularized antiracism.

There are some arguments that combating inflation combats racism, although inflation was rarely the primary focus and instead was utilized as a citation. For instance, the only two articles in which we find this perspective focused on climate change and Asian American health. Both keyed in on the Inflation Reduction Act, stating that this legislation will help alleviate the suffering experienced by marginalized communities[26] and decrease the inequities that were exacerbated by COVID-19.[27] Ironically, the Inflation Reduction Act was also criticized for failing to decrease inflation, with nonpartisan agencies such as the Congressional Budget Office concluding that inflation reduction would be negligible (Rugaber and Boak 2022). These instances point to how antiracists have not yet approached inflation as a serious space for activism but rather as a supplement for other issues that proved more attractive to antiracist authors, such as climate change.

This paucity reveals that antiracists have generally ignored inflation as an issue. Their lack of attention, relative to the stronger attention given to climate change, abortion, and even January 6, speaks to a focus of antiracists on issues favorable to political progressives. The examination of another issue—street crime—that conservatives have used in their political struggles with progressives can provide us with more clarity about how antiracists address issues favorable for political conservatives.

Street Crime

In 2022, a majority of Democrats (61%) and Republicans (95%) believed that there was more crime in the U.S. compared to 2021 (Brenan 2022). While national crime data collection is notoriously unreliable, there has been a recent increase in street crimes such as burglaries, robberies, and motor vehicle thefts (Rosenfeld, Boxerman, and Lopez 2023). Yet antiracism rhetoric is barely present in our street crime content analysis. None of the authors argued that confronting racism combats street crime (Pathway 1), supporting antiracism combats street crime (Pathway 2), or confronting street crime combats rac-

---

26. Brown and Zhu, "Climate Change Battle."
27. Krystal Ka'ai, Monica McLemore, Zhuo (Adam) Chen, Grace X. Ma, Raynald Samoa, Thu Quach, and Xinzhi Zhang, "Asian American, Native Hawaiian, and Pacific Islander Health." Health Equity 6, no. 1 (2022): 942–952, https://doi.org/10.1089/heq.2022.29015.rtd.

ism (Pathway 3). We only found evidence that street crime led to more racism (Pathway 4) in 7 out of 10 total articles.

Regarding climate change and abortion, antiracist authors often pointed out how race-neutral language is utilized to legitimate racist legislation and assumptions without being explicitly racist. Laws to build highways next to low-income, nonwhite populations would worsen the environment and create more hazards. Abortion laws would lead to more forced births, which would negatively affect Black women compared to white women. Street crime is no exception. In our content analysis, authors mentioned that terms such as "street crime" and "tough-on-crime laws" often function as colorblind tools that allow white society to discuss race without discussing race at all.[28] The omnipresence of race in the street crime discussion was well noted, and one academic researcher writes, "As to race, the research on street crime was clear: The rates of Black offending (and Black victimization) were disproportionately high. So, even as we did not talk about race, we were talking about race."[29] Racism is always present but hidden, and the work of the antiracist is to discover not if a phenomenon is racist but how.

Most articles were like the one prior, critiquing how statistics about Black men disproportionately committing more street crimes were misused and misunderstood. One article details how the actual validity of the statistic may not even be important: "If a newspaper reports street crime and rape by Black men, day after day, with menacing pictures of perpetrators and bruised white innocent victims, it may well produce a racist discourse, even if every element, in itself, is not only legitimate but also true. It is not only the elements of discourse which may or may not be racist, but the way in which it all swirls together to make a whole."[30] From this author's antiracist perspective, even a legitimately true statement can be racist, depending on its portrayal.

Statistics on the differential outcomes between white and nonwhite populations reveal that street crime is racialized to some extent, but not through the lens of antiracism. Little effort is put into envisioning antiracism techniques to reduce street crime. Calls to action abundantly present in progressive issues were nonexistent in the issue of street crime. Despite street crime being an important issue for many political offices, the lack of racialization

---

28. Akwatu Alleyne Khenti, "Three Decades of Epidemic Black Gun Homicide Victimization in Toronto: Analyzing Causes and Consequences of a Criminological Approach" (Ph.D. diss., York University, 2018), https://yorkspace.library.yorku.ca/server/api/core/bitstreams/06c161b8-4f32-4b7c-8bb1-906354554a59/content.

29. Katheryn Russell-Brown, "Black Lives Matter in Criminology? Let's Prove It." Race and Justice 11, no. 3 (2021): 328–37, https://doi.org/10.1177/2153368720983436.

30. David Hirsh, "Boycott, Divestment, and Sanctions (BDS) and Antisemitism," Academic Engagement Network Pamphlet Series No. 1, December 2016, https://academicengagement.org/wp-content/uploads/2019/09/David-Hirsh-pamphlet.pdf.

and the absence of being actively antiracist shows that popularized antiracism has not yet meaningfully engaged with street crime.

Findings

Why Might Some Issues Be Linked with Antiracism?

We found overwhelmingly more antiracist language and thought concerning issues that work to the political advantage of Democrats (climate change, January 6, abortion) than the advantage of Republicans (street crime, inflation). Antiracists likely view the Democratic Party as the more viable party to implement antiracism, given that the Democratic Party is more diverse and tends to value DEI more compared to Republicans (Mitchell 2019, Cox 2022). This perception can spur such partisan attention by antiracists.

Antiracists consistently credited the persistence of racism as a source of the problematic features connected to the issue at hand. A negative historical interpretation of the U.S. distinctly separated the rhetoric between progressive and conservative issues in Pathway 2. In progressive issues, the narrative emphasized the constant presence of racism in U.S. institutions and legislation, often tied directly to the legacies of white supremacy and slavery. Antiracism is seen as a solution that could profoundly transform the U.S. landscape inside out.

On the other hand, conservative issues were excluded from the main analysis because inflation and street crime were discussed in nonracial terms. The history of inflation was nonracial, focusing primarily on economic output and standard of living. Street crime, even though it may be more racialized than inflation, is rarely framed in a way where antiracism could be seen as a solution. If anything, the phrase "street crime" often exacerbated racism because it created stereotypes of Black men. Given that Democrats are more likely to support increased attention to the history of slavery and racism, antiracists may view this party as a more hospitable place to tell the stories of the past.

Finally, there is a great deal of similarity in how antiracist language manifested in progressive issues, despite the fundamental difference among climate change, abortion, and January 6. No matter the progressive issue, the antiracist call to action was unilaterally similar. There was an assumption that it was time to create space for nonwhite people out of fairness. Antiracist authors argued that because white society has dominated the discourse, it is now time to listen to nonwhite people as a source of solutions. There was an assumption that the nonwhite lived experience should be amplified not only for the sake of fairness but also because they have insights and solutions that white people cannot know or create on their own.

Other Characteristics: Organization Type and Political Affiliation and Activist Language

Activist language was similar regardless of organization type. Whether it was an academic article, blog, corporate response, or university forum, we consistently found a discourse that encouraged both individuals and entire institutions to take steps on the journey to become actively antiracist. This might simply be political branding, but the widespread activist language advocating for antiracist solutions highlights the increasing prominence of antiracism in our society.

An organization's political affiliations as liberal or moderate generally corresponded with antiracist rhetoric, as did websites where we could not tell their political affiliation. While there were very few conservative articles from our content analysis, the ones that were included in our final analytic sample heavily critiqued antiracist rhetoric. While the critique of antiracism from conservative discourse is expected, articles supporting and using antiracist rhetoric to affirm conservative talking points are an important development. Students for Life, a well-known pro-life organization, praises the establishment of the Center for Antiracism Research for Health Equity as admirable but states that it "would be better realized once it [the Center] is divorced from the largest abortion vendor in America."[31] Antiracism is not the problem—abortion is. Similarly, one article from *Christianity Today* goes as far as to say, "The anti-racism campaign is a model for the anti-abortion movement. The anti-abortion cause and the anti-racism cause are sibling abolition movements that protest two different cultures of exploitation and devaluation."[32] Although the evidence is sparse, we see here that antiracism does not have to have an inherently politically progressive stance but can be formed to adjust to different political opinions.

Implications

We noted earlier that antiracist rhetoric was similar among all progressive issues, despite their fundamental differences. The activist rhetoric from Pathway 1 may have the most relevant implications. Calls to be actively antiracist by sharing antiracist resources, creating space for nonwhite people by hiring

---

31. Samantha Kamman, "University of Minnesota Gets $5 Million 'Anti-racism' Grant, Ironically Involves Planned Parenthood," Students for Life of America, April 2, 2021, https://studentsforlife.org/2021/04/02/university-of-minnesota-gets-5-million-anti-racism-grant-ironically-involves-planned-parenthood/.

32. Andrea Dilley, "The Pro-Life Project Has a Playbook: Racial Justice History," *Christianity Today*, December 21, 2020, https://www.christianitytoday.com/ct/2021/january-february/abortion-pro-life-movement-playbook-racial-justice-history.html.

them in institutions and including them in national discussions, and continuing to educate oneself on antiracist principles are just a few of the ways authors called on readers to be actively antiracist. One immediate implication would be the continued rise of microactivism, which is a form of digital activism that does not necessarily involve mobilization but involves education and information through the sharing of social justice–related articles and links (Marichal 2013). While some have criticized the efficacy of this form of activism by ridiculing it as "slacktivism" or "clicktivism," we are curious to see the outcome of such calls to action by antiracists.

Another implication of the intertwining between antiracism and progressive affiliation is that antiracism—regardless of the innate value of the ideology—is more likely to act as a partisan label than a unified support for a policy. Currently, political conservatives are repelled by terms such as "woke" and "critical race theory." Antiracism may soon fall into the same category of being a way to signal partisan allegiance. The internal pressure for conservatives to remain within lines and not be outed as "woke," and the internal progressive pressure to link antiracism to events that are not overly seen as racialized, could severely limit the advancement of national discussions.

The difficulty in removing the partisan label of antiracism also applies to the individual who is antiracist first and Republican or Democrat second. Even if antiracists would like to consider conservative issues of inflation or street crime, they may be met with immense resistance from both Republicans and Democrats. Since a version of popularized antiracism is highly partisan, future antiracist work may always be considered partisan. The partisan aspect of popularized antiracism may greatly limit the ability of individual antiracists to do engage in antiracism outreach. We go into more detail about that dynamic in the final chapter. We more fully explore the implications of the partisan nature of antiracism and conclude the book by exploring possible futures for a popularized antiracism movement.

7

Conclusion

The acceptance of overt forms of racism has dramatically declined over the past few decades (Schuman et al. 1997). One might say that even white supremacists do not like to be called racist (Deggans 2020). Furthermore, to be labeled a racist today is to face tremendous social stigma (Crandall, Eshleman, and O'Brien 2002). However, evidence supporting the existence of institutional forms of racism is overwhelming (Mendez, Hogan, and Culhane 2014, Better 2007, Paradies, Truong, and Priest 2014, Patel 2022, Tate and Page 2018, Williams and Mohammed 2013, Quillian et al. 2017). There is also abundant evidence of the historical effects of racism on marginalized racial minority group members (Blanton 2011, Bailey, Feldman, and Bassett 2021, Bailey et al. 2017, Lui et al. 2006, Menendian, Gailes, and Gambhir 2021). Given this reality, movements have risen and fallen to challenge modern manifestations of racism, with the most recent movement being antiracism. Our work is not merely to examine individuals who personally identify as antiracists but also their effort to intentionally and assertively address issues of racism on a multifaceted level.

As seen in Table 4.3, education is significantly linked to higher levels of antiracism. This is not an accident, given that antiracism as a philosophy developed within academic circles. While antiracism is subject to critical inquiry among scholars, the general value of this ideology is usually taken for granted by most race scholars. Antiracists assert that the problems of racism, as they envision those problems, should be widely accepted in our general society. But in a politically polarized society, this taken-for-granted assumption is subject to challenge. Arguments concerning antiracism among academics tend to reinforce these assumptions and postulate passionate concerns about how to best implement antiracism in society. We have, on the other hand, taken on the task of analyzing those supportive of antiracism in as dispassionate a manner as possible. Issues of racial equality and equity bring about powerful emotions connected to efforts for justice and fairness. It is easy to get swept up in such efforts and make a stand on the ideological battlefield. However, our approach is to examine the nature of antiracists with an eye on how such individuals envision society. While we certainly value the interventions and writings of antiracists and those who utilize certain frameworks for their work broadly, our approach offers another perspective on the current and future trajectories of antiracism as a movement.

To be more precise, the partisan and radical nature of antiracist attitudes is key to understanding the current direction of antiracism, and the implications of this partisan element will play a major role in the potential successes and failures of antiracism. We focus on these elements as we conclude this study. We first speculate about what this partisan nature is likely to produce in a politically polarized society. Then, we look at the barriers to the possibility that antiracism finds broad support in a polarized society. Finally, we conclude this book by discussing possible research that can emerge from these current empirical efforts and discuss the final implications of our findings.

Antiracism in a Polarized Society

Recent analysis from the Pew Research Center indicates that Democrats and Republicans are further apart ideologically than at any time in the past 50 years (DeSilver 2022). Furthermore, both political parties have become more ideologically cohesive—with moderates becoming an endangered species—and more geographically isolated. There is deep polarization in our society, much of it driven by partisan choices and segmented social networks. Understanding the impact of this partisanship enables one to comprehend the reality of an antiracism not merely driven by racial concerns but also by partisan priorities. It is a mistake to consider these partisan differences to be merely about political disagreements. Given the differences in lifestyles (Bishop 2009, Cahn and Carbone 2007), religious beliefs (D'Antonio, Tuch, and Baker 2013, Yancey and Quosigk 2021, Putnam and Campbell 2012), and cultural beliefs (Castle and Stepp 2021, Cahn and Carbone 2010) between progressives and conservatives, the polarization in the United States has created divisions so deep that some individuals have seriously contemplated whether the country needs to be split into two distinct nations (Alli 2017, Muñoz 2020, Rispin 2018). Such polarization is not merely about disagreement but also about the contempt each warring faction has for the other side.

We contend that antiracism has become connected to this polarization due to the need for social and political actors to signal their allegiances and loyalties. In a polarized society, intense forms of ingroup acceptance and outgroup rejection become desirable. It becomes valuable for individuals to decide whether a person, program, or movement is to be included in their ingroup or rejected as part of their outgroup. One way that individuals can make decisions about whether to offer support or rejection for social groups is through the process of signaling (Sen 2017, Merkley and Stecula 2021, Lee and Schlesinger 2001). If we consider the political market in the United States to be dominated by the two major parties, and if most individuals perceive that they must select from these two parties, then loyalty to one party or the other is likely to drive the behavior of partisans. Political signals can act to inform individuals whether a given issue or group is part of the political framework they have accepted. Given that individuals are unable to be knowledgeable in all topics, political signaling can act as a shortcut by which an individual can decide about an issue or topic if they have limited knowledge.

Thus, when individuals consider whether to support the efforts of antiracism, the decision is made within the context of this polarization. Decisions about implementing the goals and programs linked to antiracism may be less about a sterile assessment of the viability of those goals and programs and more about the political interpretation of antiracism. Given the partisan nature of antiracism, those who identify themselves as loyal to the Democratic Party will be supportive of antiracism, while those who identify themselves as loyal to the Republican Party will reject antiracism. Once the political signal has been received and individuals have either accepted or rejected antiracism, then rationales for those decisions will be made and reinforced within polarized social networks. Antiracism will be valorized by those who interpret the political signals to support this approach and demonized by those who interpret the political signals to reject this approach.

We can simplify the United States as red (Republicans) or blue (Democrats). This is a shorthand way to discuss different pools of interest groups that create the overarching coalitions on each side of our polarized society. In this context, antiracists have been included on the blue side of the divide. Being on the blue side of the divide provides them with instant allies. One can imagine someone else who is on the blue side of the divide but is not naturally drawn toward seeking out racial justice. Let us say that a person is highly involved in fighting for publicly funded health care. While such funding may disproportionately benefit people of color, undoubtedly there exist individuals who support publicly funded health care with the general notion of health care as a right. Such individuals do not have to be particularly predisposed to deeply care about issues of racial justice, and likely some of them do not care about such issues. But with the identity of antiracists as part of the blue side, it becomes in the interest of proponents of publicly funded health care to support antiracism since the same politicians likely to promote antiracism will also be likely to support publicly supported health care. As they dig deeper into their alliances with their antiracist allies, they can find connections that substantiate the concerns of both groups, as seen in the work of academics such as that done by Metzl (2019). Thus, those on the red side of the polarization are a common enemy that needs to be defeated. In this "enemy of my enemy" approach, it becomes possible for antiracists to gain allies from those who may not normally be inclined to support issues of racial justice. Given this approach, and the ability of antiracists to find supporters among those who may not normally be inclined to deeply care about racial issues, it is fair to state that antiracists are not going away any time soon. They have access to support and resources that will ensure their continuing cultural and political power from those on the blue side for some time to come.

However, the alliance with the Democratic Party comes with costs. The red side of the U.S. is deeply antagonistic to the blue side, and this polarization will remain for the foreseeable future. Whereas individuals and groups on the blue side of polarization have an incentive to support antiracism, the incentive structure for groups linked to the red side of polarization is the opposite. Indeed, some people have created lucrative careers attacking progressive racial efforts. But if we were to remove political polarization for a moment, antiracism could be a viable and valuable framework for Republican-led priorities.[1] Consider school choice. One can argue that school choice advocates can approach antiracists with the promise of developing schools rooted in antiracist principles. Free from government and conservative political restraints, such schools would be free of the political backlash that so often comes to school boards that attempt to introduce antiracist curriculum into K–12 schools. Parents leading the charges against CRT would not have legitimacy since they simply do not have to place their children in such schools. There is a theoretical alliance between antiracists and school choice advocates that can develop over time. Yet such an alliance is not going to happen anytime soon. School choice advocates understand that a politician with leanings toward antiracism is unlikely to support their desires to alter the education system. Rather than envision the potential of recruiting antiracists as allies in their desire to promote school choice, school choice advocates will maintain an adversarial stance toward antiracism and those who advocate it. While antiracism and its supporters are not going away any time soon, neither are the detractors of antiracism.

---

1. Indeed, we have already come across literature where conservatives are finding opportunities to utilize an antiracist framework for key conservative issues on immigration and the economy (see Ufodike, Ally, and Butt 2020).

The immediate fate of antiracism is to take its place in the continuing political polarization in the United States. Whether antiracists can achieve their societal goals is tied to whether the blue side or the red side has political power at a given time. At the time of the writing of the book, the Democratic Party is in control of the Senate and the White House. Given the ability of President Biden to appoint heads of governmental departments and the ability of the Senate to confirm those appointments, he can exert changes in the government that can aid antiracists in the causes they champion. However, the Republicans control the House of Representatives. Thus, there is a limit to the type of overarching legal changes that can be made by Democrats at this time. If, during the next presidential cycle, the Democrats lose the Senate and the White House to the Republicans and cannot take the House of Representatives, then antiracists will not have anyone with their hands on the levers of power in the United States who is motivated to support them.

However, the Democrats may win back the House of Representatives and keep the White House and Senate in the next presidential cycle. It was only recently that the Democrats controlled the Senate, the House of Representatives, and the White House. In that situation, those favorable to the concerns of antiracists did not have formal restraints toward supporting antiracist measures. Such a governmental setup is distinctly more advantageous for antiracists than having Republicans in control. Yet many supporters of antiracism have complained about a lack of action by the Obama and Biden administrations (Mudde 2020, Acheson 2022, Cardoza 2022, Howard 2010). Their concerns highlight a certain limitation of what can occur even when the blue side holds all seats of power. A power shift can always be reversed in two or four years with the next election cycle. Those in power must be mindful of the fact that whatever they do may impact their ability to maintain their power. There is a reason why Republicans are hammering Democrats over issues of "wokeness" and DEI. The United States is deeply divided over issues of DEI and how to teach racial issues in our schools (Migdon 2021, Minkin 2023). Republicans may be able to use that divide to gain political power. Given that reality, any aggressive step made by the Democrats can make them vulnerable to losses in the next election. Thus, our political system encourages incremental change rather than paradigm shifts in how society can incorporate elements of antiracism into our social structures. Furthermore, any alterations made by Democrats when they have power can be removed by Republicans if they gain power back. Thus, the alterations possible within a polarized society are even more limited than what is observed due to the timidity of Democratic politicians.

The status of antiracism today is that antiracists are firmly implanted into the blue side and that those on the red side will be consistent enemies. Their bluish allies likely influence the culture through media and academia, but given the decentralized nature of modern media (Asekun-Olarinmoye et al. 2018, Krishnan 2020, Lorimer 2002), this influence is unlikely to spread to subcultures dominated by those on the red side. Incremental change is possible, especially when the Democrats are in power. But radical or revolutionary change requires support from a wider swath of Americans than they have at this current time. The current fate of antiracism is to be yet another interest group in the larger cultural and political fight that dominates the United States. It is a type of limbo where they possess the power and energy to gain some of what they want, but their desires for fundamental societal change appear to be out of their reach.

Can Antiracism Develop a Broader Appeal?

Given this current state of antiracism, one can ask whether supporters of antiracism can improve their ability to create societal change. We believe it is possible but will incorporate risky actions that we believe antiracists are unlikely to take. Given what antiracists already have, a relatively powerful position in one of the two sides in our current political debate, there are rational reasons not to take this risk. However, the degree of embeddedness of antiracism within partisan politics also places certain emotional barriers that make it unlikely for antiracists to make the necessary adjustments to gain bipartisan appeal. For antiracism to increase to the degree that its proponents desire, and for them to be able to make some of the fundamental changes they seek, they will have to break out of the partisan framework they currently operate in today. This current framework only works for antiracists when the Democrats have full, or nearly full, control of the government, and, even then, there are limits to the changes Democrats will make for fear that massive changes may allow the Republicans to criticize and wrestle power away from them. To create an atmosphere where there can be a lasting alteration, antiracists will have to learn how to appeal to nonprogressives. They will have to learn how to appeal to political independents and moderates. They may even find ways to appeal to political conservatives. It is only when they can find ways to reach such individuals that they will be in a position to make fundamental societal changes. To increase its impact on society, antiracism will have to move from being a partisan ideal to a bipartisan cause.

An example of the power of bipartisanship can be seen in the approach of the United States to the war in Ukraine (Raji, Meyer, and Caldwell 2023). At the time of this writing, both Republicans and Democrats have, for the most part, been supporting Ukraine's war with Russia. While some have balked at the level of U.S. funding for that war, for the most part, the funding of Ukraine has been bipartisan. To date, the United States has sent $35 billion for this war effort (Euronews 2023). If President Zelenskyy can not only placate individuals on both the red and blue sides of the United States but also unify them, the sky is the limit on how much aid he will receive. In a time of inflation, the willingness of the U.S. government to spend such funds on a foreign nation speaks to the degree to which Americans are willing to invest in a country many Americans know next to nothing about. Likewise, if Americans are going to invest in the change antiracists desire, then there will have to be support from both Republicans and Democrats on manifesting those changes. The partisan nature of contemporary antiracism hinders its supporters from making the very changes they so eagerly desire. For antiracism to grow and thrive, it must develop a larger tent under which more individuals can find a way to support the tenets of antiracism.

The barrier to such bipartisanship is not that antiracists would have to lessen their demands on issues that directly impact marginalized ethnic groups. Such a watering down of the core of their demands is not likely to win over those who do not identify as progressive, and thus it becomes unlikely that they will gain many new supporters and they would lose some of their more passionate supporters by seeming to go soft on calls for equity and justice. It is issues that are not directly linked to racial discrepancies that antiracists could use to make inroads into nonprogressive groups. For example, proponents of school choice have an incentive to work with antiracists to create vouchers. Such advocates can offer aid in setting up antiracist schools in a school choice system. However, the reverse is true as well. Antiracists theoretically could reach out to school choice advocates to work with them on mutually satisfying issues. They can potentially impact the new education system that may emerge as more states are adopting some version of a voucher plan. Antiracists may have hesitation since, historically and today, private schools at times are used to shelter majority group members' children from children of color and preserve their racial advantages (Clotfelter 2004).[2] However, when school choice policies are not sufficiently impacted by nonwhite perspectives, they tend to be colorblind and reinforce mechanisms of majority race privilege (Roda and Wells 2013). At the time of this writing, several states have initiated a variety of educational reforms based on school choice. Antiracists need not directly align themselves with the school choice movement, but they can either decry this inevitability or work with others to help shape it into something that can benefit their cause. If some system of school choice is going to happen in some of the red states, then working with school choice advocates to help shape the system may not only help introduce moderates and conservatives to a radical antiracism in a manner by which they can accept it but will allow antiracists to move their

---

2. However, it has been argued that vouchers have played a historical role in combating racism (Magness 2021).

perspective forward in an efficient manner (Diem, Carpenter, and Lewis-Durham 2019).

However, given the partisan and revolutionary nature of antiracism, this is unlikely to happen. Antiracists will feel pressure to fight against school choice simply because it is promoted by political conservatives. According to Beeman (2022), the focus of racial radicals is tied to other partisan interests and is not driven simply by a focus on racial issues, but rather, the critique of racism leads to a larger intersectionality multilevel critique of society. If Beeman is correct, and if antiracism is the tool of racial radicals, then a bipartisan path may not be volitionally available to antiracism since any compromises made can be seen as giving into the enemy.

Notably, school choice has not been an issue where there is a lot of discussion among antiracists. As we saw in the previous chapter, the same cannot be said about abortion, where several antiracists argue that to be an antiracist is to be pro-choice. It is in those issues where we observe the pressure of antiracists to conform to partisan values. It does not take a lot of imagination to envision a pro-life position as an antiracism position if one interprets the stopping of abortion as an attempt to save lives. Given that African Americans abort at a higher rate than European Americans, it is not surprising that this argument has already been made (Loury 2022). If antiracism means one must be pro-choice, then inevitably a certain percentage of individuals who are open and even supportive of antiracism perspectives will not be able to identify as antiracist due to their pro-life beliefs. These individuals may or may not vote for Republicans, but even if they do, if they choose to identify as antiracists, they can apply pressure within the Republican Party to become more open to support issues connected to antiracism. These individuals can move the needle from making antiracism a partisan concern into a bipartisan concern. And yet, if they must renounce their pro-life beliefs to feel comfortable within an antiracism community, then they may never be part of that community and may never become the type of advocates who can help shape a bipartisan antiracist appeal. The loss of such potential advocates is part of the costs tied to the inability of antiracists to include those who do not seek the degree of partisan-based changes they promote within their ranks.[3] The radical nature of antiracism is a barrier to attracting moderates and conservatives, but the partisan nature of the ties of antiracists makes it almost impossible for them to make the efforts necessary to recruit nonprogressives. This means that the most likely direction for antiracists is

---

3. Conservative Canadians have offered their own ideas and addressed issues connected to antiracism (Ufodike, Ally, and Butt 2020). While contemporary antiracists may dispute the value of these ideas, the fact that they are willing to attempt to address the concerns brought up by antiracists means that dialogue is possible with conservative groups in Canada.

to be a special interest group among the blues but not a bipartisan movement that can engender the societal overhaul so many of them desire.

It is plausible that the lack of legitimatization toward antiracists by nonracial radicals cripples the ability of the desired reforms of antiracists, even when they have the power to implement them, to have a powerful effect on society. The partisan identity embedded in antiracism makes it harder for nonprogressives to accept teaching that comes from an antiracist source. Nonetheless, being able to reach individuals who are not already on their blue team may be vital if antiracists can produce the societal alteration many of them want. Research has indicated that diversity programs not only have failed to lead to long-term reduction in prejudice (Lai et al. 2016) but also have engendered a backlash against marginalized racial groups (Plant and Devine 2001, Legault, Gutsell, and Inzlicht 2011) and generate perceptions of inferiority toward those minority groups (Heilman and Welle 2006). We believe that at least some of this inefficiency is linked to partisan-based resistance in which about a third to half of the nation is politically primed to resist efforts promoted by antiracists.

Beyond the issue of the larger radical desires of antiracists, a bipartisan approach does come with a huge practical risk. The very partisans currently highly supportive of antiracism may drop their support due to outreach to nonradicals or nonprogressives. Just like it is reasonable to think that pro-life individuals concerned about racial justice exist, it is also reasonable to think that some who are fighting for antiracism today will cease fighting for antiracism unless it is an explicit pro-choice movement. Indeed, efforts to reach out to nonprogressives or at least not take a stand on partisan issues that are not directly tied to racial justice may jeopardize the standing antiracists have among progressives and radicals who do not have a singular commitment to racial issues. It is not unreasonable to conclude that antiracists may lose more individuals with attempts to broaden the tent than they will gain from that broadening. There is no way to know whether antiracists have more to gain with bipartisan efforts than what they will lose or whether there are certain efforts or issues they can use to broaden their tent that are advantageous while others will be more costly to them. Indeed, the only way to find out is for antiracists to create an atmosphere that allows nonprogressives on nonracial issues to identify with antiracism. However, creating such an atmosphere brings with it the risk of loss of support, and once those steps are taken, they may not be easily retraced.

One only needs to look at the recent fate of Bud Light and Dylan Mulvaney, a transgender influencer who was hired to do a small promotion of this popular beer. By retaining Mulvaney, the beer company attempted to be "bipartisan." It already had strong shares among those with traditional and conservative perspectives. The company hoped to also bring in a fresher, younger, and hipper clientele. Yet the use of Mulvaney alienated those with conservative, traditionalist perspectives. When the company attempted to placate them, they alienated members of the LGBT movement (De Mar 2023), which was their entry to the younger clientele. The backlash against using a transgender influencer and the failure to continue to reach the younger market has resulted in a significant loss of sales for the beer company (Brooks 2023), at least for the short term. This entire episode indicates the dangers of attempting to enact a bipartisan strategy. It is quite possible that in doing so, antiracists will drive away much of their current support and still not be accommodating enough to gain significant support from nonprogressives.

Given these issues, we think it is not plausible that antiracists will develop a bipartisan strategy that will build support across political lines. This creates a natural limit to the impact they will be able to have. This is not to say that reforms to different institutions are impossible. Such reforms are especially possible in institutions, such as higher education, where political progressives, and political radicals in particular, have a great deal of lasting influence. However, the type of comprehensive societal change that some of them want is not likely to be sustainable. If antiracists gain power in any dimension where political conservatives can gain power in the future, then whatever alterations they manage to embed can, and often will, be overturned. One only needs to look at the reversal of policies at Virginia school boards after the election of Governor Youngkin to see how fast antiracist curriculum can be eliminated for the school districts in a state (Dress 2022). In his effort to root out "inherently divisive concepts," his administration produced a report that seeks to eliminate focuses on equity and reducing achievement gaps based on race (Barthel 2022). Republicans will, at some point in the future, hold the White House and the Senate. They will likely, at some point, hold power in both chambers of Congress and the presidency. While they, too, will be unable to incorporate long-term changes without winning over nonconservatives, they will be able to undo much of what antiracists gain during a Democratic administration. Given our current political system and societal polarization, the type of sweeping change many antiracists want is not plausible.

The problems antiracists face are not unique to them. In a society as polarized as the United States, building a bipartisan consensus is nearly impossible. On the one hand, to create an atmosphere for societal alteration, it is important to find support across the political spectrum. On the other hand, there may be such a powerful impulse in this society to reject their social, cultural, and political outgroup that any movement that becomes conceptually linked to one side of this polarization automatically creates enemies from the other side. Thus, there may be a natural tendency to support the status quo driven by the very nature of our polarized society. The challenges faced by antiracists may be the challenges faced by any groups seeking societal change, whether from the left or the right. The difficulties for a group to create the type of bipartisan coalition that can overcome barriers to social change are great due to how issues are politically clustered together and the pressures toward partisan loyalties. These demands may be so great that social movements that attempt such a bipartisan outreach may be wasting their efforts. But an inability to build bipartisan consensus likely limits antiracists, and others who wish to alter our society in a significant way, to minor reforms in contested areas of our society and more major alterations in political areas (i.e., blue territories such as urban areas or the coasts) where political allies can hold on to power without serious challenge.

Given this reality, we perceive that the likely future of antiracism is to be a player among the blues but unable to create the momentum for the type of societal change desired. Antiracists will be seen as a special interest group among other special interest groups. We hold out little hope that it will become one of those issues that transcend the polarized boundaries in our society, especially given the level of social conflict we have seen on racial issues over the last several years. Many antiracists will disagree with this characterization and argue that issues of racial equality should transcend partisanship. One need not agree with every claim made by antiracists to see that the fundamental racial fairness they envision is a cause that should be supported across the racial, social, and cultural spectrum. But the reality is that the partisan attitudes and radical aims of antiracists, combined with the polarization in our society, provide powerful social pressure to link antiracism to partisan interpretations of its desires as such political and cultural conservatives are going to be their natural enemies and will work to sabotage most of their efforts for some time to come. As long as such conservatives can gain social and political power from time to time, and we see no reason why that is not the case, such resistance to antiracism will inhibit the ability of antiracists to fully achieve the goals they seek. Of course, even with our knowledge of who antiracists are, this is still speculation about what may happen to this particular social and political subculture. However, in a polarized society, few partisan groups can appeal across the political barrier, and we have little reason to think that, absent a tremendous effort by antiracists to develop a more bipartisan approach, they will be an exception to that trend.

Limitations and Extensions

This study is the first to examine the association between antiracist beliefs and political affiliation in a nationally representative U.S. sample. The uniqueness of such an attempt allows this research to fill an important empirical niche. However, this study is not without limitations. One of the most obvious limitations of the antiracism attitude scale is its limited application to only the Chapman Survey of American Fears. While the use of that survey allowed us to illustrate the usefulness of this instrument with a national probability sample, the questions used on the survey do not allow for a full exploration of antiracism in comparison to other social attitudes. Specifically, issues of gender and sexuality are not included in the CSAF, making assessments of attitudes of intersectionality among antiracists impossible to verify. Other types of social attitudes on issues such as religion, abortion, economic policies, communities, technology, multiculturalism, educational policies, and more can be explored with the inclusion of the antiracism attitude scale on a variety of different survey instruments. We also suggest that further development of the scale is desirable. The scale is not beyond improvement. The issues linked to racial attitudes change over time, and part of the improvement of the antiracism attitude scale over previous attempts to assess racial attitudes is the contextualization of the scale to current racial concerns. It is viable to continue to test different statements to see how they load on the scale and explore whether we can make it a better instrument over time by contextualizing it to the current issues at a given time. We would welcome further testing and refining of the scale.

We also do not believe that our assessment of primary popular antiracism literature is complete and exhaustive. Our analysis provided us with important themes that allowed us to make a viable attempt to map out the basic themes driving antiracism. We were hesitant to include certain ideas—such as that racial minorities cannot be racist—that were not accepted in all the writings of popular antiracists.[4] However, there may be ideas or concepts we missed that provide more nuance to overall antiracist philosophy, and perhaps some of the ideals that are accepted by a majority of, but not all, antiracist advocates should be considered as well. Finally, since we are not insiders to the antiracism movement, analysis of primary antiracism literature by insiders may provide valuable insight into how antiracists conceptualize certain themes connected to their philosophy and the priorities they provide for those themes. Needless to say, there is value in further analysis of primary antiracism work.

Turning to our content analysis, we note that this analysis was cross-sectional. This makes it difficult to make strong causal inferences due to the data, and we are limited to looking at the associations between antiracist perspectives and specific social and political issues. But, while causality cannot be strongly asserted, that the depth of the commitment of antiracists to certain political issues is strong among progressives can be asserted due to the

---

4. To be specific, Kendi (2019) rejects the argument that Black people cannot be racist. According to Kendi, anyone can be racist if they act in a racist manner.

strong directionality of political issues and antiracism in abortion, climate change, and Jan. 6 compared to inflation and street crime. Over time, if the set of issues linked to Democrats changes, then we could be in a position to replicate this analysis to see if proponents of antiracism adjust their support on a given issue to match their partisan preference or if they stay consistent with their previous perspectives. It may be possible to conduct a longitudinal analysis looking at statements by antiracists in the past and comparing those statements to current perspectives. For example, in the past, Democrats tended to be more supportive of Russia than they currently are today, and thus, seeing how antiracists respond to issues connected to Russia in the past and today may be insightful. However, it is not clear how much popularized antiracism proponents labeled themselves as antiracists in the past and, even if they did, whether they dealt extensively with an issue such as foreign policy toward Russia.

Furthermore, we acknowledge that the categories used in Chapter 6 are not equal in comparability. January 6, for instance, is an event—not a concept or phenomenon. Comparing climate change to January 6 can be a difficult quantitative comparison. Despite these differences, January 6 was still an important event that, like the other issues, involved strong political divides and strong implications about race and contributed to the discussion of antiracism. Future work using a variety of different types of categories may produce deeper insight into how antiracists conceptualized different political and social issues. Finally, our analysis was conducted on Google, which has its own pros and cons compared to doing an in-depth analysis on social media platforms or exclusively in academic settings. Because the topic of antiracism is relatively new, we utilized Google for its breadth and ability to accurately capture the most popular searches for society. Our final limitation was the high exclusion of some articles due to their irrelevance. While we did initially consider continuing to look through articles until reaching N = 50 for each topic, we realized that this could be a form of bias as well since the absence of relevant articles could reveal how antiracism has not yet pervaded certain issues such as inflation.

We chose not to engage in one-on-one interviewing because we were more interested in how antiracists represent themselves to the larger society than in their internal deliberations about why they accept antiracism. Previous research on antiracists has featured interviews and ethnographies of them, adding important in-depth nuance to our understanding of antiracists, particularly white antiracists (Thompson 2001, Thompson, Schaeffer, and Brod 2003, Warren 2010, O'Brien 2001).[5] We envision value in continuing that

---

5. We did not find any ethnographies or systematic interviews of antiracists of color. Given that antiracism is supported more heavily among people of color, understanding antiracists

work, given the new directions produced by this systematic analysis. Future qualitative work can explore how partisan loyalty factors into the policy and political decisions antiracists make, as well as how antiracists envision a pathway to social alterations in a polarized society. Antiracists likely envision such change by a complete defeat of political and cultural conservatives, but perhaps there are stages of change, short of societal overhaul, that antiracists are willing to accept in the near future.

There are also questions concerning the potential behavior of antiracists. Do their racial perspectives alter how they behave toward majority group members and marginalized racial groups? Are those beliefs linked to a propensity to engage in certain types of activism? What is the relationship between antiracist attitudes and political engagement? Do antiracists merely talk the talk, or do they also walk the walk? With the antiracism attitude scale, it is feasible to assess if there are consequential effects linked to antiracism beliefs.

Finally, we do not want this work to provide an assumption that all antiracists are alike. Antiracism is not a monolith; rather, it is a movement that is diverse and constantly changing. While our current set of data does not allow us to deeply explore differences between antiracists, such an exploration is vital in our understanding of racial radicalism. Beyond individualized differences between antiracists, there are likely important differences between antiracists due to demographical and social characteristics. For example, an antiracist who is also highly religious may envision issues of racial justice and what is needed to achieve such justice from a different perspective.[6] Like most popular public ideologies, there are a variety of reasons why individuals adopt antiracism, and different types of antiracists can emerge for these distinct motivations. There is a danger that in understanding a certain type of antiracist, we may extrapolate that understanding to all antiracists. Future research can use the tools outlined in this current empirical project to first determine the level of support individuals have for antiracism and then develop other methodological tools to identify subsets of distinct types of antiracists in society.

Concerning different types of antiracists, it may be of particular interest to explore racial differences between antiracists. Given the desire of African Americans to achieve cultural and material parity with majority group members, it is fairly straightforward why the tenets of antiracism would be attrac-

---

who are not a member of the majority group is a gap in the literature that future researchers would be wise to fill.

6. Indeed, we noted an article from our content analysis in Chapter 6 where a Christian author argued that the pro-life movement and antiracist movement are siblings from the greater abolition movement. This hybridization of antiracist thought in different paradigms is something to watch closely.

tive to them. However, these incentives may not be relevant to white antiracists, especially those with higher levels of education and SES. A tremendous amount of work has gone into understanding white antiracists, but little, if any, has explored antiracists of color (O'Brien 2001, Hughey 2012b, Thompson 2001, Thompson, Schaeffer, and Brod 2003, Warren 2010). Yet we have documented that antiracism is more likely to be accepted by nonwhites than whites, which is not surprising given that this is a philosophy developed to address the plight of people of color. Given the distinct motivations of whites and nonwhites, it is highly likely that an antiracism perspective arising from a community of color is qualitatively different from one developing among majority group members. To gain a comprehensive understanding of antiracism as a public philosophy, multiple types of antiracism must be understood. Consequently, an interesting future analysis is to contrast white and Black antiracists in their motivations toward being antiracist, their attitudes toward racial solutions, and their attitudes toward partisan issues to more finely understand how antiracism impacts individuals across the racial spectrum.

Appendix A

Methodological and Statistical Findings

In this appendix, we explain the methodological and statistical findings reported in the previous chapters. We discuss the data that led us to the conclusions we made in the previous chapters. By using the appendix to discuss some of the more complicated methodological and statistical concerns, we make the main chapters of the book more accessible to the average reader.

CONSTRUCTION OF THE ANTIRACISM INDEX

In Chapter 3, we discussed the construction of the antiracism attitude index. The scale was first developed in an earlier article (Yancey 2024), and readers may want to examine that article for more details. We first performed factor analysis with varimax rotation on the 15 statements from that chapter. The books we used to legitimate the statements of that scale can be seen in Appendix B. Varimax rotation does not allow for correlation between factors and aids in finding the robust and discreet factor separate from all other factors. The 15 statements loaded onto two factors on the Amazon Mechanical Turk sample, three on the Survey Monkey sample, and two when both samples were included in the data. Complete factors and factor loadings are available in Table A.1. Potential unique differences of each sample make it less likely that the second and third loadings capture similar conceptual factors. The most potent factor for each sample is likely to capture similar conceptual dynamics, making it valuable to concentrate on only those factors in selecting workable statements. Five statements—BLM, WHITE FRAGILITY, SLAVERY, GOVERNMENT REQUEST, and BLACKS DESERVE—loaded at least .6 or higher on the first factor for the Amazon Turk and Survey Monkey samples. The fact that these five variables load highly on both samples provides confidence that they represent an ideological construct separate from the general set of variables in our study, making them potential variables in an antiracism attitude scale. However, WHITE SUPREMACY loaded at .519 with the first factor in the Amazon Mechanical Turk sample and .509 with the first fac-

TABLE A.1 FULL FACTOR LOADINGS OF AMAZON MECHANICAL TURK, SURVEY MONKEY, AND BOTH SAMPLES—VARIMAX ROTATION

	Amazon Mechanical Turk 1	Amazon Mechanical Turk 2	Survey Monkey 1	Survey Monkey 2	Survey Monkey 3	Both samples 1	Both samples 2
TRY HARD	.342	.816	.323	.782	.083	.315	.805
BLM	.756	.42	.711	.349	.239	.746	.399
RACIST SOCIETY	.691	.212	.515	.14	.118	.614	.196
QUALIFIED BLACK	.328	.502	.521	.31	.118	.405	.42
WHITE FRAGILITY	.781	.412	.666	.205	.163	.73	.367
RACISM INTENT	.359	.377	.435	.262	-.058	.363	.337
WELFARE PROGRAMS	.218	.77	.242	.744	.272	.237	.774
WHITE SUPREMACY	.519	.648	.509	.475	.204	.521	.597
PREFERENTIAL HIRING	.713	.253	.233	.155	.944	.582	.289
RACIAL INSIGHT	.266	.663	.271	.378	.143	.276	.558
SLAVERY	.697	.519	.613	.408	.209	.668	.48
SPECIAL FAVORS	.438	.811	.457	.704	.316	.452	.798
GOVERNMENT REQUEST	.765	.334	.725	.162	.208	.764	.289
BLACKS DESERVE	.712	.486	.761	.395	.209	.731	.47
NO NON-RACISTS	.249	.264	.099	.251	.343	.211	.309
Contribution	4.74	4.31	3.926	2.813	1.497	4.417	3.887
Total variation	31.602	28.735	26.17	18.755	9.979	29.447	25.915

tor in the Survey Monkey sample. Furthermore, RACIST SOCIETY loaded at .691 with the first factor in the Amazon Mechanical Tuck sample and .515 with the first factor in the Survey Monkey sample. It can be argued that our .6 cutoff is arbitrary and that WHITE SUPREMACY and RACIST SOCIETY should be included. Neither variable meets the threshold of .6 on both samples, but each is high enough to consider inclusion.

In Table A.2, we include relevant results from the first two loadings (columns 1 and 2) while also including subsequent tests with only the core five variables as well as WHITE SUPREMACY and RACIST SOCIETY. Ideally, an index will include variables that have a Cronbach's alpha score of at least .8 and construct a single factor that explains 50% of the variance. In columns 3, 4, and 5, we see the power of the five core variables in the high Cronbach's alphas (ranging from .935 to .892) and the level of variable explained (ranging from 74.276 to 63.21). Given that these variables only load on a single factor, it is clear that they make up a strong index. Expectations of Cronbach's alpha and variance explained to justify an index are met for each sample and the total of both samples. To investigate the advisability of adding WHITE SUPREMACY and RACIST SOCIETY, we added both variables to the index constructed from the Amazon Mechanical Turk sample (column 6), the Survey Monkey sample (column 7), and a combination of both samples (column 8). Adding these variables has little impact on Cronbach's alpha, decreases the total variation explained, and loads lower than any other variables in the index. While adding these variables might slightly improve the internal consistency of the index, it also slightly decreases the explanation of the data's variation. Nevertheless, the lowest variation explained in the loadings with both variables is 55.158 with the Survey Monkey sample. It is justified to include an index with WHITE SUPREMACY and RACIST SOCIETY, as those indexes meet the Cronbach's alpha and variance requirements; however, that index may not explain as much variation as one with just the five core variables.

To ensure that the potential correlation of factors did not distort these findings, we tested the variables with promax rotation. Using the .6 criteria for inclusion, four of the five variables selected by the varimax rotation were selected with the promax rotation. The SLAVERY variable failed to meet the .6 or higher criteria in both samples because it loaded on the first factor in the Survey Monkey sample at .583. However, SLAVERY loaded at .638 on the Amazon Mechanical Turk sample, and given how close this variable was to the .6 standard, which is somewhat arbitrary on the Survey Monkey sample, we assert that findings concerning the five core variables in the varimax and promax rotations are essentially the same. The full loadings of the promax rotation are available in Table A.3.

Conducting a confirmatory factor analysis is advisable to gain more confidence in the index as well as a more complete test of the value of including WHITE SUPREMACY and RACIST SOCIETY. Confirmatory factor analysis models are constructed for all seven items (the expanded model) in a structural equation model. BLACKS DESERVE is used as an a priori correlation with the latent variable to fit the model. The results of the model can be seen in Table A.4. The relative chi-square divided by degrees of freedom (PCMIN/DF) is used to assess absolute fit. That score is 3.132, below the score of 5 necessary to indicate adequate fit. However, Chi Square (CMIN) is significant in the default model ($p < .001$), suggesting a poor fit. The comparative fit index (CFI) score is .983, suggesting a good model fit. Furthermore, the root mean square of approximation (RMSEA) is .074, indicating an adequate fit; however, the PClose, which is a test of how close of a fit of the model is, is significant ($p < .05$), indicating that the model is not a good fit. The evidence that the model is a good fit is mixed. Nevertheless, the standardized regression weights for all items are significant, and squared multiple correlations ranged from .771 (BLACKS DESERVE) to .379 (RACIST SOCIETY), indicating that the items load highly on this index.

TABLE A.2 FACTOR LOADINGS OF AMAZON MECHANICAL TURK, SURVEY MONKEY, AND TOTAL SAMPLES—VARIMAX ROTATION

	Amazon Mechanical Turk	Survey Monkey	Amazon Mechanical 5-Item Scale	Survey Monkey 5-Item Scale	Both Samples 5-Item Scale	Amazon Mechanical 7-Item Scale	Survey Monkey 7-Item Scale	Both Samples 7-Item Scale
TRY HARD	.342	.323	–	–	–	–	–	–
BLM	.756	.711	.867	.85	.854	.87	.846	.852
RACIST SOCIETY	.691	.515	–	–	–	.697	.53	.625
QUALIFIED BLACK	.328	.521	–	–	–	–	–	–
WHITE FRAGILITY	.781	.666	.865	.684	.795	.877	.688	.806
RACISM INTENT	.359	.435	–	–	–	–	–	–
WELFARE PROGRAMS	.218	.242	–	–	–	–	–	–
WHITE SUPREMACY	.519	.509	–	–	–	.785	.664	.74
PREFERENTIAL HIRING	.713	.233	–	–	–	–	–	–
RACIAL INSIGHT	.266	.271	–	–	–	–	–	–
SLAVERY	.697	.613	.886	.784	.842	.859	.759	.816
SPECIAL FAVORS	.438	.457	–	–	–	–	–	–
GOVERNMENT REQUEST	.765	.725	.812	.764	.797	.829	.751	.802
BLACKS DESERVE	.712	.761	.877	.879	.878	.859	.9	.875
NO NON-RACISTS	.249	.099	–	–	–	–	–	–
Contribution	4.742	3.926	3.714	3.16	3.477	4.79	3.861	4.39
Total variation	31.602	26.17	74.276	63.21	69.536	68.422	55.158	62.713
Cronbach's alpha[1]	–	–	.935	.892	.918	.937	.89	.922

Note: [1] It was impossible to calculate Cronbach's alpha on the first two loadings due to negative correlations

TABLE A.3 FULL FACTOR LOADINGS OF AMAZON MECHANICAL TURK, SURVEY MONKEY, AND TOTAL OF BOTH SAMPLES—PROMAX ROTATION

	Amazon Mechanical Turk 1	Amazon Mechanical Turk 2	Survey Monkey 1	Survey Monkey 2	Survey Monkey 3	Total 1	Total 2
TRY HARD	.009	.878	.073	.081	-.827	-.031	.887
BLM	.77	.126	.727	.097	.086	.782	.084
RACIST SOCIETY	.798	.11	.579	-.062	.021	.72	-.108
QUALIFIED BLACK	.16	.475	.516	.146	-.006	.31	.317
WHITE FRAGILITY	.808	.101	.737	-.054	.034	.78	.05
RACISM INTENT	.269	.293	.443	.145	-.17	.3	.232
WELFARE PROGRAMS	-.13	.888	-.029	.79	.137	-.118	.892
WHITE SUPREMACY	.333	.559	.424	.347	.063	.336	.484
PREFERENTIAL HIRING	.804	-.068	.145	-.026	.936	.623	.036
RACIAL INSIGHT	-.009	.721	.171	-.051	-.337	.057	.579
SLAVERY	.638	.289	.583	-.061	-.216	.631	.239
SPECIAL FAVORS	.137	.819	.253	.642	.155	.158	.795
GOVERNMENT REQUEST	.829	.008	.826	-.139	.078	.87	-.075
BLACKS DESERVE	.675	.238	.773	.136	.039	.722	.187
NO NON-RACISTS	.185	.207	-.01	-.227	.309	.111	.286
Variation explained	54.273	6.064	44.571	4.814	5.52	50.144	5.219

TABLE A.4 SUMMARY OF ESTIMATES AND FIT ANALYSIS FROM CONFIRMATORY FACTOR ANALYSIS

	Expanded model	Original model
BLM	.854 (.73)	.853 (.728)
RACIST SOCIETY	.615 (.379)	–
WHITE FRAGILITY	.799 (.639)	.791 (.625)
WHITE SUPREMACY	.733 (.537)	–
SLAVERY	.83 (.689)	.846 (.716)
GOVERNMENT REQUEST	.8 (.64)	.797 (.634)
BLACKS DESERVE	.854 (.771)	.879 (.772)
X^2	43.841	10.815
df	14	5
CMIN	43.841	10.815
Significance of CMIN	.000	.055
PCMIN/DF	3.132	2.163
TLI	.975	.991
CFI	.983	.996
RMSEA	.074	.055
PClose	.000	.366

Source: Chapman Survey of American Fears
Note: Standardized regression weights estimates are entities, squared multiple correlations in parentheses; all regression weights are significant (p < .001)

We constructed a confirmatory factor analysis model without WHITE SUPREMACY and RACIST SOCIETY (the core model). In that model, PCMIN/DF is 2.163, which is barely insignificant in the default model (p = .055), but it is insignificant, indicating model fit. The CFI is .996, and the RMSEA is .055, with PClose insignificant (p = .366). Unlike the seven-item model, all indicators in the five-item model indicate good fit. Once again, the standardized regression weights for all items are significant, and the squared multiple correlations are even stronger in this model, ranging from .728 (BLM) to .625 (WHITE FRAGILITY). While it is debatable whether the index can be confirmed with the inclusion of WHITE SUPREMACY and RACIST SOCIETY, there are no such concerns in the five-item model. The inclusion of WHITE SUPREMACY and RACIST SOCIETY in an antiracism index should be done with caution.

CSAF RESULTS

In Chapter 4, we discussed our multivariate exploration of the data from the CSAF on predicting the antiracism attitude scale. We used Ordinary Least Squares (OLS) regression with the antiracism attitude scale as the dependent variable. The final model used the five-question index with four categories for each question, allowing respondents to score in the range of 5–20. Several social and demographic variables were included as possible predictors. Woman is a dummy variable with females as 1 and nonfemales as 0.[1] Age is the actual age of the respondent.[2] Black, Hispanic, and other race are self-identified dummy variables, with other race indicating a respondent who is not white, Black, or Hispanic. Political progressive is a seven-point scale with higher numbers indicating higher levels of political progressiveness. Education is measured on an eight-point scale. The categories for education are 1) less than high school, 2) high school incomplete, 3) high school graduate, 4) some college, no degree (includes some community college, 5) two-year associate degree, 6) four-year college or university degree, 7) some postgraduate or professional schooling, and 8) postgraduate/professional degree. Income is measured on a nine-point scale, with higher numbers indicating higher SES. Religiosity is measured on a four-point scale ranging from respondent affirming being "not religious at all" at 1 to being "very religious" at 4. Religious service attendance is measured on a nine-point scale, with higher numbers indicating more frequent attendance. Bible is word of God is a dummy variable, with the reference group being respondents who do not believe that the Bible should be taken literally. Christian, atheist/agnostic, and none (religion) are self-identified dummy variables, with those in non-Christian religions as the reference groups.

The results of our analysis can be seen in Table A.5. Gender, racial identity, political viewpoint, educational attainment, and SES are found to be significantly related to the antiracism attitude scale. The powerful standardized beta scores of Black (0.276) and political progressive (0.479) warrant special attention. The power of these standardized beta scores dwarfs the scores of the other independent variables, indicating that racial identity and political viewpoint have more powerful effect sizes than other social and demographic variables. Notably, the standardized beta score for political progressive is almost twice as large as it is for Black. T-score calculations indicate an incredibly high score of 17.462 for political progressive in comparison to an impressive but lower score of 10.562 for Black. As we argued in the main chapters, it is the case that status as an African American is a powerful predictor or support of antiracism ideology. However, the general political ideology an individual adopts is even more powerful in this given data set.

The level of missing data in our models is 6.2%, or just about the 5% threshold for needing to pay attention to missing data. We noted that almost all the missing data was due to missing data in the age variable (n = 47). Comparison of respondents with missing age data to those with stated age data indicated very little difference in their support of the antiracism attitude scale (12.738 v. 12.834: t = 0.158). Given the relatively low number of missing scores and the lack of evidence that those with missing data have a different level of acceptance of antiracism, data imputation efforts are unnecessary.

The religion measures provide an opportunity for multicollinearity. Correlations between the six religious variables (religiosity, religious service attendance, Bible is word of God, Christian, atheist/agnostic, and none [religion]) with the cases in the regression model indicated several significant correlation scores but only one above 0.35. That was between religiosity and religious service attendance ($r = 0.621$). To see if this particular relationship may suppress possible religious effects, we ran a model without religiosity and a model without religious service attendance. In the former model, religious service attendance is insignificant ($\beta = 0.031$; SE = 0.133: t = 0.935), and in the latter model, re-

---

1. Nine respondents, or .9% of the sample, indicated that they were nonbinary and were marked as 0.
2. Age ranged from 18 to 91.

TABLE A.5 REGRESSION COEFFICIENTS ASSESSING PREDICTORS OF ANTIRACISM ATTITUDE SCALE

	Antiracism attitude scale
Woman	.648*** *.08* (.205)
Age	−.009 *−.038* (.006)
Black	3.493*** *.276* (.331)
Hispanic	1.371*** *.128* (.288)
Other race	.867* *.058* (.388)
Political progressive	1.251*** *.479* (.072)
Education	.236*** *.11* (.064)
Income	−.132** *−.086* (.046)
Religiosity	.054 *.013* (.151)
Religious service attendance	.047 *.031* (.049)
Bible is word of God	.064 *.007* (.228)
Christian	−.529 *.065* (.274)
Atheist/agnostic	.298 *.018* (.499)
None (religion)	.435 *.046* (.344)
R^2	.439

Source: Chapman Survey of American Fears
Notes: Entities are unstandardized betas, standardized betas are in italics, standard errors in parentheses
* $p < .05$; ** $p < .01$; *** $p < .001$
N = 957

ligiosity is insignificant ($\beta = 0.037$; SE = 0.043: t = 1.294). Finally, we determined the variance inflation factor for the model, and the highest values are religiosity at 2.333 and none (religion) at 2.194. Since neither exceeds 4, they do not provide concerns of multicollinearity as it does not appear that correlation of the religion variables suppresses potential religious effects on antiracism.

It is plausible that these results would differ if we used the six-item index as a dependent variable. To test this possibility, we ran a model with our six-item scale as the dependent variable. These results can be seen in Table A.6. With one minor difference in that other race was no longer significant, the same findings found in the five-item model are found in the six-item model. Had we chosen to use the six-item index, we would not have reported any differences in our conclusions in Chapter 4. Ultimately, we have more confidence in the findings reported in Chapter 4 as we look at this statistical analysis. Being an African American or a political progressive is the best predictor that an individual will support antiracism. Of the two characteristics, we have reason to believe that political beliefs are more predictive than racial identity, but we understand that this is a question that needs further examination.

In Chapter 5, we looked at the differences between individuals who are strongly politically progressive and those who scored high on the antiracism attitude scale. In Table A.6, we show that those who scored high on the antiracism attitude scale are less white and younger. We now have an opportunity to see if those differences hold up after application of social and demographic controls. In Table A.7, we include logistic models that only include respondents who were designated either as scoring high on the antiracism attitude scale (at least 16 on the scale of 5–20) or as a strong political progressive (either "liberal" or "extremely liberal"). We included variables for race (Black, Hispanic, and other race, with white as the reference group), education (on a 1–8 scale), household income (on a 1–9 scale), religious preference (Christian, atheist/agnostic, and none, with non-Christian religion as the reference group), religious service attendance, Bible as word of God, and region (North-central, South, and West, with Northeast as reference group). The dependent variable is whether the respondent is designated as a high scorer on the antiracism attitude scale.

The findings indicate that African Americans and the young are more likely to score high on the antiracism attitude scale. We also found that the highly educated and non-Christians are more likely to be high scorers on the antiracism attitude scale as well. Thus, after controls, in a sample of individuals who are either highly antiracist, strongly politically progressive, or both, white people, Christians, older individuals, and the less educated are more likely to be politically progressive than antiracists. The major distinctions between antiracism and political progressiveness are due to race, age, education, and religion. We discussed the age and race differences in Chapter 5 since they emerged in our bivariate chart. However, these findings suggest that future, more sophisticated work may also explore the educational and religious dynamics that distinguish antiracists and political progressives.

Chapter 5 also allowed us to investigate the impact of antiracist attitudes on a variety of social and political issues. The full set of questions used to measure those issues can be seen in Appendix C. We documented our findings on the bivariate level in Chapter 5. We now have an opportunity to explore those results with regression models. Those OLS models can be seen in Tables A.8 through A.18. We include the same controls used in Table A.6, except, of course, we also add the antiracism attitude scale as one of the independent variables. The models allow us to assess if the results documented in Table 5.2 hold up after the application of controls and, if they do not, then determine in what ways they differ.

TABLE A.6 REGRESSION COEFFICIENTS ASSESSING PREDICTORS OF SIX-ITEM ANTIRACISM ATTITUDE SCALE

	Antiracism attitude scale
Woman	0.778*** *.085* (.228)
Age	0.01 *−.04* (.007)
Black	3.929*** *.274* (.368)
Hispanic	1.436*** *.118* (.321)
Other race	0.782 *.046* (.432)
Political progressive	1.474*** *.498* (.08)
Education	0.268*** *.111* (.071)
Income	0.118** *−.068* (.051)
Religiosity	0.092 *.02* (.160)
Religious service attendance	0.045 *.027* (.054)
Bible is word of God	0.046 *−.005* (.253)
Christian	0.652 *.071* (.306)
Atheist/agnostic	0.348 *.019* (.555)
None (religion)	0.498 *.046* (.383)
R^2	0.459

Source: Chapman Survey of American Fears
Notes: Entities are unstandardized betas, standardized betas are in italics, standard errors in parentheses
* $p < .05$; ** $p < .01$; *** $p < .001$
N = 957

TABLE A.7 LOGISTIC REGRESSION COEFFICIENTS ASSESSING PREDICTORS OF HIGH ANTIRACISTS AMONG RESPONDENTS WHO ARE STRONG POLITICAL PROGRESSIVES AND/OR HIGHLY ANTIRACIST

	Antiracism attitude scale
Woman	0.3 *.331* (.741)
Age	0.03*** *.009* (.97)
Black	1.887*** *.568* (6.603)
Hispanic	0.175 *.462* (1.191)
Other race	0.576 *.505* (.562)
Education	0.184* *.097* (1.202)
Income	0.03 *−.069* (1.03)
Religiosity	0.323 *.257* (1.382)
Religious service attendance	0.037 *.088* (.964)
Bible is word of God	0.055 *.44* (.947)
Christian	1.525** *.597* (.218)
Atheist/agnostic	1.306* *.732* (.271)

(continued)

TABLE A.7 LOGISTIC REGRESSION COEFFICIENTS ASSESSING PREDICTORS OF HIGH ANTIRACISTS AMONG RESPONDENTS WHO ARE STRONG POLITICAL PROGRESSIVES AND/OR HIGHLY ANTIRACIST (*continued*)

	Antiracism attitude scale
None (religion)	1.258* *.633* (.284)
Northcentral	0.422 *.537* (1.525)
South	0.271 *.444* (1.311)
West	0.928* *.501* (2.529)
−2 log-likelihood	272.017
Nagelkerke R^2	.218

Source: Chapman Survey of American Fears
Notes: Entities are standardized betas, standard error are in italics, odds ratio in parentheses
* $p < .05$; ** $p < .01$; *** $p < .001$
N = 319

TABLE A.8 REGRESSION COEFFICIENTS ASSESSING PREDICTORS OF VARIOUS SOCIAL ATTITUDES (ISSUES 1–5)

	Afraid of BLM	Support BLM	Afraid of illegal immigration	Afraid of immigrants	Afraid of world without white majority
Woman	.048 (.059)	.089*** (.043)	−.042 (.063)	.061 (.043)	.144*** (.05)
Age	.023 (.002)	−.02 (.001)	.122*** (.002)	.085* (.001)	−.003 (.002)
Black	.018 (.099)	−.012 (.074)	.076* (.107)	.032 (.073)	−.019 (.085)
Hispanic	.006 (.083)	.056* (.062)	.034 (.089)	.002 (.06)	−.068 (.071)
Other race	.007 (.11)	.031 (.082)	.074* (.119)	.045 (.08)	−.033 (.094)
Political progressiveness	−.108** (.023)	.28*** (.017)	−.175*** (.025)	−.212*** (.017)	−.034 (.02)
Education	.027 (.018)	−.015 (.014)	−.053 (.02)	−.08* (.013)	−.058 (.016)
Income	−.041 (.013)	−.037 (.01)	−.026 (.014)	−.014 (.01)	−.087* (.011)
Religiosity	−.065 (.043)	.049 (.032)	−.013 (.046)	−.09 (.031)	−.038 (.037)
Religious service attendance	.066 (.014)	−.038 (.01)	.036 (.015)	−.078 (.01)	−.037 (.012)
Bible is word of God	−.058 (.065)	.047* (.048)	−.001 (.07)	.043 (.047)	−.037 (.055)
Christian	.078 (.079)	−.003 (.058)	.134*** (.084)	.03 (.057)	.089* (.067)
Atheist/agnostic	.023 (.141)	−.004 (.105)	.029 (.152)	−.004 (.103)	.000 (.121)
None (religion)	.039 (.098)	.005 (.072)	.076 (.105)	.05 (.071)	.089* (.083)
Antiracism attitude scale	−.407*** (.009)	.581*** (.007)	−.385*** (.01)	−.187*** (.007)	−.257*** (.008)
R^2	.225	.635	.308	.149	.131
N	936	957	954	946	954

Source: Chapman Survey of American Fears
Notes: Entities are standardized betas, standard error in parentheses
* $p < .05$; ** $p < .01$; *** $p < .001$

TABLE A.9 REGRESSION COEFFICIENTS ASSESSING PREDICTORS OF VARIOUS SOCIAL ATTITUDES (ISSUES 6–10)

	Afraid of white supremacy	Afraid of being a victim of hate crime	Afraid of Muslims	Voted Trump	Voted Biden
Woman	0.082** (.071)	0.116*** (.065)	0.026 (.044)	0.172 (.216)	0.057 (.185)
Age	0.091** (.002)	0.005 (.002)	0.087* (.001)	0.009 (.007)	0.041*** (.0006)
Black	0.013 (.119)	0.289*** (.111)	0.035 (.074)	2.21*** (.677)	1.221*** (.308)
Hispanic	0.038 (.1)	0.26*** (.092)	0.024 (.062)	1.181*** (.348)	0.999*** (.245)
Other race	0.089** (.136)	0.218*** (.123)	0.047 (.083)	0.315 (.39)	0.262 (.338)
Political progressiveness	0.197*** (.028)	0.097 (.026)	0.102* (.017)	0.674*** (.091)	0.658*** (.079)
Education	0.098** (.022)	0.061 (.02)	0.002 (.014)	0.03 (.07)	0.287*** (.059)
Income	0.042 (.016)	0.081* (.015)	0.092* (.01)	0.056 (.05)	0.023 (.042)
Religiosity	0.013 (.052)	0.018 (.048)	0.053 (.032)	0.164 (.163)	0.046 (.14)
Religious service attendance	0.053 (.017)	0.024 (.015)	0.000 (.01)	0.076 (.048)	0.069 (.045)
Bible is word of God	0.014 (.078)	0.012 (.072)	0.002 (.049)	0.393* (.23)	0.275 (.208)
Christian	0.008 (.096)	0.024 (.087)	0.003 (.059)	0.642** (.277)	0.085 (.242)
Atheist/agnostic	0.014 (.169)	0.014 (.158)	0.05 (.106)	0.763 (.607)	0.608 (.439)
None (religion)	0.023 (.119)	0.044 (.109)	0.035 (.073)	0.281 (.37)	0.785** (.312)
Antiracism attitude scale	0.266*** (.011)	0.028 (.01)	0.213*** (.007)	0.39*** (.039)	0.281*** (.312)
R^2	.221	.209	.086	#	#
N	908	957	935	957	957

Source: Chapman Survey of American Fears
Notes: Entities are standardized betas, standard error in parentheses
* p < .05; ** p < .01; *** p < .001
# R^2 not calculated in logistic model

TABLE A.10 REGRESSION COEFFICIENTS ASSESSING PREDICTORS OF VARIOUS SOCIAL ATTITUDES (ISSUES 11–15)

	Afraid of right-wing extremists	Afraid of left-wing extremists	Trump to blame for Jan 6 violence	Biden legitimate winner of 2020 election	Can not know who won 2020 election because of election fraud
Woman	.034 (.074)	.085* (.079)	−.006 (.053)	−.078*** (.054)	−.104*** (.06)
Age	.115*** (.002)	.055 (.002)	.169*** (.002)	.132*** (.002)	.113*** (.002)
Black	−.038 (.127)	.059 (.136)	.055* (.089)	.04 (.091)	−.054 (.102)
Hispanic	.023 (.108)	.069 (.116)	.095*** (.074)	.1*** (.076)	.006 (.085)
Other race	.069* (.139)	.057 (.149)	.015 (.099)	.015 (.101)	−.023 (.113)
Political progressiveness	.192*** (.03)	−.154*** (.032)	.18*** (.021)	.238*** (.021)	.263*** (.024)
Education	.105** (.023)	.012 (.024)	.028 (.016)	.091*** (.017)	.129*** (.019)
Income	−.04 (.017)	−.015 (.018)	−.011 (.012)	−.001 (.012)	.064* (.013)
Religiosity	.05 (.054)	−.031 (.058)	.079* (.039)	−.108*** (.039)	−.021 (.044)
Religious service attendance	−.073 (.018)	−.023 (.019)	−.032 (.012)	.083** (.013)	.072* (.014)
Bible is word of God	.007 (.081)	−.018 (.086)	.077*** (.058)	.094*** (.059)	.085** (.066)
Christian	.038 (.1)	.039 (.106)	−.098*** (.07)	−.052 (.072)	−.061 (.08)
Atheist/agnostic	.091* (.172)	.044 (.184)	−.012 (.127)	.03 (.13)	.016 (.145)
None (religion)	.073 (.124)	.012 (.131)	−.099 (.088)	.005 (.09)	.019 (.1)
Antiracism attitude scale	.311*** (.012)	−.21*** (.013)	.597*** (.008)	.489*** (.008)	.388*** (.009)
R^2	.259	.102	.564	.51	.379
N	788	790	957	957	957

Source: Chapman Survey of American Fears
Notes: Entities are standardized betas, standard error in parentheses
* $p < .05$; ** $p < .01$; *** $p < .001$

TABLE A.11 REGRESSION COEFFICIENTS ASSESSING PREDICTORS OF VARIOUS SOCIAL ATTITUDES (ISSUES 16-20)

	Jan 6 protestors are patriots	Need new laws to protect against voter fraud	Afraid of widespread voter fraud	Afraid of air pollution	Afraid of water pollution
Woman	−.069* (.053)	−.083*** (.057)	.059* (.069)	−.004 (.058)	−.061* (.063)
Age	.057 (.002)	.132*** (.002)	−.003 (.002)	−.002 (.002)	.014 (.002)
Black	−.066* (.09)	−.048 (.096)	−.114*** (.117)	−.012 (.099)	−.015 (.107)
Hispanic	−.077* (.075)	−.062* (.08)	−.089** (.097)	.004 (.082)	.048 (.09)
Other race	−.047 (.1)	−.053 (.107)	.037 (.13)	−.008 (.11)	.078* (.119)
Political progressiveness	.272*** (.021)	.3*** (.023)	−.217*** (.027)	.261*** (.023)	.191*** (.025)
Education	.131*** (.016)	.179*** (.018)	−.083* (.021)	−.159*** (.018)	−.125*** (.02)
Income	.069 (.012)	.04 (.013)	−.008 (.015)	−.109*** (.013)	−.131*** (.014)
Religiosity	.047 (.039)	.028 (.042)	.005 (.05)	−.021 (.043)	.032 (.046)
Religious service attendance	−.01 (.012)	.035 (.013)	−.039 (.016)	−.078* (.014)	−.127** (.015)
Bible is word of God	.02 (.058)	.026 (.063)	−.076* (.076)	−.012 (.064)	.01 (.07)
Christian	.037 (.071)	−.114*** (.076)	.142*** (.092)	−.082* (.078)	−.038 (.084)
Atheist/agnostic	.041 (.128)	.061 (.137)	.018 (.166)	−.047 (.141)	−.041 (.153)
None (religion)	.017 (.088)	−.015 (.095)	.041 (.115)	−.13*** (.097)	−.078 (.105)
Antiracism attitude scale	.189*** (.008)	.324*** (.009)	−.288*** (.011)	.229*** (.009)	.187*** (.01)
R^2	.193	.383	.226	.239	.174
N	957	957	954	957	956

Source: Chapman Survey of American Fears
Notes: Entities are standardized betas, standard error in parentheses
* $p < .05$; ** $p < .01$; *** $p < .001$

TABLE A.12 REGRESSION COEFFICIENTS ASSESSING PREDICTORS OF VARIOUS SOCIAL ATTITUDES (ISSUES 21–25)

	Afraid of animal and plant extinction	Afraid of climate change	Afraid of climate change affecting where I live	Climate Change Index (4–16 range)	Afraid of pandemic
Woman	.08** (.063)	.06* (.06)	.054 (.062)	.044 (.17)	.015 (.062)
Age	−.012 (.002)	−.035 (.002)	−.021 (.002)	.092*** (.005)	.028 (.002)
Black	−.089** (.107)	−.088** (.101)	−.034 (.106)	−.045 (.289)	−.029 (.106)
Hispanic	.037 (.089)	.006 (.085)	.143*** (.088)	.044 (.241)	.141*** (.088)
Other race	−.023 (.119)	.001 (.113)	.001 (.118)	.071** (.321)	.014 (.118)
Political progressiveness	.266*** (.025)	.323*** (.024)	.209*** (.025)	.257*** (.068)	.149*** (.025)
Education	−.047 (.02)	−.031 (.019)	−.032 (.019)	.067* (.053)	−.095** (.019)
Income	−.138*** (.014)	−.1** (.013)	−.085* (.014)	−.047 (.038)	−.163*** (.014)
Religiosity	.024 (.046)	.016 (.044)	.022 (.046)	−.01 (.125)	.026 (.046)
Religious service attendance	−.1** (.015)	−.072* (.014)	−.092* (.015)	−.064* (.04)	−.025 (.015)
Bible is word of God	.018 (.09)	.033 (.066)	.033 (.069)	.033 (.188)	.047 (.069)
Christian	−.04 (.084)	−.017 (.08)	.038 (.083)	.041 (.227)	.076 (.083)
Atheist/agnostic	−.012 (.152)	.044 (.145)	.009 (.151)	.017 (.412)	.004 (.151)
None (religion)	−.017 (.105)	.036 (.1)	.014 (.104)	.035 (.284)	.016 (.104)
Antiracism attitude scale	.189*** (.01)	.363*** (.009)	.321*** (.01)	.388 (.027)	.262*** (.01)
R^2	.224	.375	.29	.449	.203
N	956	957	957	957	954

Source: Chapman Survey of American Fears
Notes: Entities are standardized betas, standard error in parentheses
* p < .05; ** p < .01; *** p < .001

TABLE A.13 REGRESSION COEFFICIENTS ASSESSING PREDICTORS OF VARIOUS SOCIAL ATTITUDES (ISSUES 26-30)

	Afraid of catching Covid	Lost friend because of Covid	Spent more time alone because of Covid	Got into arguments more because of Covid	Prepared household more because of Covid
Woman	.06* (.056)	−.016 (.056)	.035 (.057)	−.028 (.062)	.045 (.05)
Age	.14*** (.002)	.053 (.002)	−.014 (.002)	−.159*** (.002)	.109** (.002)
Black	−.009 (.094)	.015 (.095)	−.047 (.097)	−.1** (.105)	.041 (.086)
Hispanic	.176*** (.079)	.03 (.079)	.03 (.081)	−.017 (.087)	.138*** (.071)
Other race	.097** (.105)	.033 (.106)	−.04 (.107)	−.116*** (.116)	.03 (.095)
Political progressiveness	.087* (.022)	.006 (.022)	.051 (.023)	.036 (.025)	.03 (.02)
Education	−.017 (.017)	−.000 (.017)	.112** (.018)	.048 (.019)	−.086* (.016)
Income	−.147*** (.012)	−.106** (.012)	−.135*** (.013)	.01 (.014)	−.005 (.011)
Religiosity	.048 (.041)	.049 (.041)	−.096* (.042)	.095 (.045)	.000 (.037)
Religious service attendance	−.031 (.013)	.016 (.013)	.081 (.013)	.024 (.015)	.1* (.012)
Bible is word of God	.043 (.061)	.029 (.062)	.005 (.063)	.024 (.068)	−.023 (.056)
Christian	−.018 (.074)	−.113* (.075)	−.024 (.076)	−.015 (.082)	−.066 (.067)
Atheist/agnostic	−.02 (.135)	−.046 (.136)	.04 (.138)	.042 (.149)	−.023 (.122)
None (religion)	.02 (.093)	−.023 (.094)	.016 (.095)	−.028 (.103)	−.073 (.084)
Antiracism attitude scale	.312*** (.009)	.121** (.009)	.187*** (.009)	.054 (.01)	.194*** (.008)
R^2	.204	.042	.102	.053	.085
N	957	957	957	957	957

Source: Chapman Survey of American Fears
Notes: Entities are standardized betas, standard error in parentheses
* p < .05; ** p < .01; *** p < .001

TABLE A.14 REGRESSION COEFFICIENTS ASSESSING PREDICTORS OF VARIOUS SOCIAL ATTITUDES (ISSUES 31–35)

	Afraid of economic collapse	Afraid of not having enough money in the future	Afraid of being unemployed	Afraid of not being able to pay rent or mortgage	Afraid of not being able to pay college debt
Woman	.054 (.066)	.041 (.065)	.012 (.089)	−.014 (.082)	.035 (.082)
Age	−.06 (.002)	−.246*** (.002)	−.053 (.003)	−.288*** (.002)	−.34*** (.002)
Black	.018 (.113)	−.008 (.11)	.016 (.145)	.021 (.139)	.1** (.14)
Hispanic	.154*** (.094)	.17*** (.092)	.093* (.114)	.153*** (.116)	.11*** (.116)
Other race	.022 (.125)	.02 (.123)	.027 (.154)	.041 (.155)	.007 (.155)
Political progressiveness	−.014 (.027)	.074* (.026)	−.054 (.036)	.089* (.033)	−.034 (.033)
Education	−.035 (.021)	−.042 (.02)	−.152** (.028)	−.063 (.026)	.102** (.026)
Income	−.071 (.015)	−.257*** (.015)	−.218*** (.02)	−.217*** (.018)	.022 (.018)
Religiosity	−.005 (.049)	−.059 (.048)	−.117* (.066)	−.016 (.06)	.002 (.06)
Religious service attendance	−.077 (.016)	−.104** (.015)	.019 (.021)	−.055 (.019)	−.026 (.019)
Bible is word of God	.043 (.073)	−.012 (.072)	.027 (.099)	.002 (.091)	−.003 (.091)
Christian	.065 (.089)	−.001 (.087)	.089 (.118)	.015 (.109)	.039 (.11)
Atheist/agnostic	.037 (.161)	−.02 (.157)	.045 (.212)	−.009 (.98)	−.03 (.199)
None (religion)	−.01 (.111)	−.072 (.109)	−.001 (.146)	−.053 (.137)	.032 (.137)
Antiracism attitude scale	.031 (.011)	.089* (.01)	.205*** (.014)	.062 (.013)	.121** (.013)
R^2	.058	.265	.168	.266	.21
N	957	956	616	957	957

Source: Chapman Survey of American Fears
Notes: Entities are standardized betas, standard error in parentheses
* p < .05; ** p < .01; *** p < .001

TABLE A.15 REGRESSION COEFFICIENTS ASSESSING PREDICTORS OF VARIOUS SOCIAL ATTITUDES (ISSUES 36-40)

	Afraid of not being able to pay medical bill	Afraid of U.S. becoming involved in another world war	Afraid of biological warfare	Afraid of terrorist attack	Afraid of North Korea using nuclear weapons
Woman	.021 (.07)	.137*** (.065)	.098** (.068)	.129*** (.068)	.192*** (.068)
Age	−.143*** (.002)	−.000 (.000)	−.053 (.002)	.014 (.002)	.107** (.002)
Black	−.066 (.12)	−.006 (.111)	.022 (.115)	.025 (.115)	−.003 (.116)
Hispanic	.022 (.1)	.113** (.092)	.127*** (.096)	.149*** (.096)	.133*** (.097)
Other race	.062 (.133)	.043 (.123)	.01 (.127)	.045 (.128)	.03 (.129)
Political progressiveness	.061 (.028)	.004 (.026)	.029 (.027)	.006 (.027)	−.006 (.027)
Education	−.05 (.022)	−.076* (.02)	−.031 (.021)	−.05 (.021)	−.069 (.021)
Income	−.149*** (.016)	−.072 (.015)	−.101** (.015)	−.118** (.015)	−.128*** (.015)
Religiosity	−.059 (.052)	.025 (.048)	.064 (.05)	.05 (.05)	−.051 (.05)
Religious service attendance	−.051 (.017)	−.14*** (.015)	−.136** (.016)	−.076 (.016)	−.035 (.016)
Bible is word of God	.026 (.078)	.037 (.072)	.013 (.075)	.023 (.075)	.084* (.075)
Christian	.054 (.094)	.085 (.087)	.029 (.09)	.087* (.09)	.045 (.091)
Atheist/agnostic	.003 (.171)	.06 (.158)	−.03 (.163)	.006 (.164)	−.107** (.165)
None (religion)	−.122** (.118)	.028 (.109)	−.073 (.113)	−.02 (.113)	−.022 (.114)
Antiracism attitude scale	.141*** (.011)	.046 (.01)	.004 (.011)	.017 (.011)	.058 (.011)
R^2	.118	.073	.071	.08	.118
N	957	954	954	957	957

Source: Chapman Survey of American Fears
Notes: Entities are standardized betas, standard error in parentheses
* $p < .05$; ** $p < .01$; *** $p < .001$

TABLE A.16 REGRESSION COEFFICIENTS ASSESSING PREDICTORS OF VARIOUS SOCIAL ATTITUDES (ISSUES 41–45)

	Afraid of Iran using nuclear weapons	Afraid of gun legislation	Local gov should use curfews during protests	National Guard should be used during protests	We need national law enforcement reform
Woman	.2*** (.07)	−.034 (.068)	.135*** (.054)	.081** (.053)	−.035 (.051)
Age	.088* (.002)	−.035 (.002)	.218*** (.002)	.135*** (.002)	−.088** (.002)
Black	.024 (.12)	.037 (.116)	−.031 (.092)	−.069* (.089)	.121*** (.086)
Hispanic	.177*** (.1)	−.005 (.097)	.064 (.077)	.014 (.075)	.045 (.072)
Other race	.026 (.133)	−.033 (.129)	.04 (.102)	.031 (.099)	.001 (.096)
Political progressiveness	−.105** (.028)	−.228*** (.027)	−.139*** (.022)	−.18*** (.021)	.209*** (.02)
Education	−.036 (.022)	−.165*** (.021)	−.046 (.017)	−.07 (.016)	−.041 (.016)
Income	−.087* (.016)	.003 (.015)	−.065 (.012)	−.009 (.012)	−.061 (.011)
Religiosity	.012 (.052)	.064 (.05)	.022 (.04)	.016 (.039)	−.097* (.037)
Religious service attendance	−.059 (.017)	−.088* (.016)	.000 (.013)	−.085* (.012)	−.003 (.012)
Bible is word of God	.04 (.078)	−.013 (.075)	−.007 (.06)	.052 (.058)	−.068* (.056)
Christian	.046 (.094)	.071 (.091)	.075 (.072)	.079 (.07)	−.043 (.068)
Atheist/agnostic	−.051 (.17)	.032 (.165)	−.063 (.131)	.007 (.127)	−.069* (.123)
None (religion)	.031 (.118)	.078 (.114)	.009 (.09)	.002 (.088)	−.06 (.085)
Antiracism attitude scale	−.007 (.011)	−.296*** (.011)	.014 (.009)	−.128** (.008)	.305*** (.008)
R^2	.107	.284	.133	.161	.331
N	957	957	957	957	957

Source: Chapman Survey of American Fears
Notes: Entities are standardized betas, standard error in parentheses
* p < .05; ** p < .01; *** p < .001

TABLE A.17 REGRESSION COEFFICIENTS ASSESSING PREDICTORS OF VARIOUS SOCIAL ATTITUDES (ISSUES 46–50)

	We need to defund the police	Afraid of police brutality	Afraid of murder by stranger	Afraid of being mugged	Afraid of suffering from random shooting
Woman	−.013 (.046)	.046 (.064)	.215*** (.065)	.223*** (.061)	.21*** (.065)
Age	−.239*** (.001)	−.151*** (.002)	−.103** (.002)	−.05 (.002)	−.48*** (.002)
Black	.019 (.078)	.234*** (.109)	.126*** (.111)	.102** (.103)	.078* (.11)
Hispanic	.025 (.065)	.192*** (.091)	.231*** (.093)	.24*** (.086)	.194*** (.092)
Other race	−.043 (.087)	.139*** (.121)	.129*** (.124)	.109*** (.115)	.146*** (.123)
Political progressiveness	.142*** (.016)	.112** (.026)	.063 (.026)	−.011 (.024)	.064 (.026)
Education	−.046 (.04)	−.075* (.02)	−.132*** (.02)	.005 (.019)	−.115** (.02)
Income	−.037 (.01)	−.114*** (.014)	−.06 (.015)	−.087* (.014)	−.08* (.014)
Religiosity	−.084* (.034)	−.025 (.047)	.094* (.048)	.06 (.045)	−.021 (.048)
Religious service attendance	.043 (.011)	.038 (.015)	−.051 (.015)	−.046 (.014)	.016 (.015)
Bible is word of God	−.033 (.051)	−.052 (.071)	−.008 (.072)	−.027 (.067)	.019 (.072)
Christian	−.005 (.061)	.004 (.086)	.085* (.087)	−.015 (.081)	.04 (.087)
Atheist/agnostic	.032 (.111)	−.023 (.155)	−.002 (.159)	−.039 (.148)	.022 (.157)
None (religion)	.006 (.077)	.023 (.107)	.116** (.109)	−.017 (.102)	.005 (.108)
Antiracism attitude scale	.351*** (.007)	.124*** (.01)	.04 (.01)	.054 (.01)	.09* (.01)
R^2	.361	.279	.21	.154	.211
N	957	957	957	957	957

Source: Chapman Survey of American Fears
Notes: Entities are standardized betas, standard error in parentheses
* p < .05; ** p < .01; *** p < .001

TABLE A.18 REGRESSION COEFFICIENTS ASSESSING PREDICTORS OF VARIOUS SOCIAL ATTITUDES (ISSUES 51–53)

	Afraid of being a victim of breaking and entering	Afraid of being a victim of property theft	Afraid of being a victim of gang violence
Woman	.192*** (.063)	.17*** (.061)	.119*** (.068)
Age	−.03 (.002)	−.036 (.002)	.047 (.002)
Black	.04 (.107)	.025 (.104)	.079* (.115)
Hispanic	.187*** (.089)	.164*** (.087)	.236*** (.096)
Other race	.05 (.118)	.011 (.115)	.128*** (.128)
Political progressiveness	.027 (.025)	.089* (.024)	−.022 (.027)
Education	−.068 (.02)	−.083* (.019)	−.028 (.021)
Income	−.079* (.014)	−.076* (.014)	−.159*** (.015)
Religiosity	.034 (.046)	.009 (.045)	−.058 (.05)
Religious service attendance	−.029 (.015)	.002 (.014)	−.007 (.016)
Bible is word of God	.078* (.069)	.029 (.068)	.05 (.075)
Christian	.088* (.084)	.104* (.082)	.011 (.091)
Atheist/agnostic	.039 (.152)	−.003 (.146)	−.105** (.164)
None (religion)	.039 (.105)	.047 (.102)	−.017 (.113)
Antiracism attitude scale	.063 (.01)	−.012 (.01)	−.026 (.011)
R^2	.121	.099	.115
N	956	956	957

Source: Chapman Survey of American Fears
Notes: Entities are standardized betas, standard error in parentheses
* $p < .05$; ** $p < .01$; *** $p < .001$

For the most part, the results in Table 5.2 are found in Tables A.8 through A.18. However, there are some variations worth noting. Concerning the overt racial dependent variables, both political ideology and antiracism attitudes continue to be significant predictors. What is of interest is the more powerful impact indicated by the antiracism attitude scale relative to political ideology. Note the greater size of the standardized betas of the antiracism attitude scale relative to political ideology as it concerns afraid of BLM (−0.407 v. −0.108), support BLM (0.581 v. 0.28), afraid of illegal immigration (0.385 v. −0.175), and afraid of Muslims (−0.213 v. −0.102). As pointed out in footnote 7 in chapter 5 the t-score of the antiracism attitude scale is also higher than for political progressiveness for these models as well. Furthermore, it should be noted that, once again, political ideology is not connected to being afraid of a world without a white majority, but antiracism is significantly linked to not having that fear. Political ideology is still significant and matters greatly, but the effect sizes for the antiracism attitude scale are greater, and those attitudes matter more. This should be expected in a direct measurement of racial attitudes, although such a distinction does not show up in the bivariate results. However, we observe a similar effect in the assessment of January 6. Although the scores of strong political progressives and high antiracists are close at the bivariate level in the regression models, the standardized betas of the antiracism attitude scale are higher than political ideology for Trump to blame for Jan. 6 violence (0.597 v. 0.18) and Biden legitimate winner of 2020 election (0.489 v. 0.238). Surprisingly attitudes shaped by antiracism may be more powerful explanations for attitudes toward January 6 than overall political orientation. Furthermore, the bivariate difference between the scores of strong political progressives and high antiracists on the issue of voter fraud disappears in the multivariate models as the antiracism attitude scale produces higher t-scores and political ideology on the variable of afraid of widespread voter fraud (−7.51 v. −5.826).

Criminal justice is also a racialized issue. However, attitudes toward antiracism are not significantly tied to whether local governments should use curfews in the regression models, unlike the bivariate assessment. The higher fear of being murdered by strangers for both political liberals and antiracists, as well as the fear of suffering from a random shooting for political progressives, disappears in the multivariate models as well. In the regression models, political progressives are significantly more fearful of property theft, unlike the null finding in the bivariate analysis. Perhaps the most relevant difference from the bivariant findings is that in the regression models, there was not a significant difference between strong political progressives and high antiracists on whether to defund the police. In the multivariate model, both political ideology and attitudes toward antiracism are significant, but the standardized betas (0.351 v. 0.142) and t-scores (10.08 v. 4.209) of the antiracism attitude scale are much higher than for political ideology, indicating the larger effects of attitudes toward antiracism on whether a respondent wants to defund the police. Such a result is in keeping with the racialized nature that has developed within the debate about our criminal justice system.

Interestingly, although political progressives at the bivariate level were more likely to lose friends, spend more time alone, get into arguments, and prepare their households because of Covid, those differences did not hold in the regression models. The social and demographic characteristics of political progressives, rather than their political ideals, may account for their actions surrounding Covid. While there were some differences in the multivariate and bivariate results in the areas of environmentalism, economic fears, and foreign policy, they are not relevant enough for additional attention. Overall, the findings in the bivariate table are similar to the findings in the multivariate model, with a few exceptions. The basic findings in Chapter 5 concerning the ties of antiracism to partisan interest hold up after relevant social and demographic controls.

ASSESSMENT OF ANTIRACIST WEBSITES

We provide a table with the basic information from the websites used in the analysis in Chapter 6. That information is posted in Table A.19. In that table, we indicate the location, coding, and organization of the websites. This is done in the interest of transparency. The information is public, although it is likely that some of the websites will eventually become outdated. However, enough websites should remain viable so that scholars can conduct their own tests of validity of how the websites were coded.

Note on column headings:

Organization type: academic = 1, industry = 2, government = 3, media outlet = 4, community-org = 5, other = 6

Is there a direct link with antiracism and content analysis subject?: Yes = 1, No = 0

Pathway 1: Yes = 1, No = 0
Pathway 2: Yes = 1, No = 0
Pathway 3: Yes = 1, No = 0
Pathway 4: Yes = 1, No = 0

Political affiliation: Liberal = 1, Conservative = 2, Can't Tell = 3

Type of article: Analysis = 1, Activist = 2, Other = 3

TABLE A.19 CODING OF WEBSITES USED IN CONTENT ANALYSIS

Content analysis of climate change articles

ID	Pub. date	Name	Website	Organization type	Is there a direct link with antiracism and climate change?	Pathway 1	Pathway 2	Pathway 3	Pathway 4	Political affiliation	Type of article
1	2020	Friends of the Earth	https://friendsoftheearth.uk/about/climate-justice-and-antiracism	5	1	1	0	0	1	1	2
2	2022	Boston University	https://www.bu.edu/articles/2022/climate-change-battle-must-include-environmental-justice/	1	1	1	1	1	1	1	2
3	2021	Foreign Policy	https://foreignpolicy.com/2021/07/21/the-racial-violence-of-climate-change/	4	1	1	1	0	1	3	1
4	2020	Glamour	https://www.glamour.com/story/want-to-be-an-environmentalist-start-with-anti-racism	4	1	1	0	0	1	1	2
5	2022	Harvard University	https://www.hks.harvard.edu/faculty-research/policy-topics/environment-energy/climate-change-multiplier-racial-inequities-warns	1	1	1	0	0	1	1	2
6	2020	Pacific RISA	https://www.pacificrisa.org/2020/06/02/climate-and-racial-justice-resources/	1	1	1	0	1	1	1	2

7	2020	Families for Climate	https://www.familiesforclimate.org/antiracism-resources	5	1	1	1	1	1	2
8	2021	University of Connecticut	https://today.uconn.edu/2021/09/new-faculty-bring-antiracism-and-the-environment-to-the-forefront/	1	1	0	0	0	1	3
9	2020	Colorado College	https://www.coloradocollege.edu/newsevents/newsroom/2023/contesting-climate-change-class-connects-students-in-a-shared-desire-for-justice.html	1	1	1	1	1	1	3
10	2023	King's College London	https://www.kcl.ac.uk/blm-and-the-struggle-to-centre-racial-justice-in-the-climate-movement	1	1	1	0	1	1	2
11	2021	University of Miami	https://news.miami.edu/stories/2021/01/u-link-team-launches-climate-and-racial-justice-talks.html	1	1	1	0	1	1	2
12	2023	Science Communication Digest	https://www.scicommbites.org/post/climate-change-white-supremacy-colonialism-heteronormativity-an-unsettling-connection	1	1	0	1	0	3	2
13	2022	VTDigger	https://vtdigger.org/2022/01/17/youth-activists-say-legislature-must-combat-climate-change-systemic-racism/	4	1	1	0	0	1	1
14	2022	Fox News	https://www.foxnews.com/politics/wisconsin-dem-senate-candidate-chaired-state-taskforce-pushed-climate-antiracism-curriculum	4	1	1	0	1	2	1
15	2022	Oxford Academic	https://academic.oup.com/tbm/article/12/4/526/6591609	1	1	1	1	1	3	2
16	2021	Layla F. Saad	http://laylafsaad.com/good-ancestor-podcast/ep047-mikaela-loach	4	1	1	0	0	3	2

(continued)

TABLE A.19 CODING OF WEBSITES USED IN CONTENT ANALYSIS (continued)

Content analysis of climate change articles

ID	Pub. date	Name	Website	Organization type	Is there a direct link with antiracism and climate change?	Pathway 1	Pathway 2	Pathway 3	Pathway 4	Political affiliation	Type of article
17	2023	James Madison University Libraries	https://guides.lib.jmu.edu/bookdisplays/climatejustice	1	1	0	0	0	1	1	2
18	2021	Clinical Problem Solving	https://clinicalproblemsolving.com/2021/11/22/episode-209-antiracism-in-medicine-series-episode-12-our-land-is-our-health-addressing-anti-indigenous-racism-in-medicine/	1	1	0	0	0	1	3	2
19	2020	Fridays For Future	https://fridaysforfuture-heidelberg.de/en/act-for-justice-2/	5	1	1	0	0	1	1	2
20	2021	Mary Ann Liebert	https://www.liebertpub.com/doi/10.1089/env.2021.0034	1	1	1	1	0	1	3	1
21	2022	Network for Public Health Law	https://www.networkforphl.org/news-insights/taking-action-to-address-the-human-health-impacts-of-climate-change/	2	1	0	0	0	1	3	2
22	2020	Sierra Club	https://www.sierraclub.org/michael-brune/2020/05/christian-cooper-antiracism-outdoors	2	1	1	1	0	0	1	2
23	2021	Wednesday Journal	https://www.oakpark.com/2021/08/03/why-antiracism-is-key-to-sustainability/	4	1	0	1	0	1	3	2
24	2020	Penguin Publishing	https://www.penguin.co.uk/articles/2020/06/ibram-x-kendi-definition-of-antiracist	6	1	0	1	0	1	3	2
25	2023	Washington Hebrew Congregation	https://www.whctemple.org/faith-in-action/diversity-equity-inclusion-and-justice-dei/antiracism-resources/	5	1	0	0	0	1	3	2

26	2022	Alliance of Baptists	https://allianceofbaptists.org/environmental-justice-is-racial-justice/	5	1	0	1	0	1	1	2
27	2020	Columbia University	https://news.climate.columbia.edu/2020/08/21/environmental-sciences-anti-racism/	1	1	1	0	1	1	1	2
28	2023	University of Southern California	https://keck.usc.edu/jedi-west/initiatives/	1	1	0	0	0	1	1	2
29	2023	American Journal of Public Health	https://ajph.aphapublications.org/doi/full/10.2105/AJPH.2022.307114	1	1	1	0	0	1	1	2
30	2019	The Guardian	https://www.theguardian.com/environment/2019/oct/04/extinction-rebellion-race-climate-crisis-inequality	4	1	0	0	0	1	1	1
31	2020	American University	https://www.american.edu/about/sustainability/campus-greening/social-sustainability.cfm	1	1	1	0	0	1	1	2
32	2021	American Psychological Association	https://psycnet.apa.org/record/2020-79656-001	1	1	0	0	0	1	3	1
33	2021	Open Society Foundation	https://www.opensocietyfoundations.org/voices/where-roma-rights-and-environmental-justice-meet	4	1	1	0	0	1	1	2
34	2022	University of Denver	https://libguides.du.edu/c.php?g=1046908&p=7746544	1	1	0	1	0	1	1	2
35	2020	Northwestern University	https://devsci.northwestern.edu/462-2/antiracism-resources/	1	1	0	0	0	1	1	2

(continued)

TABLE A.19 CODING OF WEBSITES USED IN CONTENT ANALYSIS (*continued*)

Content analysis of climate change articles

ID	Pub. date	Name	Website	Organization type	Is there a direct link with antiracism and climate change?	Pathway 1	Pathway 2	Pathway 3	Pathway 4	Political affiliation	Type of article
36	2020	*K-12 Dive: K-12 Education News*	https://www.k12dive.com/news/how-3-school-systems-started-their-antiracism-practices/588307/	4	1	1	0	0	0	3	1
37	2020	*Washington Area Bicyclist Association*	https://waba.org/antiracism/	5	1	0	0	0	0	1	2
38	2021	*Bloomberg*	https://www.bloomberg.com/news/features/2021-05-27/addressing-racism-inside-climate-science	4	1	1	0	0	1	1	1
39	2022	University of Michigan	https://lsa.umich.edu/ncid/news-events/all-news/antiracism-collaborative/arc-funding-resources/antiracism-grant-announcement-2022.html	1	1	1	0	0	0	1	2
40	2021	Climate Generation	https://climategen.org/blog/tag/yea/	2	1	0	0	0	1	1	2
41	2022	Wikipedia	https://en.wikipedia.org/wiki/How_to_Be_an_Antiracist	6	1	0	0	0	0	3	1

Content analysis of abortion articles

ID	Pub. date	Name	Website	Organization type	Is there a direct link with antiracism and abortion?	Pathway 1	Pathway 2	Pathway 3	Pathway 4	Political affiliation	Type of article
1	2022	*New England Journal of Medicine*	https://www.nejm.org/doi/full/10.1056/NEJMp2209737	1	1	0	1	1	1	3	2
2	2022	Boston University	https://www.bu.edu/antiracism-center/2022/06/20/five-things-you-should-know-about-abortion-in-america/	1	1	1	1	0	1	1	2
3	2019	*Yes Magazine*	https://www.yesmagazine.org/social-justice/2019/07/04/abortion-ban-fear-white-extinction-babies	4	1	0	1	0	1	1	1
4	2023	University of Minnesota	https://carhe.umn.edu/events/person-place-and-policy-understanding-health-equity-implications-changing-abortion	1	1	0	0	0	0	1	3
5	2021	Harvard University	https://harvardlawreview.org/wp-content/uploads/2021/04/134-Harv.-L.-Rev.-2025.pdf	1	1	1	0	0	1	1	1
6	2022	*Nebraska Public Media*	https://nebraskapublicmedia.org/news/news-articles/abortion-bans-could-have-far-reaching-impacts-on-the-black-community-in-the-midwest/	4	1	1	0	0	1	3	1
7	2020	American College of Obstetricians and Gynecologists	https://www.acog.org/news/news-articles/2020/08/joint-statement-obstetrics-and-gynecology-collective-action-addressing-racism	1	1	1	0	0	1	1	2
8	2023	Loeb & Loeb	https://www.loeb.com/en/newsevents/news/2023/02/loeb-aids-pro-bono-partner-law-firm-antiracism-alliance-lfaa	2	1	0	1	0	1	1	2

(continued)

TABLE A.19 CODING OF WEBSITES USED IN CONTENT ANALYSIS (continued)

Content analysis of abortion articles

ID	Pub. date	Name	Website	Organization type	Is there a direct link with antiracism and abortion?	Pathway 1	Pathway 2	Pathway 3	Pathway 4	Political affiliation	Type of article
9	2021	Crooked	https://crooked.com/podcast/antiracist-healthcare-w-prof-ibram-x-kendi/	4	1	0	0	0	1	1	2
10	2022	SAGE Journals	https://journals.sagepub.com/doi/pdf/10.1177/10497322211097622	1	1	1	1	0	0	3	2
11	2021	Students for Life	https://studentsforlife.org/2021/04/02/university-of-minnesota-gets-5-million-anti-racism-grant-ironically-involves-planned-parenthood/	5	1	0	1	0	1	2	2
12	2023	Minnesota Department of Health	https://www.health.state.mn.us/people/womeninfants/womenshealth/childbirthact.html	3	1	0	0	0	1	3	2
13	2023	CNN	https://www.cnn.com/2023/02/01/health/medication-abortion-survey-kff/index.html	4	1	0	0	0	0	1	1
14	2022	Boston Globe	https://www.bostonglobe.com/2022/05/C5/opinion/right-an-abortion-can-be-saved/	4	1	0	0	0	1	1	2
15	2022	Health Services Research	https://onlinelibrary.wiley.com/doi/10.1111/1475-6773.14108?af=R	1	1	0	0	0	1	3	1
16	2022	Sahan Journal	https://sahanjournal.com/health/asha-hassan-university-of-minnesota-roe-v-wade-abortion-supreme-court/	4	1	0	0	0	1	3	1
17	2023	She Seeks Non-fiction	https://sheseeksnonfiction.blog/tag/abortion-rights/	6	1	1	1	0	1	1	1

18	2020	Christianity Today	https://www.christianitytoday.com/ct/2021/january-february/abortion-pro-life-movement-playbook-racial-justice-history.html	4	1	0	0	0	2	2
19	2022	Journal of the American Medical Association	https://jamanetwork.com/journals/jama/fullarticle/2797864	1	1	1	0	0	3	2
20	2022	Represent Collaborative	https://representcollaborative.com/stories/5-things-friday-may-6	5	1	1	1	0	1	2
21	2023	Nurturely	https://nurturely.org/reproductive-justice-is-perinatal-equity/	2	1	0	1	1	3	2
22	2020	National Council of Jewish Women	https://www.ncjw.org/act/action-resources/antiracism-resources/	5	1	0	0	1	1	2
23	2021	University of Connecticut	https://today.uconn.edu/2021/09/new-faculty-bring-antiracism-and-the-environment-to-the-forefront/	1	1	0	0	0	1	3
24	2022	Hello Hello Books	https://hellohellobooks.com/social-justice/reading-group-info	6	1	0	0	0	3	2
25	2022	SciLine	https://www.sciline.org/disparities/pregnancy-related-death/	4	1	0	0	1	3	2
26	2016	SisterSong	https://www.instagram.com/sistersong_woc/?hl=en	5	1	0	0	0	1	2
27	2023	Holy Trinity Lutheran Church	https://www.htchicago.org/artbooks	5	1	0	0	0	1	2

(continued)

TABLE A.19 CODING OF WEBSITES USED IN CONTENT ANALYSIS (continued)

Content analysis of abortion articles

ID	Pub. date	Name	Website	Organization type	Is there a direct link with antiracism and abortion?	Pathway 1	Pathway 2	Pathway 3	Pathway 4	Political affiliation	Type of article
28	2021	Population Reference Bureau	https://www.prb.org/resources/black-women-over-three-times-more-likely-to-die-in-pregnancy-postpartum-than-white-women-new-research-finds/	2	1	1	0	0	1	1	1
29	2022	Evolve Family Services	https://evolveservices.org/blog/roe-v-wade-the-impact-on-people-of-color/	5	1	1	0	0	1	3	2
30	2019	Peggy Jack Baskin Foundation	https://baskinfoundation.org/resources/abortion-activism-and-access-resources/	6	1	1	0	0	1	1	2
31	2022	*Milwaukee Independent*	http://www.milwaukeeindependent.com/syndicated/abortion-bans-expose-white-anxiety-reproduction-people-color/	4	1	0	1	0	1	3	1

Content analysis: January 6 riots

ID	Pub. date	Name	Website	Organization type	Is there a direct link with antiracism and the Jan. 6 riots?	Pathway 1	Pathway 2	Pathway 3	Pathway 4	Political affiliation	Type of article
1	2021	Boston University	https://www.bu.edu/articles/2021/pov-january-6-insurrection-has-evolved-into-a-racist-relapse/	1	0	1	0	1	1	2	2
2	2021	*Vox*	https://www.vox.com/22227102/anti-racism-ibram-kendi	4	1	1	0	1	1	2	2
3	2022	New America	https://www.newamerica.org/political-reform/reports/equity-and-racial-justice-where-do-they-fit-in-a-national-security-strategy/reimagining-us-foreign-policy-as-an-anti-racist-endeavor-by-sneha-nair/	2	1	1	0	0	1	1	1

#	Year	Source	URL							
4	2021	Eric Pernell	https://www.ericapernell.com/white-supremacy-capitol-attack	1	1	1	0	1	4	2	2
5	2023	University of California	https://www.bjcl.org/assets/files/1.-Outlaw_The-Line-That-I-Did-Not-Know-I-Had_Final-Draft_2023-02-21-050445_cuer.pdf	1	0	1	0	1	4	1	1
6	2021	CATESOL	https://www.catesol.org/response_to_jan_6_insurrection.php	1	1	1	0	0	4	1	1
7	2021	Access of West Michigan	https://accessofwestmichigan.org/2021/02/01/reflection-and-statement-on-antiracism-and-recent-events/	5	1	1	0	1	1	2	2
8	2022	University of St. Louis	https://scholarship.law.slu.edu/cgi/viewcontent.cgi?article=2312&context=jj	1	0	1	0	0	1	1	1
9	2021	Beacon Broadside	https://www.beaconbroadside.com/broadside/2021/03/the-democracy-aaron-sorkin-has-in-mind-is-missing-antiracism.html	4	0	1	0	0	4	1	1
10	2021	Eagle Rock School	https://eaglerockschool.org/eagle-rocks-statement-on-the-events-of-january-6-2021/	1	0	1	0	1	4	2	2
11	2021	Columbia University	https://blogs.law.columbia.edu/revolution1313/6-13/	1	0	1	0	0	1	2	2
12	2022	Harvard University	https://www.cambridge.org/core/journals/journal-of-law-and-religion/article/continuous-action-toward-justice/EBFD03D0FE0B8FE63762D8082B8850BF	1	0	1	0	1	1	2	2
13	2022	Journal of Applied Social Psychology	https://onlinelibrary.wiley.com/doi/pdf/10.1111/jasp.12865	1	0	1	0	0	1	1	1
14	2022	University of Michigan	https://lsa.umich.edu/ncid/news-events/all-news/antiracism-collaborative/arc-students/2022-awardees-grad-student-research-grants.html	1	0	0	0	0	1	2	2

(continued)

TABLE A.19 CODING OF WEBSITES USED IN CONTENT ANALYSIS (continued)

Content analysis: January 6 riots

ID	Pub. date	Name	Website	Organization type	Is there a direct link with antiracism and the Jan. 6 riots?	Pathway 1	Pathway 2	Pathway 3	Pathway 4	Political affiliation	Type of article
15	2022	Brooklyn Law Review	https://brooklynworks.brooklaw.edu/cgi/viewcontent.cgi?article=2296&context=blr	1	0	1	0	1	4	2	2
16	2021	Loyola Law	https://lawecommons.luc.edu/cgi/viewcontent.cgi?article=1698&context=facpubs	1	0	1	0	0	4	1	1
17	2021	Bulwark	https://www.thebulwark.com/app/uploads/2021/07/FIELD-What-the-Hell-Happened-to-the-Claremont-Institute-1.pdf	4	0	1	0	0	2	1	1
18	2021	Unherd	https://unherd.com/2021/03/antiracism-is-too-middle-class/	4	0	1	0	0	1	1	1

Content analysis: inflation articles

ID	Pub. date	Name	Website	Organization type	Is there a direct link with antiracism and inflation?	Pathway 1	Pathway 2	Pathway 3	Pathway 4	Political affiliation	Type of article
1	2022	Independent Institute	https://www.independent.org/news/article.asp?id=14138	2	1	0	0	0	0	2	1
2	2022	Harvard University	https://www.cambridge.org/core/journals/perspectives-on-politics/article/from-freedom-now-to-black-lives-matter-retrieving-king-and-randolph-to-theorize-contemporary-white-antiracism/BAA21ABFEE8F72DC7AF06B99940F68A2	1	1	0	0	0	0	1	1
3	2022	University of Nevada, Las Vegas	https://scholarship.shu.edu/cgi/viewcontent.cgi?article=1839&context=shlr	1	1	0	0	0	0	3	1

	Pub. date	Name	Website								
4	2022	Boston University	https://www.bu.edu/articles/2022/climate-change-battle-must-include-environmental-justice/	1	1	0	0	1	0	1	2
5	2022	American Institute for Economic Research	https://www.aier.org/article/a-parents-guide-to-kendis-antiracist-baby/	2	1	0	0	0	0	2	2
6	2022	New Yorker	https://www.newyorker.com/news/annals-of-inquiry/the-marxist-who-antagonizes-liberals-and-the-left	4	1	0	0	0	0	1	1
7	2022	Health Equity	https://www.ncbi.nlm.nih.gov/pmc/articles/PMC9811829/	3	1	0	0	1	0	3	2
8	2021	Times of San Diego	http://timesofsandiego.com/opinion/2021/10/24/cal-state-faculty-slammed-by-inflation-as-presidents-get-hefty-raises/	4	1	0	0	0	0	3	1

Content analysis: street crime articles

ID	Pub. date	Name	Website	Organization type	Is there a direct link with antiracism and street crime?	Pathway 1	Pathway 2	Pathway 3	Pathway 4	Political affiliation	Type of article
1	2021	SAGE Journals	https://journals.sagepub.com/doi/10.1177/21533687209 83436	1	1	0	0	0	1	3	2
2	2023	City Journal	https://www.city-journal.org/article/the-great-abdication/	4	1	0	0	0	1	2	1
3	2018	University of Nevada, Las Vegas	https://digitalscholarship.unlv.edu/cgi/viewcontent.cgi?article=4223&context=thesesdissertations	1	1	0	0	0	1	3	1
4	2020	University of California Berkeley	https://repository.uchastings.edu/cgi/viewcontent.cgi?article=2807&context=faculty_scholarship	1	1	0	0	0	1	3	1

(continued)

TABLE A.19 CODING OF WEBSITES USED IN CONTENT ANALYSIS *(continued)*

Content analysis: street crime articles

ID	Pub. date	Name	Website	Organization type	Is there a direct link with antiracism and street crime?	Pathway 1	Pathway 2	Pathway 3	Pathway 4	Political affiliation	Type of article
5	2021	Fair for All	https://www.fairforall.org/content/newsletters/2021-03-24.html	5	1	0	0	0	0	2	1
6	2021	Freedom and Reason	https://andrewaustin.blog/2021/05/02/the-myth-of-racist-criminal-justice-persists-at-the-denial-of-human-agency-and-logic/	6	1	0	0	0	0	2	1
7	2020	University of Wisconsin	https://search.proquest.com/openview/ab32245a2e8aaaa09908c76bd1831235/1?pq-origsite=gscholar&cbl=18750&diss=y	1	1	0	0	0	0	1	1
8	2018	York University	https://yorkspace.library.yorku.ca/xmlui/bitstream/handle/10315/34979/Khenti_Akwatu_A_2018_Phd.pdf?sequence=2&isAllowed=y	1	1	0	0	0	1	3	1
9	2016	University of London	https://academicengagement.org/wp-content/uploads/2019/09/David-Hirsh-pamphlet.pdf	1	1	0	0	0	1	3	1
10	2016	Book (Black Feminist Thought)	https://negrasoulblog.files.wordpress.com/2016/04/patricia-hill-collins-black-feminist-thought.pdf	1	1	0	0	0	1	1	1

We made certain to carefully describe our methodology for the qualitative analysis in Chapter 6. For the most part, the work was done by the second author (Oh) under the direction of the first author (Yancey). However, the second author possessed more knowledge about how Google searches work, and with our combined knowledge, we were able to conduct this research. Perhaps there are alternative ways to conduct searches for websites, and those alternatives may turn up websites missed by this research. In addition to future research focusing on different social and political topics, the use of contrasting ways to locate websites can prove to be valuable in extending our knowledge on this topic.

Appendix B

Antiracism Literature

DiAngelo, Robin. 2018. *White Fragility: Why It's So Hard for White People to Talk about Racism*. Beacon Press.
Eddo-Lodge, Reni. 2020. *Why I'm No Longer Talking to White People about Race*. Bloomsbury Publishing.
Fidel, Kondwani. 2020. *The Antiracist: How to Start the Conversation about Race and Take Action*. Hot Books
Jewell, Tiffany. 2020. *This Book Is Anti-racist*. Frances Lincoln.
Kendi, Ibram X. 2019. *How to Be an Antiracist*. One World.
Kivel, Paul, 2017. *Uprooting Racism: How White People Can Work for Racial Justice*. New Society Publishers.
Oluo, Ijeoma. 2019. *So You Want to Talk about Race*. Hachette UK.
Saad, Layla F. 2020. *Me and White Supremacy: Combat Racism, Change the World, and Become a Good Ancestor*. Sourcebooks.

Appendix C

Selected Questions from Chapman Survey of American Fears

RACIALIZED ISSUES

Afraid of BLM—How afraid are you of the following: Black Lives Matter (BLM)?#
Support of BLM—Please indicate your level of agreement with the following statements: I support the Black Lives Matter (BLM) movement.@
Afraid of illegal immigration—How afraid are you of the following events: Illegal immigration?#
Afraid of immigrants—How afraid are you of the following: Immigrants?#
Afraid of world without white majority—How afraid are you of the following events: Whites no longer being the majority in the US?#
Afraid of white supremacy—How afraid are you of the following: White supremacists?#
Afraid of being a victim of hate crime—How afraid are you of being the victim of the following crimes: Racial/hate crime?#
Afraid of Muslims—How afraid are you of the following: Muslims?#

PARTISAN POLITICAL ATTITUDES

Voted Trump/Voted Biden—Who did you vote for in the 2020 Presidential election?
Donald Trump, the Republican nominee
Joseph Biden, the Democratic nominee
Someone else
Did not vote
Afraid of right-wing extremists—How afraid are you of the following: Right wing extremists?#
Afraid of left-wing extremists—How afraid are you of the following: Left wing extremists?#

\# — Responses are "Very afraid," "Afraid," "Slightly afraid," and "Not afraid."
@ — Responses are "Strongly disagree," "Disagree," "Agree," and "Strongly agree."

POLITICAL ISSUE—JAN 6.

Trump to blame for Jan. 6 violence—Donald Trump is to blame for the violent events that occurred on January 6th, 2021.@

Biden legitimate winner of 2020 election—Joseph Biden was the legitimate winner of the 2020 U.S. presidential election.@

Can not know who won 2020 election because of election fraud—Because of widespread election fraud, we'll never know who won the 2020 presidential election.@

Jan 6 protesters are patriots—The protesters who attacked the U.S. Capitol on January 6th, 2021 were patriots.@

Need new laws to protect against voter fraud—We need new voting laws because there is too much voter fraud.@

Afraid of widespread voter fraud—How afraid are you of the following events: Widespread voter fraud?#

POLITICAL ISSUE—ENVIRONMENTALISM

Afraid of air pollution—How afraid are you of the following: Air pollution?#

Afraid of water pollution—How afraid are you of the following: Pollution of drinking water?#

Afraid of animal and plant extinction—How afraid are you of the following: Extinction of plant and animal species?#

Afraid of climate change—How afraid are you of the following: Global warming and climate change?#

Afraid of climate change affecting where I live—How afraid are you of the following events: Climate change impacting where I live?#

Climate Change Index (4–16 range)

Please indicate your level of agreement with the following statements.

Climate change is causing more frequent and severe floods.@

Climate change is causing more frequent and severe wildfires.@

Climate change is causing more frequent and severe droughts.@

Climate change is causing more frequent and severe hurricanes.@

ATTITUDES TOWARD COVID

Afraid of pandemic—How afraid are you of the following events: A new pandemic or a major epidemic?#

Afraid of catching Covid—How afraid are you of the following: Catching the coronavirus (COVID-19)?#

Lost friend because of Covid—Please indicate your level of agreement with the following statements: I have lost friendships because of COVID-19.@

Spent more time alone because of Covid—Please indicate your level of agreement with the following statements: I have spent more time alone because of COVID-19.@

Got into arguments more because of Covid—Please indicate your level of agreement with the following statements: I have had arguments with friends or family because of COVID-19.@

Prepared household more because of Covid—Please indicate your level of agreement with the following statements: I have done more to prepare my household for emergencies and disasters because of COVID-19.@

ECONOMIC FEARS

Afraid of economic collapse—How afraid are you of the following events: Economic/financial collapse?#

Afraid of not having enough money in the future—How afraid are you of the following: Not having enough money for the future?#

Afraid of being unemployed—How afraid are you of the following: Being unemployed?#

Afraid of not being able to pay rent or mortgage—How afraid are you of the following: Not having enough money to pay my rent or mortgage?#

Afraid of not being able to pay college debt—How afraid are you of the following: Not being able to pay off the college debt of myself or a family member?#

Afraid of not being able to pay medical bill—How afraid are you of the following: High medical bills?#

FOREIGN POLICY FEARS

Afraid of US becoming involved in another world war—How afraid are you of the following events: The US becoming involved in another world war?#

Afraid of biological warfare—How afraid are you of the following events: Biological warfare?#

Afraid of terrorist attack—How afraid are you of the following events: A terrorist attack?#

Afraid of North Korea using nuclear weapons—How afraid are you of the following events: North Korea using nuclear weapons?#

Afraid of Iran using nuclear weapons—How afraid are you of the following events: Iran using nuclear weapons?#

Afraid of Russia using nuclear weapons—How afraid are you of the following events: Russia using nuclear weapons?#

CRIMINAL JUSTICE CONCERNS

Afraid of gun legislation—How afraid are you of the following: Government restrictions on firearms and ammunition?#

Local gov should use curfews during protests—Please indicate your level of agreement with the following statements: Local governments should enact curfews during protests?@

National Guard should be used during protests—Please indicate your level of agreement with the following statements: The National Guard should be called in to cities to stop protests when needed.@

We need national law enforcement reform—Please indicate your level of agreement with the following statements: Our nation needs to reform the entire system of law enforcement.@

We need to defund the police—Please indicate your level of agreement with the following statements: We should defund the police.@

Afraid of police brutality—How afraid are you of being the victim of the following crimes: Police brutality?#

Afraid of murder by stranger—How afraid are you of being the victim of the following crimes: Murder by a stranger?#

Afraid of being mugged—How afraid are you of being the victim of the following crimes: Mugging?#

Afraid of suffering from random shooting—How afraid are you of <u>being the victim</u> of the following crimes: Random/mass shooting?#

Afraid of being a victim of breaking and entering—How afraid are you of <u>being the victim</u> of the following crimes: Break-ins?#

Afraid of being a victim of property theft—How afraid are you of <u>being the victim</u> of the following crimes: Theft of property?#

Afraid of being a victim of gang violence—How afraid are you of <u>being the victim</u> of the following crimes: Gang violence?#

References

Acheson, Ray. 2022. *Abolishing State Violence: A World Beyond Bombs, Borders, and Cages.* Haymarket Books.

Aiyetoro, Adjoa A., and Adrienne D. Davis. 2009. "Historic and Modern Social Movements for Reparations: The National Coalition of Blacks for Reparations in America (N'Cobra) and Its Antecedents." *Texas Wesleyan Law Review* 16:687–766.

Alberta Civil Liberties Research Centre. 2020. "Anti-racism Defined." November 1, 2020. https://web.archive.org/web/20201101022553/http://www.aclrc.com/antiracism-defined.

Alcendor, Donald J. 2020. "Racial Disparities-Associated COVID-19 Mortality among Minority Populations in the US." *Journal of Clinical Medicine* 9 (8): 2442.

Alexander, Bryant Keith. 2016. "Introduction: 'Hands Up! Don't Shoot!': Policing Race in America." *Cultural Studies ↔ Critical Methodologies* 16 (3): 239–244.

Alexander, Michelle. 2010. *The New Jim Crow: Mass Incarceration in the Age of Colorblindness.* New Press.

Allen, Upton, Tya Collins, George J. Sefa Dei, Frances Henry, Awad Ibrahim, Carl James, Johanne Jean-Pierre, Audrey Kobayashi, Kathy Lewis, Renisa Mawani, Kwame McKenzie, Akwasi Owusu-Bempah, Rinaldo Walcott, and Njoki N. Wane. 2021. *Impacts of COVID-19 in Racialized Communities.* Royal Society of Canada. https://doi.org/10.14288/1.0398437.

Alli, Shawn. 2017. "Calexit: Yes, California Should Become Its Own Country." https://www.shawnalli.com/calexit-yes-california-should-become-its-own-country.html.

Altemeyer, Bob. 1988. *Enemies of Freedom: Understanding Right-Wing Authoritarianism.* Wiley.

Alvarez, Michael, and Tara Butterfield. 1998. "The Revolution against Affirmative Action in California: Politics, Economics, and Proposition 209." *State Politics and Policy Quarterly* 4 (May). https://doi.org/10.1177/153244000400400101.

Angermeyer, Matthias C., and Herbert Matschinger. 2005. "Labeling—Stereotype—Discrimination." *Social Psychiatry and Psychiatric Epidemiology* 40 (5): 391–395.

Arat-Koç, Sedef. 2014. "Rethinking Whiteness, 'Culturalism,' and the Bourgeoisie in the Age of Neoliberalism." In *Theorizing Anti-racism: Linkages in Marxism and Critical Race Theories*, edited by Abigail B. Bakan and Enakshi Dua, 311–339. University of Toronto Press.

Arbatli, Ekim, and Dina Rosenberg. 2021. "United We Stand, Divided We Rule: How Political Polarization Erodes Democracy." *Democratization* 28 (2): 285–307. https://doi.org/10.1080/13510347.2020.1818068.

Asekun-Olarinmoye, Olusesan, Oluwakemi Oriola, Olushewa Akilla, and Shade Ade-Johnson. 2018. "Media Systems: A Comparative Analysis of Britain, the United States, Canada and France." *Research on Humanities and Social Sciences* 8 (2): 15–23.

Atske, Sara. 2021. "The Internet and the Pandemic." Pew Research Center. September 1, 2021. https://www.pewresearch.org/internet/2021/09/01/the-internet-and-the-pandemic/.

Ayris, Alex. 2021. "'They'd Vote against Jesus Christ Himself': Trump's 'White Evangelicals,' the Construction of a Contested Identity, and the Need for a New Narrative." *Journal of Church and State* 63 (4): 648–670.

Badenhorst, Pauli, James Jupp, Jenna Min Shim, Timothy J. Lensmire, Zachary A. Casey, Samuel J. Tanner, Veronica Watson, and Erin Miller. 2022. "Doesn't Your Work Just Re-Center Whiteness? The Fallen Impossibilities of White Allyship." *Journal of Curriculum Theorizing* 37 (3): 47–71.

Bader, Christopher, Joseph O. Baker, L. Edward Day, and Ann Gordon. 2020. *Fear Itself: The Causes and Consequences of Fear in America*. New York University Press.

Bailey, Zinzi D., Justin M. Feldman, and Mary T. Bassett. 2021. "How Structural Racism Works—Racist Policies as a Root Cause of US Racial Health Inequities." *New England Journal of Medicine* 384 (8): 768–773.

Bailey, Zinzi D., Nancy Krieger, Madina Agénor, Jasmine Graves, Natalia Linos, and Mary T. Bassett. 2017. "Structural Racism and Health Inequities in the USA: Evidence and Interventions." *The Lancet* 389 (10077): 1453–1463.

Bakan, Abigail B. 2008. "Marxism and Antiracism: Rethinking the Politics of Difference." *Rethinking Marxism* 20 (2): 238–256.

———. 2014. "Race, Class, and Colonialism: Reconsidering the 'Jewish Question.'" In *Theorizing Anti-racism: Linkages in Marxism and Critical Race Theories*, edited by Abigail B. Bakan and Enakshi Dua, 252–279. University of Toronto Press.

Bannerji, Himani. 2014. "Marxism and Anti-racism in Theory and Practice: Reflections and Interpretations." In *Theorizing Anti-racism: Linkages in Marxism and Critical Race Theories*, edited by Abigail B. Bakan and Enakshi Dua, 127–141. University of Toronto Press.

Barrie, Christopher. 2020. "Searching Racism after George Floyd." *Socius* 6:2378023120971507.

Barthel, Margaret. 2022. "Youngkin Administration Rescinds Racial Equity Resources for Schools." DCist. February 25, 2022. https://dcist.com/story/22/02/25/youngkin-critical-race-theory-report/.

Bartolovich, Crystal, and Neil Lazarus, eds. 2002. *Marxism, Modernity and Postcolonial Studies*. Cambridge University Press. https://doi.org/10.1017/CBO9780511483158.

Bateman, David A. 2016. "Race, Party, and American Voting Rights." *The Forum* 14 (1): 39–65. https://doi.org/10.1515/for-2016-0005.

Bayless, Beau, Kimberly Hampton, and Keaton Jones. 2022. "Understanding Teachers' Views Regarding Critical Race Theory and the Surrounding Debate in Utah High Schools." In *Inquiry of the Public Sort*, Vol. 2, edited by David P. Carter, article 3. Pressbooks.

Beeman, Angie. 2022. *Liberal White Supremacy: How Progressives Silence Racial and Class Oppression*. University of Georgia Press.

Bell, Derrick. 1973. *Race, Racism, and American Law*. Little, Brown.

———. 2018. *Faces at the Bottom of the Well: The Permanence of Racism*. Hachette UK.

Benedetti, Christopher, and Annette M. Holba. 2022. "Finding 'Pity' within the 'Haggle and Nag' Rhetoric around Critical Race Theory." *Nonpartisan Education Review/Essays* 18 (3): 1–13. https://nonpartisaneducation.org/Review/Essays/v18n3.htm.

Benson, Devyn Spence. 2016. *Antiracism in Cuba: The Unfinished Revolution*. University of North Carolina Press.

Benson, Keith E. 2022. "Crying, 'Wolf!' The Campaign against Critical Race Theory in American Public Schools as an Expression of Contemporary White Grievance in an Era of Fake News." *Journal of Education and Learning* 11 (4): 1–14.

Bentley, Frank R., Nediyana Daskalova, and Brooke White. 2017. "Comparing the Reliability of Amazon Mechanical Turk and Survey Monkey to Traditional Market Research Surveys." In *Proceedings of the 2017 CHI Conference Extended Abstracts on Human Factors in Computing Systems*, 1092–1099. Association for Computing Machinery. https://doi.org/10.1145/3027063.3053335.

Berman, Gabrielle, and Yin Paradies. 2010. "Racism, Disadvantage and Multiculturalism: Towards Effective Anti-racist Praxis." *Ethnic and Racial Studies* 33 (2): 214–232.

Better, Shirley. 2007. *Institutional Racism: A Primer on Theory and Strategies for Social Change*. Rowman and Littlefield Publishers.

Beyer, Sylvia. 2022. "College Students' Political Attitudes Affect Negative Stereotypes about Social Groups." *Social Sciences* 11 (8): 321.

Binkin, Martin. 2011. *Blacks and the Military*. Rowman and Littlefield Publishers.

Bishop, Bill, and Robert G. Cushing. 2008. *The Big Sort: Why the Clustering of Like-Minded America Is Tearing Us Apart*. Houghton Mifflin Harcourt.

Blaisdell, Benjamin. 2021. "Counternarrative as Strategy: Embedding Critical Race Theory to Develop an Antiracist School Identity." *International Journal of Qualitative Studies in Education* 1:1–21.

Blanton, Ryan. 2011. "Chronotopic Landscapes of Environmental Racism." *Journal of Linguistic Anthropology* 21(S1):E76–E93.

Bogues, Anthony. 2014. "CLR James and WEB Du Bois: Black Jacobins and Black Reconstruction, Writing Heresy and Revisionist Histories." In *Theorizing Anti-racism: Linkages in Marxism and Critical Race Theories*, edited by Abigail B. Bakan and Enakshi Dua, 148–183. University of Toronto Press.

Bonilla-Silva, Eduardo. 2001. *White Supremacy and Racism in the Post–Civil Rights Era*. Lynne Rienner.

———. 2006. *Racism without Racists: Color-Blind Racism and the Persistence of Racial Inequality in the United States*. Rowman and Littlefield Publishers.

———. 2013. "'New Racism,' Color-Blind Racism, and the Future of Whiteness in America." In *White Out*, edited by Ashley W. Doane and Eduardo Bonilla-Silva, 268–281. Routledge.

Bonnett, Alastair. 2000. *Anti-racism*. Routledge.

Boxell, Levi. 2020. "Demographic Change and Political Polarization in the United States." *Economics Letters* 192:109187. https://doi.org/10.1016/j.econlet.2020.109187.

Boysen, Guy A., Rebecca L. Chicosky, and Erin E. Delmore. 2020. "Dehumanization of Mental Illness and the Stereotype Content Model." *Stigma and Health* 8 (2): 150–158.

Bracey, Glenn E. 2015. "Toward a Critical Race Theory of State." *Critical Sociology* 41 (3): 553–572.

Brah, Avtar, and Ann Phoenix. 2004. "Ain't I a Woman? Revisiting Intersectionality." *Journal of International Women's Studies* 5 (3): 75–86.

Brenan, Megan. 2022. "Record-High 56% in U.S. Perceive Local Crime Has Increased." Gallup. October 28, 2022. https://news.gallup.com/poll/404048/record-high-perceive-local-crime-increased.aspx.

Brooks, Khristopher J. 2023. "Bud Light Is No Longer America's Best-Selling Beer: Here's Why." CBS News. June 15, 2023. https://www.cbsnews.com/news/bud-light-no-longer-best-selling-beer-boycott-sales/.

Bui, Ngoc H., James J. Garcia, Monique J. Williams, and Alexandra M. Burrel. 2022. "A Model for Anti-racism Training in Higher Education." *Journal of Faculty Development* 36 (3): 41–48.

Burke, Meghan. 2018. *Colorblind Racism*. John Wiley and Sons.

Cahn, Naomi, and June Carbone. 2007. "Red Families v. Blue Families." GWU Law School Public Law Research Paper 343, George Washington University, Washington, D.C.

———. 2010. *Red Families v. Blue Families: Legal Polarization and the Creation of Culture*. Oxford University Press.

Calliste, Agnes. 1996. "Antiracism Organizing and Resistance in Nursing: African Canadian Women." *Canadian Review of Sociology/Revue Canadienne de Sociologie* 33 (3): 361–90. https://doi.org/10.1111/j.1755-618X.1996.tb02457.x.

Cardoza, Nicole. 2022. "What 'Defunding the Police' Actually Means." *Anti-racism Daily*. March 4, 2022. https://the-ard.com/2022/03/04/defunding-the-police-anti-racism-daily/.

Caron, Christian. 2022. "Partisan Strategy and the Adoption of Same-Day Registration in the American States." *State Politics and Policy Quarterly* 22 (2): 140–160.

Carr, Leslie G. 1997. *"Colorblind" Racism*. Sage.

Carter, Ray. 2021. "Tulsa Library Paid 'White Fragility' Author $15,000." OCPA. May 24, 2021. https://www.ocpathink.org/post/tulsa-library-paid-white-fragility-author-15-000.

Case, Alissa, and Bic Ngo. 2017. "'Do We Have to Call It That?' The Response of Neoliberal Multiculturalism to College Antiracism Efforts." *Multicultural Perspectives* 19 (4): 215–222.

Casey, Zachary A. 2016. *A Pedagogy of Anticapitalist Antiracism: Whiteness, Neoliberalism, and Resistance in Education*. State University of New York Press.

Castle, Jeremiah J., and Kyla K. Stepp. 2021. "Partisanship, Religion, and Issue Polarization in the United States: A Reassessment." *Political Behavior*: 43:1311–1335.

Chan, Jason. 2017. "Racial Identity in Online Spaces: Social Media's Impact on Students of Color." *Journal of Student Affairs Research and Practice* 54 (2): 163–174. https://doi.org/10.1080/19496591.2017.1284672.

Chandler, Jesse, Cheskie Rosenzweig, Aaron J. Moss, Jonathan Robinson, and Leib Litman. 2019. "Online Panels in Social Science Research: Expanding Sampling Methods beyond Mechanical Turk." *Behavior Research Methods* 51 (5): 2022–2038.

Chapman University Earl Babbie Research Center. 2022. *The Chapman University Survey of American Fears, Wave 8*. Chapman University Earl Babbie Research Center.

Chester, Andrea, and Di Bretherton. 2009. "Impression Management and Identity Online." In *Oxford Handbook of Internet Psychology*, edited by Adam Joinson, Katelyn

Y. A. McKenna, Tom Postmes, and Ulf-Dietrich Reips, 223–236. Oxford University Press.

Cigler, Allan J., Burdett A. Loomis, and Anthony J. Nownes. 2015. *Interest Group Politics*. CQ Press.

Clarke, Averil Y., and Leslie McCall. 2013. "Intersectionality and Social Explanation in Social Science Research." *Du Bois Review: Social Science Research on Race* 10 (2): 349–363.

Clifford, Scott, Ryan M. Jewell, and Philip D. Waggoner. 2015. "Are Samples Drawn from Mechanical Turk Valid for Research on Political Ideology?" *Research and Politics* 2 (4): 2053168015622072.

Closson, Rosemary B. 2010. "An Exploration of Critical Race Theory." In *The Handbook of Race and Adult Education*, edited by Vanessa Sheared, Juanita Johnson-Bailey, Scipio A. J. Colin III, Elizabeth Peterson, and Stephen D. Brookfield, 173–185. Jossey-Bass

Clotfelter, Charles T. 2004. "Private Schools, Segregation, and the Southern States." *Peabody Journal of Education* 79 (2): 74–97.

Cole, Luke W., and Sheila R. Foster. 2001. *From the Ground Up: Environmental Racism and the Rise of the Environmental Justice Movement*. New York University Press.

Combahee River Collective. 2014. "A Black Feminist Statement." *Women's Studies Quarterly* 42 (3/4): 271–280.

Comer, Krista. 2021. "Staying with the White Trouble of Recent Feminist Westerns." *Western American Literature* 56 (2): 101–123.

Cowlishaw, Gillian K. 2000. "Censoring Race in 'Post-colonial' Anthropology." *Critique of Anthropology* 20 (2): 101–123.

Cox, Daniel. 2022. "The Democratic Party's Transformation: More Diverse, Educated, and Liberal but Less Religious." Survey Center on American Life, July 22. https://www.americansurveycenter.org/research/the-democratic-partys-transformation-more-diverse-educated-and-liberal-but-less-religious/files/2622/the-democratic-partys-transformation-more-diverse-educated-and-liberal-but-less-religious.html.

Coyle, Michael J. 2010. "Notes on the Study of Language: Towards Critical Race Criminology." *Western Criminology Review* 11 (1): 11–19.

Crandall, Christian S., Amy Eshleman, and Laurie O'Brien. 2002. "Social Norms and the Expression and Suppression of Prejudice: The Struggle for Internalization." *Journal of Personality and Social Psychology* 82 (3): 359–378.

Crenshaw, Kimberlé Williams. 2010. "Twenty Years of Critical Race Theory: Looking Back to Move Forward." *Connecticut Law Review* 43:1253–1354.

———. 2019. "Unmasking Colorblindness in the Law: Lessons from the Formation of Critical Race Theory." In *Seeing Race Again*, edited by Kimberle Williams Crenshaw, 52–84. University of California Press.

Crenshaw, Kimberlé Williams, Neil Gotanda, Gary Peller, and Kendall Thomas. 1995. *Critical Race Theory: The Key Writings That Formed the Movement*. New Press.

Daniels, Jessie. 2009. *Cyber Racism: White Supremacy Online and the New Attack on Civil Rights*. Rowman and Littlefield Publishers.

D'Antonio, William V., Steven A. Tuch, and Josiah R. Baker. 2013. *Religion, Politics, and Polarization: How Religiopolitical Conflict Is Changing Congress and American Democracy*. Rowman and Littlefield Publishers.

Deggans, Eric. 2020. "'Not Racist' Is Not Enough: Putting in the Work to Be Anti-racist." NPR. August 24, 2020. https://www.npr.org/2020/08/24/905515398/not-racist-is-not-enough-putting-in-the-work-to-be-anti-racist.

Dei, George Jerry Sefa, Joe L. Kincheloe, Gurpreet Singh Johal, and Shirley R. Steinberg. 2005. *Critical Issues in Anti-racist Research Methodologies*. Peter Lang.

Delgado, Richard, and Jean Stefancic. 2000. *Critical Race Theory: The Cutting Edge*. Temple University Press.

———. 2023. *Critical Race Theory: An Introduction*. New York University Press.

De Lissovoy, Noah, and Anthony L. Brown. 2013. "Antiracist Solidarity in Critical Education: Contemporary Problems and Possibilities." *Urban Review* 45:539–560.

De Mar, Charlie. 2023. "Chicago LGBTQ Bars Drop Anheuser-Busch Products after Company Distances Itself from Dylan Mulvaney." CBS News. May 5, 2023. https://www.cbsnews.com/chicago/news/chicago-lgbtq-bars-anheuser-busch-dylan-mulvaney/.

Demaske, Chris. 2009. "Critical Race Theory." Free Speech Center. August 7, 2009. https://www.mtsu.edu/first-amendment/article/1254/critical-race-theory.

DeNavas-Walt, Carmen. 2010. *Income, Poverty, and Health Insurance Coverage in the United States (2005)*. Diane Publishing.

Denney, Matthew G. T., and Ramon Garibaldo Valdez. 2021. "Compounding Racialized Vulnerability: COVID-19 in Prisons, Jails, and Migrant Detention Centers." *Journal of Health Politics, Policy and Law* 46 (5): 861–887.

DeSilver, Drew. 2022. "The Polarization in Today's Congress Has Roots That Go Back Decades." Pew Research Center. March 10, 2022. https://www.pewresearch.org/short-reads/2022/03/10/the-polarization-in-todays-congress-has-roots-that-go-back-decades/.

Dhamoon, Rita. 2015. "A Feminist Approach to Decolonizing Anti-racism: Rethinking Transnationalism, Intersectionality, and Settler Colonialism." *Feral Feminisms* 4 (1): 20–37.

DiAngelo, Robin. 2018. *White Fragility: Why It's So Hard for White People to Talk about Racism*. Beacon Press.

———. 2021. *Nice Racism: How Progressive White People Perpetuate Racial Harm*. Beacon Press.

Dias, Felipe A. 2021. "The Racial Gap in Employment and Layoffs during COVID-19 in the United States: A Visualization." *Socius* 7:23780231209883397.

Dick, Hannah. 2017. "Not without Precedent: Populist White Evangelical Support for Trump." *Berkeley Journal of Sociology* 61:26–31.

Diem, Sarah, Bradley W. Carpenter, and Tiffanie Lewis-Durham. 2019. "Preparing Antiracist School Leaders in a School Choice Context." *Urban Education* 54 (5): 706–731. https://doi.org/10.1177/0042085918783812.

Dixson, Adrienne D., and Celia Rousseau Anderson. 2018. "Where Are We? Critical Race Theory in Education 20 Years Later." *Peabody Journal of Education* 93 (1): 121–131.

Doherty, Carroll, and Vianney Gomez. 2022. "By a Wide Margin, Americans View Inflation as the Top Problem Facing the Country Today." Pew Research Center. May 12, 2022. https://www.pewresearch.org/short-reads/2022/05/12/by-a-wide-margin-americans-view-inflation-as-the-top-problem-facing-the-country-today/.

Donnor, Jamel K. 2005. "Towards an Interest-Convergence in the Education of African-American Football Student Athletes in Major College Sports." *Race Ethnicity and Education* 8 (1): 45–67.

Dress, Brad. 2022. "Youngkin Signs Executive Orders Banning Critical Race Theory, Lifting Mask Mandate in Virginia Public Schools." The Hill. January 15, 2022. https://thehill.com/homenews/state-watch/589923-youngkin-signs-executive-orders-banning-critical-race-theory-lifting/.

Dua, Enakshi. 2014. "Not Quite a Case of the Disappearing Marx: Tracing the Place of Material Relations in Postcolonial Theory." In *Theorizing Anti-racism: Linkages in*

Marxism and Critical Race Theories, edited by Abigail B. Bakan and Enakshi Dua, 63–91. University of Toronto Press.

Dunivin, Zackary Okun, Harry Yaojun Yan, Jelani Ince, and Fabio Rojas. 2022. "Black Lives Matter Protests Shift Public Discourse." *Proceedings of the National Academy of Sciences* 119 (10): e2117320119.

Dunn, Kevin, James Forrest, Rogelia Pe-Pua, Maria Hynes, and Karin Maeder-Han. 2009. "Cities of Race Hatred?: The Spheres of Racism and Anti-racism in Contemporary Australian Cities." *Cosmopolitan Civil Societies: An Interdisciplinary Journal* 1 (1): 1–14.

Duveen, Gerard, and Barbara Lloyd. 1986. "The Significance of Social Identities." *British Journal of Social Psychology* 25 (3): 219–230.

Dyson, Michael Eric, and David L. Jagerman, 2000. *I May Not Get There with You: The True Martin Luther King, Jr.* Simon and Schuster: New York.

Eddo-Lodge, Reni. 2020. *Why I'm No Longer Talking to White People about Race*. Bloomsbury Publishing.

Edirmanasinghe, Natalie, Emily Goodman-Scott, Stephanie Smith-Durkin, and Shuntay Z. Tarver. 2022. "Supporting All Students: Multitiered Systems of Support from an Antiracist and Critical Race Theory Lens." *Professional School Counseling* 26 (1): 2156759X221109154.

Edsall, Thomas B. 2021. "Republicans Are Once Again Heating Up the Culture Wars." *New York Times*, November 10, 2021. https://www.nytimes.com/2021/11/10/opinion/republicans-democrats-crt.html.

Elias, Sean. 2015. "Racism, Overt." In *The Wiley Blackwell Encyclopedia of Race, Ethnicity, and Nationalism*, edited by John Stone, Dennis M. Rutledge, Anthony D. Smith, Polly S. Rizova, Xiaoshuo Hou, and Michael J. Rya, 1–3. John Wiley and Sons.

Ellefsen, Rune, Azin Banafsheh, and Sveinung Sandberg. 2022. "Resisting Racism in Everyday Life: From Ignoring to Confrontation and Protest." *Ethnic and Racial Studies* 45 (16): 435–457.

Emeka, Amon. 2018. "Where Race Matters Most: Measuring the Strength of Association between Race and Unemployment across the 50 United States." *Social Indicators Research* 136 (2): 557–573.

Encheva, Petrova Mariya. 2017. "Safety in the Dialectics of Mental State, Socio-psychological Process and Social Phenomenon." *Globalization, the State and the Individual* 14 (2): 187–192

Euronews. 2023. "The US Announces New €2.3 Billion Military Aid Package for Ukraine." April 5, 2023. https://www.euronews.com/2023/04/05/the-us-announces-new-23-billion-military-aid-package-for-ukraine.

Ezell, Jerel M., Samira Salari, Clinton Rooker, and Elizabeth C. Chase. 2021. "Intersectional Trauma: COVID-19, the Psychosocial Contract, and America's Racialized Public Health Lineage." *Traumatology* 27 (1): 78–85.

Fabrigar, Leandre R., and Duane T. Wegener. 2011. *Exploratory Factor Analysis*. Oxford University Press.

Fagelson, David. 2002. "Perfectionist Liberalism, Tolerance and American Law." *Res Publica* 8 (1): 41–70. https://doi.org/10.1023/A:1014280625713.

Feagin, Joe R., and Vera Hernan. 2000. *White Racism: The Basics*. Routledge.

Feigenbaum, Harvey B., and Jeffrey R. Henig. 1997. "Privatization and Political Theory." *Journal of International Affairs* 50 (2): 338–355.

Feuerstein, Abe. 2022. "School Curriculum in the News: Black Lives Matter and the Continuing Struggle for Culturally Responsive Education." *Current Issues in Education* 23 (1): 1–33.

Fidel, Kondwani. 2020. *The Antiracist*. Hot Books.
Fields, Barbara J. 2001. "Whiteness, Racism, and Identity." *International Labor and Working-Class History* 60:48–56.
Finlay, Christopher J. 2006. "Violence and Revolutionary Subjectivity: Marx to Žižek." *European Journal of Political Theory* 5 (4): 373–397.
Flanagan, Maureen A. 2016. "Progressives and Progressivism in an Era of Reform." *Oxford Research Encyclopedia of American History*. August 5, 2016. https://oxfordre.com/americanhistory/display/10.1093/acrefore/9780199329175.001.0001/acrefore-9780199329175-e-84.
Forbes-Erickson, D. Amy-Rose. 2022. "Performance 'Art'–Dismantling Structural Racism in Colonial Monuments." *NaKaN—A Journal of Cultural Studies* 1 (1): 1–14. https://nakanjournal.com/performance-art-dismantling-structural-racism-in-colonial-monuments/.
Ford, Chandra L., and Collins O. Airhihenbuwa. 2010. "Critical Race Theory, Race Equity, and Public Health: Toward Antiracism Praxis." *American Journal of Public Health* 100 (S1): S30–S35.
Ford, Richard T. 2005. "Political Identity as Identity Politics." *Journal of Unbound* 53 (1): 53–57.
Forman, Tyrone A., and Amanda E. Lewis. 2015. "Beyond Prejudice? Young Whites' Racial Attitudes in Post–Civil Rights America, 1976 to 2000." *American Behavioral Scientist* 59 (11): 1394–1428.
Fourlas, George N. 2021. "The 'Unknown' Middle Easterner: Post-racial Anxieties and Anti-MENA Racism throughout Colonized Space-Time." *Critical Philosophy of Race* 9 (1): 48–70.
Garam, Bernadette Kwee, and Jeneve Brooks. 2010. "Students' Perceptions of Race and Ethnic Relations Post Obama's Election: A Preliminary Analysis." *Race, Gender and Class* 17 (3/4): 64–80.
Gardiner, Simon, and Louisa Riches. 2016. "Racism and Homophobia in English Football: The Equality Act, Positive Action and the Limits of Law." *International Journal of Discrimination and the Law* 16 (2–3): 102–121.
Garner, Steve. 2007. *Whiteness: An Introduction*. Routledge.
Gillborn, David. 2006. "Critical Race Theory and Education: Racism and Anti-racism in Educational Theory and Praxis." *Discourse: Studies in the Cultural Politics of Education* 27 (1): 11–32.
Gilmore, Glenda Elizabeth. 2019. *Gender and Jim Crow: Women and the Politics of White Supremacy in North Carolina, 1896–1920*. University of North Carolina Press.
Goffman, Erving. 1959. *The Presentation of Self in Everyday Life*. Doubleday.
Goldberg, David Theo. 2021. "The War on Critical Race Theory." *Boston Review*, May 7, 2021. http://bostonreview.net/race-politics/david-theo-goldberg-war-critical-race-theory.
Gonzales Rose, Jasmine B. 2016. "Toward a Critical Race Theory of Evidence." *Minnesota Law Review* 101:2243–2312.
Gooden, Amoaba, and Charmaine Crawford. 2016. "Teaching Black Canada(s) across Borders: Insights from the Caribbean and United States." *Southern Journal of Canadian Studies* 7:3–18.
Gooding-Williams, Robert. 2010. *In the Shadow of Du Bois: Afro-modern Political Thought in America*. Harvard University Press.
Grace, Breanne Leigh, and Katie Heins. 2021. "Redefining Refugee: White Christian Nationalism in State Politics and Beyond." *Ethnic and Racial Studies* 44 (4): 555–575. https://doi.org/10.1080/01419870.2020.1767799.

Graham, B. 2007. "Toward a Critical Race Theory of Political Science." In *African American Perspectives on Political Science*, edited by Wilbur C. Rich, 212–231. Temple University Press.

Graham, Louis, Shelly Brown-Jeffy, Robert Aronson, and Charles Stephens. 2011. "Critical Race Theory as Theoretical Framework and Analysis Tool for Population Health Research." *Critical Public Health* 21 (1): 81–93.

Greene, Kyra R. 2011. "Why We Need More Marxism in the Sociology of Race." *Souls* 13 (2): 149–174.

Grosfoguel, Ramón. 2011. "Decolonizing Post-colonial Studies and Paradigms of Political-Economy: Transmodernity, Decolonial Thinking, and Global Coloniality." *Transmodernity: Journal of Peripheral Cultural Production of the Luso-Hispanic World* 1 (1). https://doi.org/10.5070/T411000004.

Hadden, Bernadette R., Willie Tolliver, Fabienne Snowden, and Robyn Brown-Manning. 2016. "An Authentic Discourse: Recentering Race and Racism as Factors That Contribute to Police Violence against Unarmed Black or African American Men." *Journal of Human Behavior in the Social Environment* 26 (3–4): 336–349.

Hage, Ghassan. 2012. *White Nation: Fantasies of White Supremacy in a Multicultural Society*. Routledge.

Hagerman, Margaret Ann. 2017. "White Racial Socialization: Progressive Fathers on Raising 'Antiracist' Children." *Journal of Marriage and Family* 79 (1): 60–74. https://doi.org/10.1080/14755610.2011.557015.

Hainmueller, Jens, and Michael J. Hiscox. 2010. "Attitudes toward Highly Skilled and Low-Skilled Immigration: Evidence from a Survey Experiment." *American Political Science Review* 104 (1): 61–84.

Hamadi, Lutfi. 2014. "Edward Said: The Postcolonial Theory and the Literature of Decolonization." *European Scientific Journal* 2:39–46

Hamilton, Denise. 2022. "The Diversity Backlash Is Underway. Here's How to Resist It." Centre for the New Economy and Society. October 11, 2022. https://www.weforum.org/agenda/2022/10/the-diversity-backlash-here-s-how-to-resist-it/.

Hamilton, James T. 1995. "Testing for Environmental Racism: Prejudice, Profits, Political Power?" *Journal of Policy Analysis and Management* 14 (1): 107–132.

Han, JooHee. 2018. "Who Goes to College, Military, Prison, or Long-Term Unemployment? Racialized School-to-Labor Market Transitions among American Men." *Population Research and Policy Review* 37 (4): 615–640.

Hatch, Anthony Ryan. 2007. "Critical Race Theory." In *The Blackwell Encyclopedia of Sociology*, edited by George Ritzer. Blackwell Publishing.

Hatemi, Peter K., Rose McDermott, Lindon J. Eaves, Kenneth S. Kendler, and Michael C. Neale. 2013. "Fear as a Disposition and an Emotional State: A Genetic and Environmental Approach to Out-Group Political Preferences." *American Journal of Political Science* 57 (2): 279–293.

Hawkesworth, Mary. 2010. "From Constitutive Outside to the Politics of Extinction: Critical Race Theory, Feminist Theory, and Political Theory." *Political Research Quarterly* 63 (3): 686–696.

Hawkman, Andrea M., and Sarah Diem. 2022. "The Big Lie(s): Situating the January 6th Coup Attempt within White Supremacist Lies." *Cultural Studies ↔ Critical Methodologies* 22 (5): 490–504. https://doi.org/10.1177/15327086221094883.

Heilman, Madeline E., and Brian Welle. 2006. "Disadvantaged by Diversity? The Effects of Diversity Goals on Competence Perceptions 1." *Journal of Applied Social Psychology* 36 (5): 1291–1319.

Henderson, Jason. 2009. "The Spaces of Parking: Mapping the Politics of Mobility in San Francisco." *Antipode* 41 (1): 70–91.

Henderson, Sheree, and Rebecca Wells. 2021. "Environmental Racism and the Contamination of Black Lives: A Literature Review." *Journal of African American Studies* 25: 134–151.

Hill, Terrence, Andrew Mannheimer, and J. Micah Roos. 2021. "Measuring White Fragility." *Social Science Quarterly* 102 (4): 1812–1829.

Ho, Arnold K., Jim Sidanius, Nour Kteily, Jennifer Sheehy-Skeffington, Felicia Pratto, Kristin E. Henkel, Rob Foels, and Andrew L. Stewart. 2015. "The Nature of Social Dominance Orientation: Theorizing and Measuring Preferences for Intergroup Inequality using the new SDO₇ Scale." *Journal of Personality and Social Psychology* 109 (6): 1003–1028.

Hoffower, Hillary. 2020. "What It Really Means to Be an Anti-racist, and Why It's Not the Same as Being an Ally." Business Insider. June 8, 2020. https://www.businessinsider.com/what-is-anti-racism-how-to-be-anti-racist-2020-6.

Hojnacki, Marie. 1997. "Interest Groups' Decisions to Join Alliances or Work Alone." *American Journal of Political Science* 41 (1): 61–87.

Holton, Robert J. 1981. "Marxist Theories of Social Change and the Transition from Feudalism to Capitalism." *Theory and Society* 10 (6): 833–867.

Hooijer, Gerda, and Desmond King. 2022. "The Racialized Pandemic: Wave One of COVID-19 and the Reproduction of Global North Inequalities." *Perspectives on Politics* 20 (2): 507–527.

Housee, Shirin. 2012. "What's the Point? Anti-racism and Students' Voices against Islamophobia." *Race Ethnicity and Education* 15 (1): 101–120.

Howard, Philip S. S. 2010. "Turning out the Center: Racial Politics and African Agency in the Obama Era." *Journal of Black Studies* 40 (3): 380–394.

Hübinette, Tobias. 2013. "Swedish Antiracism and White Melancholia: Racial Words in a Post-racial Society." *Ethnicity and Race in a Changing World* 4 (1): 24–33.

Hughes, Coleman. 2019. "Martin Luther King, Colorblind Radical." *Wall Street Journal*, January 17, 2019. https://www.wsj.com/articles/martin-luther-king-colorblind-radical-11547769741.

Hughey, Matthew W. 2012a. "Stigma Allure and White Antiracist Identity Management." *Social Psychology Quarterly* 75 (3): 219–241.

———. 2012b. *White Bound: Nationalists, Antiracists, and the Shared Meanings of Race*. Stanford University Press.

Hunter, James Davison. 1992. *Culture Wars: The Struggle to Control the Family, Art, Education, Law, and Politics in America*. Basic Books.

———. 2018. "The American Culture War." In *The Limits of Social Cohesion*, edited by Peter L. Berger, 1–37. Routledge.

Huq, Rupa. 2008. "Youth Culture and Antiracism in New Britain: From the Margins to the Mainstream?" *International Journal of Sociology* 38 (2): 43–53.

Hylton, Kevin. 2010. "How a Turn to Critical Race Theory Can Contribute to Our Understanding of 'Race', Racism and Anti-racism in Sport." *International Review for the Sociology of Sport* 45 (3): 335–354.

Iati, Marisa. 2021. "What Is Critical Race Theory, and Why Do Republicans Want to Ban It in Schools." *Washington Post*, May 29, 2021. https://www.washingtonpost.com/education/2021/05/29/critical-race-theory-bans-schools/.

Ignatiev, Noel, and John Garvey. 2014. *Race Traitor*. Routledge.

Islam, Namira. 2018. "Soft Islamophobia." *Religions* 9 (9): article 280.

Iyengar, Shanto, Yphtach Lelkes, Matthew Levendusky, Neil Malhotra, and Sean J. West-wood. 2019. "The Origins and Consequences of Affective Polarization in the United States." *Annual Review of Political Science* 22:129–146.
Jackson, Sarah J. 2018. "Progressive Social Movements and the Internet." In *Oxford Research Encyclopedia of Communication*, edited by Dana Cloud. Oxford University Press. https://doi.org/10.1093/acrefore/9780190228613.013.644.
Jardina, Ashley. 2019. *White Identity Politics*. Cambridge University Press.
Jensen, Robert. 2005. *The Heart of Whiteness: Confronting Race, Racism and White Privilege*. City Lights Books.
Jewell, Tiffany. 2020. *This Book Is Anti-racist*. Frances Lincoln.
Jiang, Julie, Emily Chen, Shen Yan, Kristina Lerman, and Emilio Ferrara. 2020. "Political Polarization Drives Online Conversations about COVID-19 in the United States." *Human Behavior and Emerging Technologies* 2 (3): 200–211.
Johnson, Vida B. 2021. "White Supremacy's Police Siege on the United States Capitol." *Brooklyn Law Review* 87:557–608.
Jones, Robert P. 2020. "White Christian America Needs a Moral Awakening." *The Atlantic*, July 28, 2020.
———. 2021. *White Too Long: The Legacy of White Supremacy in American Christianity*. Simon and Schuster.
Jussim, Lee. 2017. "Précis of Social Perception and Social Reality: Why Accuracy Dominates Bias and Self-Fulfilling Prophecy." *Behavioral and Brain Sciences* 40. https://doi.org/10.1017/S0140525X1500062X.
Kam, Cindy D., and Camille D. Burge. 2018. "Uncovering Reactions to the Racial Resentment Scale across the Racial Divide." *Journal of Politics* 80 (1): 314–320.
Kamenetz, Anya. 2021. "A Look at the Groups Supporting School Board Protesters Nationwide." NPR. October 26, 2021. https://www.npr.org/2021/10/26/1049078199/a-look-at-the-groups-supporting-school-board-protesters-nationwide.
Kantack, Benjamin R., and Collin E. Paschall. 2022. "Perceptions of Policy Problems and Solutions: Climate Change and Structural Racism." *Public Understanding of Science* 32 (2): 247–256.
Katz, Phyllis A., and Dalmas A. Taylor. 2013. *Eliminating Racism: Profiles in Controversy*. Springer Science and Business Media.
Kelman, Mark. 1999. *Strategy or Principle?: The Choice between Regulation and Taxation*. University of Michigan Press.
Kendi, Ibram X. 2016. *Stamped from the Beginning: The Definitive History of Racist Ideas in America*. Hachette UK.
———. 2019. *How to Be an Antiracist*. One World.
Kennedy, Brian, and Courtney Johnson. 2020. "More Americans See Climate Change as a Priority, but Democrats Are Much More Concerned than Republicans." Pew Research Center. February 28, 2020. https://www.pewresearch.org/short-reads/2020/02/28/more-americans-see-climate-change-as-a-priority-but-democrats-are-much-more-concerned-than-republicans/.
Kerr, John, Costas Panagopoulos, and Sander van der Linden. 2021. "Political Polarization on COVID-19 Pandemic Response in the United States." *Personality and Individual Differences* 179:110892.
Kimura, Keisuke. 2021. "'Yellow Perils,' Revived: Exploring Racialized Asian/American Affect and Materiality through Hate Discourse over the COVID-19 Pandemic." *Journal of Hate Studies* 17 (1): 133–145.

Kinder, Donald R., and Lynn M. Sanders. 1996. *Divided by Color: Racial Politics and Democratic Ideals.* University of Chicago Press.

Kivel, Paul. 2017. *Uprooting Racism: How White People Can Work for Racial Justice.* New Society Publishers.

Kluegel, James R. 1990. "Trends in Whites' Explanations of the Black-White Gap in Socioeconomic Status, 1977–1989." *American Sociological Review* 55 (4): 512–525.

Knowles, Ryan T., and Andrea M. Hawkman. 2020. "Anti-racist Quantitative Research: Developing, Validating, and Implementing Racialized Teaching Efficacy and Racial Fragility Scales." *Urban Review* 52 (2): 238–262.

Koran, Mario. 2022. "In Kiel, Wisconsin, Attack on 'Critical Race Theory' Ignores Bullying of Black Student." Wisconsin Watch. October 14, 2022. https://wisconsinwatch.org/2022/10/in-kiel-wisconsin-attack-on-critical-race-theory-ignores-bullying-of-black-student/.

Kousser, J. Morgan. 2000. *Colorblind Injustice: Minority Voting Rights and the Undoing of the Second Reconstruction.* University of North Carolina Press.

Krishnan, Armin. 2020. "Blockchain Empowers Social Resistance and Terrorism through Decentralized Autonomous Organizations." *Journal of Strategic Security* 13 (1): 41–58.

Kubota, Ryuko. 2015. "Race and Language Learning in Multicultural Canada: Towards Critical Antiracism." *Journal of Multilingual and Multicultural Development* 36 (1): 3–12.

———. 2021. "Critical Antiracist Pedagogy in ELT." *ELT Journal.* 75 (3): 237–246.

Lai, Calvin K., Allison L. Skinner, Erin Cooley, Sohad Murrar, Markus Brauer, Thierry Devos, Jimmy Calanchini, Y. Jenny Xiao, Christina Pedram, and Christopher K. Marshburn. 2016. "Reducing Implicit Racial Preferences: II. Intervention Effectiveness across Time." *Journal of Experimental Psychology: General* 145 (8): 1001–1016.

Lally, Kevin. 2022. *Whiteness and Antiracism: Beyond White Privilege Pedagogy.* Teachers College Press.

Langrehr, Kimberly J., Laurel B. Watson, Alexa Keramidas, and Sarah Middleton. 2021. "The Development and Initial Validation of the White Fragility Scale." *Journal of Counseling Psychology* 68 (4): 404–417.

Larson, Samantha June. 2022. "An Antiracist Index for State Level Assessment." *State and Local Government Review* 0160323X221089639.

Laughter, Judson, and Heather Hurst. 2022. "Critical AntiRacist Discourse Analysis (CARDA)." *Urban Education* 59 (6): 1651–1675.

Lawrence, Bonita, and Enakshi Dua. 2005. "Decolonizing Antiracism." *Social Justice* 32 (4): 120–143.

Lee, Sun Young, Marko Pitesa, Stefan Thau, and Madan M. Pillutla. 2015. "Discrimination in Selection Decisions: Integrating Stereotype Fit and Interdependence Theories." *Academy of Management Journal* 58 (3): 789–812.

Lee, Taeku, and Mark Schlesinger. 2001. "Signaling in Context: Elite Influence and the Dynamics of Public Support for Clinton's Health Security Act." Available at SSRN: https://doi.org/10.2139/ssrn.284023.

Legault, Lisa, Jennifer N. Gutsell, and Michael Inzlicht. 2011. "Ironic Effects of Antiprejudice Messages: How Motivational Interventions Can Reduce (but Also Increase) Prejudice." *Psychological Science* 22 (12): 1472–1477.

Lennard, Natasha. 2021. "Gov. Ron DeSantis Wants to Defund Florida Universities That Teach Anti-racism." The Intercept. June 27, 2021. https://theintercept.com/2021/06/27/desantis-florida-universities-white-supremacy-antiracism/.

Lentin, Alana. 2011. "What Happens to Anti-racism When We Are Post Race?" *Feminist Legal Studies* 19:159–168.

Levitz, Eric. 2022. "Ibram X. Kendi Does Not Run the Democratic Party." *New York*, Intelligencer, February 17, 2022. https://nymag.com/intelligencer/2022/02/ibram-x-kendi-does-not-run-the-democratic-party.html.
Lim, Chaeyoon, Carol Ann MacGregor, and Robert D. Putnam. 2010. "Secular and Liminal: Discovering Heterogeneity among Religious Nones." *Journal for the Scientific Study of Religion* 49 (4): 586–618.
Lipka, Michael. 2022. "A Closer Look at Republicans Who Favor Legal Abortion and Democrats Who Oppose It." Pew Research Center. June 17, 2022. https://www.pewresearch.org/short-reads/2022/06/17/a-closer-look-at-republicans-who-favor-legal-abortion-and-democrats-who-oppose-it/.
Lippold, Julia V., Julia I. Laske, Svea A. Hogeterp, Éilish Duke, Thomas Grünhage, and Martin Reuter. 2020. "The Role of Personality, Political Attitudes and Socio-demographic Characteristics in Explaining Individual Differences in Fear of Coronavirus: A Comparison over Time and across Countries." *Frontiers in Psychology* 11:552305.
Lockhart, Jonathan. 2021. "Critical Race Theory—The Right's Latest Target in the Culture Wars." *Green Left Weekly*, no. 1313, 17.
Lorimer, Rowland. 2002. "Mass Communication: Some Redefinitional Notes." *Canadian Journal of Communication* 27 (1): 63–72.
Loughnan, Steve, Nick Haslam, Robbie M. Sutton, and Bettina Spencer. 2014. "Dehumanization and Social Class: Animality in the Stereotypes of 'White Trash,' 'Chavs,' and 'Bogans.'" *Social Psychology* 45 (1): 54–61.
Loury, Glenn. 2022. "Cruelty in the Name of 'Antiracism.'" November 29, 2022. https://glennloury.substack.com/p/cruelty-in-the-name-of-antiracism.
Loutzenheiser, Lisa W. 2001. "If I Teach about These Issues They Will Burn Down My House: The Possibilities and Tensions of Queered, Antiracist Pedagogy." In *Troubling Intersections of Race and Sexuality: Queer Students of Color and Anti-oppressive Education*, edited by Kevin K. Kumashiro, 195–214. Rowman and Littlefield.
Love, Bettina L, and Brandelyn Tosolt. 2010. "Reality or Rhetoric? Barack Obama and Post-racial America." *Race, Gender and Class* 17 (3/4): 19–37.
Loyola, Mario. 2021. "The Race-Marxists Finally Went Too Far." Competitive Enterprise Institute. November 11, 2021. https://cei.org/opeds_articles/the-race-marxists-finally-went-too-far/.
Lugo, Sujei. 2016. "A Latino Anti-racist Approach to Children's Librarianship." *Teacher Librarian* 44 (1): 24–27.
Lui, Meizhu, Barbara J. Robles, Betsy Leondar-Wright, Rose M. Brewer, and Rebecca Adamson. 2006. *The Color of Wealth: The Story behind the US Racial Wealth Divide*. New Press.
Luo, Michael. 2020. "American Christianity's White-Supremacy Problem." *New Yorker*, September 2, 2020.
Macoun, Alissa. 2016. "Colonising White Innocence: Complicity and Critical Encounters." In *The Limits of Settler Colonial Reconciliation: Non-Indigenous People and the Responsibility to Engage*, edited by Sarah Maddison, Tom Clark, and Ravi de Costa, 85–102. Springer.
Magness, Phillip. 2021. "School Choice's Antiracist History." *Wall Street Journal*, October 18. https://www.wsj.com/articles/school-choice-antiracist-history-integration-funding-segregation-11634568700.
Major, Brenda, Pamela J. Sawyer, and Jonathan W. Kunstman. 2013. "Minority Perceptions of Whites' Motives for Responding without Prejudice: The Perceived Internal and External Motivation to Avoid Prejudice Scales." *Personality and Social Psychology Bulletin* 39 (3): 401–414.

Manhattan Institute. 2021. *Woke Schooling: A Toolkit for Concerned Parents.* Manhattan Institute.

Manning, Jimmie. 2020. "Examining Whiteness in Interpersonal Communication Textbooks." *Communication, Culture and Critique* 13 (2): 254–258.

Marable, Manning. 1990. "Socialist Vision and Political Struggle for the 1990s." *Rethinking Marxism* 3 (3–4): 27–36.

———. 2010. "Katrina's Unnatural Disaster: A Tragedy of Black Suffering and White Denial." *Souls* 8 (1): 1–8.

Marichal, Jose. 2013. "Political Facebook Groups: Micro-Activism and the Digital Front Stage." *First Monday* 18 (12). https://doi.org/10.5210/fm.v18i12.4653.

Marshburn, Christopher K., Abigail M. Folberg, Chelsea Crittle, and Keith B. Maddox. 2021. "Racial Bias Confrontation in the United States: What (If Anything) Has Changed in the COVID-19 Era, and Where Do We Go from Here?" *Group Processes and Intergroup Relations* 24 (2): 260–269.

Martin, Jordan. 2021. "Breonna Taylor: Transforming a Hashtag into Defunding the Police." *Journal of Criminal Law and Criminology* 111 (4): 995–1034.

Mayer, Jeremy D. 2015. "Reagan and Race: Prophet of Color Blindness, Baiter of the Backlash." In *Deconstructing Reagan: Conservative Mythology and America's Fortieth President*, edited by Kyle Longley, Jeremy Mayer, Michael Schaller, and John W. Sloan, 88–107. Routledge.

Mazzocco, Philip J. 2017. *The Psychology of Racial Colorblindness.* Springer.

McCauley, Clark R., Lee J. Jussim, and Yueh-Ting Lee. 1995. *Stereotype Accuracy: Toward Appreciating Group Differences.* American Psychological Association.

McConahay, John B. 1986. "Modern Racism, Ambivalence, and the Modern Racism Scale." In *Prejudice, Discrimination, and Racism*, edited by John F. Dovidio and Samuel L. Gaertner, 9–125. Academic Press.

McDermott, Monika L., and Cornell Belcher. 2014. "Barack Obama and Americans' Racial Attitudes: Rallying and Polarization." *Polity* 46 (3): 449–469.

McEwan, Cheryl. 2008. *Postcolonialism and Development.* Routledge.

McGhee, Heather. 2022. *The Sum of Us: What Racism Costs Everyone and How We Can Prosper Together.* One World.

McKanders, Karla M. 2020. "Immigration and Racial Justice: Enforcing the Borders of Blackness." *Georgia State University Law Review* 37:1139–1176.

McKee, Megan, and Anne Pedersen. 2018. "Efficacy as a Predictor of Bystander Anti-racism in Support of Indigenous Australians." *Australian Community Psychologist* 29 (2): 38–55.

McKenzie, Sam. 2019. "Hold Your Applause for Gillibrand's Words on Whiteness and White Privilege." August 3, 2019. https://sammckenziejr.medium.com/hold-your-applause-for-gillibrands-words-on-whiteness-and-white-privilege-401c13d5f54b.

McRae, Elizabeth Gillespie. 2018. *Mothers of Massive Resistance: White Women and the Politics of White Supremacy.* Oxford University Press.

Mendez, Dara D., Vijaya K. Hogan, and Jennifer F. Culhane. 2014. "Institutional Racism, Neighborhood Factors, Stress, and Preterm Birth." *Ethnicity and Health* 19 (5): 479–499.

Menendian, Stephen, Arthur Gailes, and Samir Gambhir. 2021. *The Roots of Structural Racism: Twenty-First Century Racial Residential Segregation in the United States.* Othering and Belonging Institute.

Merkley, Eric, and Dominik A. Stecula. 2021. "Party Cues in the News: Democratic Elites, Republican Backlash, and the Dynamics of Climate Skepticism." *British Journal of Political Science* 51 (4): 1439–1456.

Metzl, Jonathan M. 2019. *Dying of Whiteness: How the Politics of Racial Resentment Is Killing America's Heartland.* Basic Books.

Middlebrook, Jeb Aram. 2019. "Organizing a Rainbow Coalition of Revolutionary Solidarity." *Journal of African American Studies* 23 (4): 405–434.

Migdon, Brook. 2021. "Nearly Half of Republicans Polled Say Schools Shouldn't Teach History of Racism." Changing America. November 10, 2021. https://thehill.com/changing-america/enrichment/education/581029-nearly-half-of-republicans-polled-say-schools-shouldnt/.

Migliori, Chiara M. 2022. *Religious Rhetoric in US Right-Wing Politics: Donald Trump, Intergroup Threat and Nationalism.* Springer.

Miller, Erin T. 2020. "Christianity and Whiteness." In *Encyclopedia of Critical Whiteness Studies in Education,* edited by Zachary A. Casey, 98–105. Brill.

Miller, Kevin P., Marylynn B. Brewer, and Nathan L. Arbuckle. 2009. "Social Identity Complexity: Its Correlates and Antecedents." *Group Processes and Intergroup Relations* 12 (1): 79–94.

Miller, Ryan A. 2017. "'My Voice Is Definitely Strongest in Online Communities': Students Using Social Media for Queer and Disability Identity-Making." *Journal of College Student Development* 58 (4): 509–525. https://doi.org/10.1353/csd.2017.0040.

Milligan, Susan. 2022. "Three-Quarters of Republicans Sympathize with Jan. 6 Rioters: Poll." *U.S. News and World Report,* January 4, 2022. https://www.usnews.com/news/politics/articles/2022-01-04/three-quarters-of-republicans-sympathize-with-jan-6-rioters-poll.

Milner, H. Richard, IV. 2008. "Critical Race Theory and Interest Convergence as Analytic Tools in Teacher Education Policies and Practices." *Journal of Teacher Education* 59 (4): 332–346.

Milner, H. Richard, IV, F. Alvin Pear III, and Ebony O. McGee. 2013. "Critical Race Theory, Interest Convergence, and Teacher Education." In *Handbook of Critical Race Theory in Education,* edited by Lynn, Marvin and Adrieene D. Dixson, 359–374. Routledge.

Minkin, Rachel. 2023. "Diversity, Equity and Inclusion in the Workplace." Pew Research Center. May 17, 2023. https://www.pewresearch.org/social-trends/2023/05/17/diversity-equity-and-inclusion-in-the-workplace/.

Mishra, Vijay, and Bob Hodge. 2005. "What Was Postcolonialism?" *New Literary History* 36 (3): 375–402.

Mitchell, Travis. 2019. "Americans See Advantages and Challenges in Country's Growing Racial and Ethnic Diversity." Pew Research Center. May 8, 2019. https://www.pewresearch.org/social-trends/2019/05/08/americans-see-advantages-and-challenges-in-countrys-growing-racial-and-ethnic-diversity/.

Mohai, Paul, and Bunyan Bryant. 2019. "Environmental Racism: Reviewing the Evidence." In *Race and the Incidence of Environmental Hazards,* edited by Bunyan Bryant and Paul Mohai, 163–176. Routledge.

Montanaro, Domenico. 2022. "Republicans Have the Advantage with Voters in 2022 Elections, Poll Finds." NPR. April 29, 2022. https://www.npr.org/2022/04/29/1095366671/npr-pbs-newshour-marist-survey-republicans-biden-democrats-midterms.

Moody, Josh. 2021. "Nebraska Governor Criticizes University Diversity Initiative." Inside Higher Education. November 23, 2021. https://www.insidehighered.com/quicktakes/2021/11/23/nebraska-governor-criticizes-university-diversity-initiative.

Moon, Dreama, and Lisa A. Flores. 2000. "Antiracism and the Abolition of Whiteness: Rhetorical Strategies of Domination among 'Race Traitors.'" *Communication Studies* 51 (2): 97–115.

Morava, Maria, and Scottie Andrew. 2021. "The Black Lives Matter Foundation Raised $90 Million in 2020, and Gave Almost a Quarter of It to Local Chapters and Organizations." CNN. February 25, 2021. https://www.cnn.com/2021/02/25/us/black-lives-matter-2020-donation-report-trnd/index.html.

Moschel, Mathias. 2007. "Color Blindness or Total Blindness? The Absence of Critical Race Theory in Europe." *Rutgers Race and the Law Review* 9 (1): 57–127.

Mudde, Cas. 2020. "Why Antiracism Protests Are Achieving More Progress under Trump than Obama." *The Guardian*, June 18, 2020. https://www.theguardian.com/commentisfree/2020/jun/18/why-antiracist-protests-are-achieving-more-progress-under-trump-than-obama.

Mude, William, Victor M. Oguoma, Tafadzwa Nyanhanda, Lillian Mwanri, and Carolyne Njue. 2021. "Racial Disparities in COVID-19 Pandemic Cases, Hospitalisations, and Deaths: A Systematic Review and Meta-analysis." *Journal of Global Health* 11:05015. https://doi.org/10.7189/jogh.11.05015.

Mukherjee, Roopali. 2016. "Antiracism Limited: A Pre-history of Post-race." *Cultural Studies* 30 (1): 47–77.

Müller, Carolin. 2021. "Anti-racism in Europe: An Intersectional Approach to the Discourse on Empowerment through the EU Anti-Racism Action Plan 2020–2025." *Social Sciences* 10 (4): 137.

Muñoz, Vincent Phillip. 2020. "Divided We Fall: America's Secession Threat and How to Restore Our Nation." *First Things*, December, 1–5.

Myers, Peter C. 2019. "The Case for Color-Blindness." Heritage Foundation. https://www.heritage.org/civil-society/report/the-case-color-blindness.

Mynott, Ed. 2002. "Nationalism, Racism and Immigration Control: From Anti-racism to Anti-capitalism." In *From Immigration Controls to Welfare Controls*, edited by Steve Cohen, Beth Humphries, and Ed Mynott, 11–29. Routledge.

Newkirk, Pamela. 2019. *Diversity, Inc.: The Failed Promise of a Billion-Dollar Business*. Hachette UK.

Ng, Roxana. 1993. "'A Woman out of Control': Deconstructing Sexism and Racism in the University." *Canadian Journal of Education/Revue Canadienne de l'éducation* 18 (3): 189–205.

Nguyen-Truong, Connie Kim Yen, Sara F. Waters, Meenakshi Richardson, Natasha Barrow, Joseph Seia, Deborah U. Eti, and Keara Funchess Rodela. 2023. "An Antiracism Community-Based Participatory Research with Organizations Serving Immigrant and Marginalized Communities, Including Asian Americans and Native Hawaiians/Pacific Islanders in the United States Pacific Northwest: Qualitative Description Study with Key Informants." *Asian/Pacific Island Nursing Journal* 7:e43150.

Nicholls, Heidi. 2022. "Antiracism amidst Empire? Understanding the United States' Relationship to Whiteness." *Sociology Compass* 16 (9): e13017.

Nichols, John. 2020. *The Fight for the Soul of the Democratic Party: The Enduring Legacy of Henry Wallace's Anti-fascist, Anti-racist Politics*. Verso Books.

Nishiyama, Takayuki. 2022. "Political Division and Identity Politics in the United States." *Seikei Hogaku* (95): 139–158.

Nomani, Asra Q. 2021. "Barrington, RI Paid Ibram Kendi $15,000 for 1-Hour Zoom Talk." Asra Investigates. May 23, 2021. https://asrainvestigates.substack.com/p/barrington-ri-paid-ibram-kendi-15000.

O'Brien, Eileen. 2001. *Whites Confront Racism: Antiracists and Their Paths to Action*. Rowman and Littlefield Publishers.

———. 2009. "From Antiracism to Antiracisms." *Sociology Compass* 3 (3): 501–512.

O'Brien, Kerry, Walter Forrest, Dermot Lynott, and Michael Daly. 2013. "Racism, Gun Ownership and Gun Control: Biased Attitudes in US Whites May Influence Policy Decisions." *PLOS One* 8 (10): e77552.

Oh, Euna, Chun-Chung Choi, Helen A. Neville, Carolyn J. Anderson, and Joycelyn Landrum-Brown. 2010. "Beliefs about Affirmative Action: A Test of the Group Self-Interest and Racism Beliefs Models." *Journal of Diversity in Higher Education* 3 (3): 163–176. https://doi.org/10.1037/a0019799.

Oliver, Melvin L., and Thomas M. Shapiro. 2006. *Black Wealth, White Wealth: A New Perspective on Racial Inequality.* Taylor and Francis.

Oluo, Ijeoma. 2019. *So You Want to Talk about Race.* Hachette UK.

Osamudia, James. 2022. "White Injury and Innocence: On the Legal Future of Antiracism Education." *Virginia Law Review* 108 (8): 1689–1757.

Oxford Analytica. 2021. "Critical Race Theory Will Fuel US Political Divisions." *Emerald Expert Briefings.* https://doi.org/10.1108/OXAN-DB263215.

Oyinlade, A. Olu. 2013. "Affirmative Action Support in an Organization: A Test of Three Demographic Models." *SAGE Open* 3 (4): 2158244013516156.

Pacini-Ketchabaw, Veronica. 2014. "Postcolonial and Anti-racist Approaches to Understanding Play." In *The SAGE Handbook of Play and Learning in Early Childhood,* edited by Liz Brooker, Susan Edwards and Mindy Blaise, 67–78. Sage.

Paradies, Yin. 2005. "Anti-Racism and Indigenous Australians." *Analyses of Social Issues and Public Policy* 5 (1): 1–28.

———. 2016. "Whither Anti-racism?" *Ethnic and Racial Studies* 39 (1): 1–15.

Paradies, Yin, Mandy Truong, and Naomi Priest. 2014. "A Systematic Review of the Extent and Measurement of Healthcare Provider Racism." *Journal of General Internal Medicine* 29:364–387.

Patel, Nimisha. 2022. "Dismantling the Scaffolding of Institutional Racism and Institutionalising Anti-racism." *Journal of Family Therapy* 44 (1): 91–108.

Pedersen, Anne, Iain Walker, and Mike Wise. 2005. "'Talk Does Not Cook Rice': Beyond Anti-racism Rhetoric to Strategies for Social Action." *Australian Psychologist* 40 (1): 20–31.

Pennycook, Gordon, Jonathon McPhetres, Bence Bago, and David G. Rand. 2022. "Beliefs about COVID-19 in Canada, the United Kingdom, and the United States: A Novel Test of Political Polarization and Motivated Reasoning." *Personality and Social Psychology Bulletin* 48 (5): 750–765.

Perry, Samuel L., Kenneth E. Frantz, and Joshua B. Grubbs. 2021. "Who Identifies as Antiracist? Racial Identity, Color-Blindness, and Generic Liberalism." *Socius* 7:23780231 211052945.

Pew Research Center. 2022. "Midterm Voting Intentions Are Divided, Economic Gloom Persists." https://www.pewresearch.org/politics/2022/10/20/midterm-voting-intentions-are-divided-economic-gloom-persists/October 20.

Picca, Leslie Houts, and Joe R. Feagin. 2020. *Two-Faced Racism: Whites in the Backstage and Frontstage.* Routledge.

Pieterse, Alex L., Shawn O. Utsey, and Matthew J. Miller. 2016. "Development and Initial Validation of the Anti-racism Behavioral Inventory (ARBI)." *Counselling Psychology Quarterly* 29 (4): 356–381.

Pindi, Gloria Nziba, and Antonio Tomas De La Garza. 2018. "'The Colonial Jesus': Deconstructing White Christianity." In *Interrogating the Communicative Power of Whiteness,* edited by Dawn Marie D. McIntosh, Dreama G. Moon, and Thomas K. Nakayama, 218–238. Routledge.

Plant, E. Ashby, and Patricia G. Devine. 2001. "Responses to Other-Imposed Pro-Black Pressure: Acceptance or Backlash?" *Journal of Experimental Social Psychology* 37 (6): 486–501.
Polletta, Francesca, and Alex Maresca. 2021. "Claiming Martin Luther King, Jr. for the Right: The Martin Luther King Day Holiday in the Reagan Era." *Memory Studies* 16 (2): 386–402.
Poole, Keith T., and Howard Rosenthal. 1984. "The Polarization of American Politics." *Journal of Politics* 46 (4): 1061–1079.
Postmes, Tom, Anna Rabinovich, Thomas Morton, and Martijn van Zomeren. 2013. "Toward Sustainable Social Identities: Including Our Collective Future into the Self-Concept." In *Encouraging Sustainable Behavior*, edited by Hans C. M. van Trip, 185–201. Psychology Press.
Power, Marcus. 2006. "Anti-racism, Deconstruction and 'Overdevelopment.'" *Progress in Development Studies* 6 (1): 24–39.
Pratto, Felicia, Jim Sidanius, Lisa M. Stallworth, and Bertram F. Malle. 1994. "Social Dominance Orientation: A Personality Variable Predicting Social and Political Attitudes." *Journal of Personality and Social Psychology* 67 (4): 741–763.
Pressman, Jeremy, and Elannah Devin. 2023. "Profile: The Diffusion of Global Protests after George Floyd's Murder." *Social Movement Studies* 23 (4): 1–8.
Prior, Markus. 2013. "Media and Political Polarization." *Annual Review of Political Science* 16 (1): 101–127. https://doi.org/10.1146/annurev-polisci-100711-135242.
PRRI. 2021. "Dramatic Partisan Differences on Blame for January 6 Riots." September 15, 2021. https://www.prri.org/research/dramatic-partisan-differences-on-blame-for-january-6-riots/.
Putnam, Robert D., and David E. Campbell. 2012. *American Grace: How Religion Divides and Unites Us*. Simon and Schuster.
Quillian, Lincoln, Devah Pager, Ole Hexel, and Arnfinn H Midtbøen. 2017. "Meta-analysis of Field Experiments Shows No Change in Racial Discrimination in Hiring over Time." *Proceedings of the National Academy of Sciences* 114 (41): 10870–10875.
Rabaka, Reiland. 2006. "WEB DuBois's 'The Comet' and Contributions to Critical Race Theory: An Essay on Black Radical Politics and Anti-racist Social Ethics." *Ethnic Studies Review* 29 (1): 22–48.
Raji, Tobi, Meyer Theodoric Meyer, and Leigh Ann Caldwell. 2023. "A Bipartisan Show of Force on Ukraine." *Washington Post*, February 17, 2023. https://www.washingtonpost.com/politics/2023/02/17/bipartisan-show-force-ukraine/.
Rapoport, Robyn, and Christian Kline. 2022. *Methodological Report: American Fear Survey*. SSRS.
Rashid, Kamau. 2011. "'To Break Asunder along the Lesions of Race': The Critical Race Theory of WEB Du Bois." *Race Ethnicity and Education* 14 (5): 585–602.
Ray, Victor. 2022. "Critical Race Theory's Merchants of Doubt." *Time*, August 1, 2022. https://time.com/6202664/critical-race-theorys-merchants-of-doubt/.
Razack, Sherene H. 2021. "Whiteness, Christianity, and Anti-Muslim Racism" In *Routledge Handbook of Critical Studies in Whiteness*, edited by Shona Hunter and Christi van der Westhuizen, 43–53. Routledge.
Reed, Adolph. 2017. "Revolution as 'National Liberation' and the Origins of Neoliberal Antiracism." *Socialist Register* 53:299–322.
———. 2018. "Antiracism: A Neoliberal Alternative to a Left." *Dialectical Anthropology* 42 (2): 105–115.
Rich, Camille Gear. 2010. "Marginal Whiteness." *California Law Review* 98 (5): 1497–1593.

Rispin, Chloe M. 2018. "Could California Secede? A Philosophical." *Independent Student Journal: International Relations* 1:50–58.

Roda, Allison, and Amy Stuart Wells. 2013. "School Choice Policies and Racial Segregation: Where White Parents' Good Intentions, Anxiety, and Privilege Collide." *American Journal of Education* 119 (2): 261–293.

Rosenfeld, Richard, Bobby Boxerman, and Ernesto Lopez. 2023. *Pandemic, Social Unrest, and Crime in U.S. Cities: Year-End 2022 Update*. Council on Criminal Justice.

Rucker, Julian M., and Jennifer A. Richeson. 2021. "Toward an Understanding of Structural Racism: Implications for Criminal Justice." *Science* 374 (6565): 286–290.

Rufo, Christopher F. 2021. "What Critical Race Theory Is Really About." *New York Post*, May 6, 2021. https://nypost.com/2021/05/06/what-critical-race-theory-is-really-about/.

Rugaberfsch, Christopher, and Josh Boak. 2022. "Inflation Reduction Act May Have Little Impact on Inflation." Associated Press, August 16, 2022. https://apnews.com/article/inflation-biden-health-congress-climate-and-environment-63df07e15002c01fb560a6f0e69fcb03.

Ruwe, Dalitso. 2022. "Black Minds Matter: Repression of Critical Race Theory and Racial Violence against Black Students." *Journal of Critical Race Inquiry* 9 (2): 73–92.

Saad, Layla F. 2020. *Me and White Supremacy: Combat Racism, Change the World, and Become a Good Ancestor*. Sourcebooks.

Sanchez, James Chase. 2018. "Trump, the KKK, and the Versatility of White Supremacy Rhetoric." *Journal of Contemporary Rhetoric* 8 (1/2): 44–56.

Sanchez, Ray M. 2021. "An Anti-antiracism Manifesto." Minding the Campus. May 29, 2021. https://www.mindingthecampus.org/2021/05/29/an-anti-antiracism-manifesto/.

Sangillo, Gregg. 2019. "Antiracism in Action: Ibram Kendi Offers Hard Truths and Real Solutions." American University. August 20, 2019. https://www.american.edu/ucm/news/20190820-kendi-antiracism.cfm.

San Juan, Epifanio, Jr. 2002. "Postcolonialism and the Problematic of Uneven Development." In *Marxism, Modernity and Postcolonial Studies*, edited by Crystal Bartolovich and Neil Lazaus, 221–239. Cambridge University Press.

———. 2005. "From Race to Class Struggle: Marxism and Critical Race Theory." *Nature, Society, and Thought* 18 (3): 333–356.

Saran, A. K. 1963. "The Marxian Theory of Social Change." *Inquiry* 6 (1–4): 70–128.

Schaff, Adam. 1973. "Marxist Theory on Revolution and Violence." *Journal of the History of Ideas* 34 (2): 263–270.

Schaffner, Brian, Ansolavehere Stephen, and Sam Luks. 2021. *Cooperative Election Study Common Content 2020*. Harvard Dataverse.

Schulzke, Marcus. 2013. "The Politics of New Atheism." *Politics and Religion* 6 (4): 778–799.

Schuman, Howard, Charlotte Steeh, Lawrence Bobo, and Maria Krysan. 1997. *Racial Attitudes in America: Trends and Interpretations*. Harvard University Press.

Sears, David O. 1988. "Symbolic Racism." In *Eliminating Racism*, edited by Phyllis A. Katz and Dalmas A. Taylor, 53–84. Springer.

Seidel, Andrew L. 2019. *The Founding Myth: Why Christian Nationalism Is Un-American*. Sterling.

Sen, Maya. 2017. "How Political Signals Affect Public Support for Judicial Nominations: Evidence from a Conjoint Experiment." *Political Research Quarterly* 70 (2): 374–393.

Sewing, Joy. 2022. "Raising Antiracist Children Is about Teaching Equality." *Houston Chronicle*, June 24, 2022. https://www.houstonchronicle.com/lifestyle/article/Antiracist-children-17255255.php.

Sikkink, David, and Michael O. Emerson. 2008. "School Choice and Racial Segregation in US Schools: The Role of Parents' Education." *Ethnic and Racial Studies* 31 (2): 267–293.

Simmons, Jonathan. 2019. "Politics, Individualism, and Atheism: An Examination of the Political Attitudes of Atheist Activists in a Canadian City." *Secularism and Nonreligion* 8 (2): 1–9.

Sinanan, Kerry. 2020. "BLM 2020: Breathing, Resistance, and the War against Enslavement." Age of Revolutions. June 10, 2020. https://ageofrevolutions.com/2020/06/10/blm-2020-breathing-resistance-and-the-war-against-enslavement.

Siu, Lok, and Claire Chun. 2020. "Yellow Peril and Techno-orientalism in the Time of Covid-19: Racialized Contagion, Scientific Espionage, and Techno-economic Warfare." *Journal of Asian American Studies* 23 (3): 421–440.

Smith, Christen A. 2017. "Battling Anti-Black Genocide in Brazil: For over a Decade, Antiracist Movements in Brazil Have Sought Justice for the Killing of Black Brazilians by State Forces." *NACLA Report on the Americas* 49 (1): 41–47.

Snyder, Ian. 2020. "What Does It Mean to Be an Anti-racist?" National League of Cities. July 21, 2020. https://www.nlc.org/article/2020/07/21/what-does-it-mean-to-be-an-anti-racist/.

Solomos, John. 1995. "Racism and Anti-racism in Great Britain: Historical Trends and Contemporary Issues." In *Racism and Anti-racism in World Perspective*, edited by Benjamin P. Bowser, 157–180. Sage.

Srivastava, Sarita. 2005. "'You're Calling Me a Racist?' The Moral and Emotional Regulation of Antiracism and Feminism." *Signs: Journal of Women in Culture and Society* 31 (1): 29–62.

Srivastava, Sarita, and Margot Francis. 2006. "The Problem of 'Authentic Experience': Storytelling in Anti-racist and Anti-homophobic Education." *Critical Sociology* 32 (2–3): 275–307.

Stanford University. 2020. "Say Their Names Green Library Exhibit Supporting the Black Lives Matter Movement." August 3, 2020. https://exhibits.stanford.edu/saytheirnames/feature/330-names.

Stanojević, Aleksandar, and Jože Benčina. 2019. "The Construction of an Integrated and Transparent Index of Wellbeing." *Social Indicators Research* 143 (3): 995–1015.

Stepman, Jarrett. 2020. "3 Key Concepts That Woke 'Antiracists' Believe." Daily Signal. August 10, 2020. https://www.dailysignal.com/2020/08/10/3-key-concepts-that-woke-anti-racists-believe/.

Taguieff, Pierre-André. 2020. "On Antiracism." In *Theories of Race and Racism*, edited by Les Back and John Solomos, 138–162. Routledge.

Tate, Shirley Anne, and Damien Page. 2018. "Whiteliness and Institutional Racism: Hiding behind (Un)conscious Bias." *Ethics and Education* 13 (1): 141–155.

Taylor, Kathryn, and Deidra C. Crews. 2021. "Toward Antiracist Reimbursement Policy in End-Stage Kidney Disease: From Equality to Equity." *Journal of the American Society of Nephrology* 32 (10): 2422–2424.

Tesler, Michael. 2016. *Post-racial or Most-racial? Race and Politics in the Obama Era*. University of Chicago Press.

Tesler, Michael, and David O. Sears. 2010. *Obama's Race: The 2008 Election and the Dream of a Post-racial America*. University of Chicago Press.

Thompson, Becky W. 2001. *A Promise and a Way of Life: White Antiracist Activism*. University of Minnesota Press.

Thompson, Cooper, Emmett Schaeffer, and Harry Brod. 2003. *White Men Challenging Racism: 35 Personal Stories*. Duke University Press.

Ting-Toomey, Stella. 2005. "Identity Negotiation Theory: Crossing Cultural Boundaries." In *Theorizing about Intercultural Communication*, edited by William B. Gudykunst, 211–233. Sage.

Tomkin, Anastasia Reesa. 2020. "Unpacking the False Allyship of White Racial Justice Leaders." *Nonprofit Quarterly*, December 14, 2020. https://nonprofitquarterly.org/unpacking-the-false-allyship-of-white-racial-justice-leaders/.

Toombs, Charles. 2022. "Antiracism, Social Justice, and the California Faculty Association." American Association of University Professors. *Organizing Matters* 108 (1). https://www.aaup.org/article/antiracism-social-justice-and-california-faculty-association#.Y679vHbMKUk.

Toosi, Negin R., Kristin Layous, and Gretchen M. Reevy. 2021. "Recognizing Racism in George Floyd's Death." *Analyses of Social Issues and Public Policy* 21 (1): 1184–1201. https://doi.org/10.1111/asap.12282.

Tsong, Yuying, Sapna B. Chopra, and Hsiu-Lan Cheng. 2022. "Racial Healing during the COVID-19 and Anti-Asian Pandemics through Critical Consciousness Informed antiracist Parenting Practices (CCIARP)." *Asian American Journal of Psychology* 13 (4): 385–393.

Turner, Jack. 2012. *Awakening to Race: Individualism and Social Consciousness in America*. University of Chicago Press.

Turner, Ronald. 1996. "The Dangers of Misappropriation: Misusing Martin Luther King, Jr.'s Legacy to Prove the Colorblind Thesis." *Michigan Journal of Race and Law* 2 (1): 101–130.

Turner Kelly, Bridget. 2005. "History of Antiracism Education: Lessons for Today's Practitioners." *Vermont Connection* 26 (1): article 6.

Twine, France Winddance, and Kathleen M. Blee. 2001. *Feminism and Antiracism: International Struggles for Justice*. New York University Press.

Ufodike, Akolisa, Susanna Ally, and Louis Butt. 2020. "Conservative Party Can Lead on Anti-racism Policy—A Blueprint." *MacLean's*, August 10, 2020. https://macleans.ca/opinion/conservative-party-policy-can-be-anti-racist-a-blueprint/.

Valdes, Francisco, Jerome McCristal Culp, and Angela Harris. 2002. *Crossroads, Directions and a New Critical Race Theory*. Temple University Press.

Vanderbilt, Sandra. 2023. "Bridging the Conversational Chasm: White Antiracist Confrontations in Personal Spaces." *Educational Theory* 72 (6): 777–792.

Van Dijk, Teun A. 2021. *Antiracist Discourse: Theory and History of a Macromovement*. Cambridge University Press.

Verba, Sidney, and Gary R. Orren. 1985. *Equality in America: The View from the Top*. Harvard University Press.

Voci, Alberto. 2006. "The Link between Identification and In-Group Favouritism: Effects of Threat to Social Identity and Trust-Related Emotions." *British Journal of Social Psychology* 45 (2): 265–284. https://doi.org/10.1348/014466605x52245.

Waldron, Ingrid R. G. 2020. "The Wounds That Do Not Heal: Black Expendability and the Traumatizing Aftereffects of Anti-Black Police Violence." *Equality, Diversity and Inclusion: An International Journal* 40 (1): 29–40.

Wallace, Carey. 2021. "White American Christianity Needs to Be Honest about Its History of White Supremacy." *Time*, January 14, 2021.

Warren, Mark R. 2010. *Fire in the Heart: How White Activists Embrace Racial Justice*. Oxford University Press.

Watson, Christian. 2023. "DEI Proponents Should Not Celebrate Martin Luther King, Jr. Day." *Newsweek*, January 12, 2023. https://www.newsweek.com/dei-proponents-should-not-celebrate-martin-luther-king-jr-day-opinion-1772691.

Wellman, Mariah L. 2022. "Black Squares for Black Lives? Performative Allyship as Credibility Maintenance for Social Media Influencers on Instagram." *Social Media + Society* 8 (1): 1–10.
West, Traci C. 2020. "Ending Gender Violence: An Antiracist Intersectional Agenda for Churches." *Review and Expositor* 117 (2): 199–203.
Whitehead, Andrew, and Samuel L. Perry. 2020. *Taking America Back for God: Christian Nationalism in the United States*. Oxford University Press.
Whitley, Bernard E., Jr. 1999. "Right-Wing Authoritarianism, Social Dominance Orientation, and Prejudice." *Journal of Personality and Social Psychology* 77 (1): 126–134.
Williams, Dana M., and Suzanne R. Slusser. 2014. "Americans and Iraq, Twelve Years Apart: Comparing Support for the US Wars in Iraq." *Social Science Journal* 51 (2): 231–239.
Williams, David R., and Selina A. Mohammed. 2013. "Racism and Health I: Pathways and Scientific Evidence." *American Behavioral Scientist* 57 (8): 1152–1173.
Williamson, David A., and George Yancey. 2013. *There Is No God: Atheists in America*: Rowman and Littlefield Publishers.
Wilson, David C., and Darren W. Davis. 2011. "Reexamining Racial Resentment: Conceptualization and Content." *Annals of the American Academy of Political and Social Science* 634 (1): 117–133.
Yancey, George. 2024. "Finding Antiracists: Construction of an Antiracism Scale." *Sociological Focus* 57 (2): 230–251.
Yancey, George, and Ashlee R. Quosigk. 2021. *One Faith No Longer: The Transformation of Christianity in Red and Blue America*. New York University Press.
Yanco, Jennifer J. 2014. *Misremembering Dr. King: Revisiting the Legacy of Martin Luther King Jr.* Indiana University Press: Bloomington.
Yang, Janet Z., Haoran Chu, and LeeAnn Kahlor. 2019. "Fearful Conservatives, Angry Liberals: Information Processing Related to the 2016 Presidential Election and Climate Change." *Journalism and Mass Communication Quarterly* 96 (3): 742–766.
Young, Robert J. C. 1998. "Ideologies of the Postcolonial." *Interventions: International Journal of Postcolonial Studies* 1 (1): 4–8.
Zakrisson, Ingrid. 2005. "Construction of a Short Version of the Right-Wing Authoritarianism (RWA) Scale." *Personality and Individual Differences* 39 (5): 863–872.
Zamalin, Alex. 2019. *Antiracism: An Introduction*. New York University Press.

Index

Abortion, 62, 95, 97–98, 103–106, 108–112, 121, 126
Activists, 18, 20, 27, 28n2, 99–101; civil rights; 82; climate change, 102–103; language, 112
Affirmative action, 4
African Americans, 8, 10, 14–16, 39, 59–61, 63, 83, 121, 127; men, 110–111; progressive, 65–66; women, 104, 105 n18, 110
Afro-Modern tradition, 16
Allies, 7–8, 24, 26, 36, 63, 116–117, 124
Amazon Mechanical Turk, 8, 43
Antiracist attitude, 9, 51, 59 n6, 105, 127
Antiracists, 4, 18, 20–26, 31–32, 34, 38, 50–52, 97, 107–109, 111, 113, 119–124, 127–28; compared to political progressives, 70–74, 79–83, 90–93, 123; and Democrat party, 116–118; popularized, 7, 34, 125; white, 20, 126, 128
Arbery, Ahmaud, 1, 20, 22
Asian Americans, 16, 39, 109
Australia, 24, 40

Backlash, 27, 117, 122
Biden, Joe, 79, 88, 107, 118
Bigotry, 24, 32–33
Bipartisan, 119–124
Black Lives Matter, 4, 42 n5, 47, 83; protests, 22, 30, 107; variable; 41–42, 45, 47, 52, 83 n7

Canada, 24, 121 n3
Capitalism, 24, 35, 66
Center for Antiracism Research, 4, 99, 106 n16, 112
Chapman Survey of Fears, 9, 52, 54, 70–71, 125
Christian nationalism, 27, 54–55
Christianity, 62
Civil rights movement, 15
Climate change, 10, 89 n8. 95, 97–99, 101–103, 108–111, 126
Colorblindness, 3, 15, 21–23, 34, 67
Counternarrative, 14–15, 23
Covid, 1, 80–81, 89, 92, 109
Crime, 10, 95; racial hate, 74, 79, 83; fear of; 82, 91; street; 95, 97–98, 109–111, 126
Criminal justice, 74, 81–82, 90–91
Critical theory, 8, 13
Critical race theory, 5, 8, 12–14, 28–29, 64, 113; scholars, 22
Culture war, 61–62, 64

198 / Index

DEI, 28, 111, 118
Democrats, 7, 79, 93, 95, 97, 101, 104, 106, 108–109, 111, 113, 115–116, 118–120, 126
DiAngelo, Robin, 8, 38–39

Education, 4, 10, 14, 51, 65–66, 120; antiracist, 26
Enlightenment movement, 15, 22
Environmental racism, 80
Environmentalism, 80, 91–92

Factor analysis, 8–9, 45
Feminism, 104
Feminist, 19, 24, 166,
Floyd, George, 1, 20, 22
Foreign policy, 74, 81, 90–93, 107

Gender, 72, 125
Google, 2, 97–98, 126
Great Britain, 24
Great Replacement theory, 105

Hate crime, 74, 79, 83
Hispanic-Americans, 16
Homophobia, 17, 72

Immigration, 83, 93, 117 n1
Income, 65, 81 n6
Inflation, 10, 93, 97–98, 108–109, 111, 126
Internet, 26, 54 n2, 96

January 6, 10, 74, 79–80, 88, 92–93, 97–98, 106–109, 111, 126; riots, 80, 106–108

Kendi, Ibram, 8, 29, 38–39, 70 n1, 102, 125 n4
King Jr., Martin Luther, 3
King, Rodney, 2

LGBT, 123
Liberals, 5, 7, 22, 56, 58–61, 65–66, 100–101, 112, 137, 152, 154, 165,
Lived experience, 14, 22–23, 104, 111

Macrolevel approach, 17
Marginalized, 8, 14–15, 18, 22–24, 33, 35, 38–39, 50, 63–64, 96, 108–109, 114, 120, 122, 127,
Marxism, 8, 13, 18–19, 26
Media, 1–2, 100–101, 118–119
Microaggression, 14, 37

Microlevel approach, 17–18, 96, 113
Middle Easterners, 16
Modernity, 15, 19
Multicultural, 21–23, 25, 74
Mulvaney, Dylan, 122–123

Non-Black racial groups, 20, 39

Obama, Barack, 20, 107, 118
Ontario Anti-Racism Secretariat, 30
Overt racial issues, 74, 83, 88, 92

Partisan identity, 7, 10, 122
Polarization, 27, 115–118, 123; racial; 21; political; 67–68, 89, 98
Political conservatives, 10–11, 22, 51, 56, 60, 64–65, 67, 109, 113, 119
Political identity; 7, 10, 61, 63, 66–67, 69, 93, 96
Political progressives, 9–10, 61–64, 67, 69; compared to antiracists; 70–74, 79–83, 90–93, 123; white, 65
Postcolonialism, 8, 15–16, 19
Post-racial, 3, 20–21, 25
Prejudice, 18 n2, 63, 122

Queer, 96

Racial justice, 5, 13, 23, 36, 38, 40, 70, 105–106, 116–117, 122, 127
Racial radicalism, 51, 127
Racial resentment scale, 54–55
Racialized identity, 67
Racism, 4–6, 13, 15, 17–19, 21–22, 25, 30, 39, 47, 62–63, 67, 111, 114; anti-Black, 17, 40; institutional, 6; modern, 14, 16; multifaceted, 32–34, 42, 45–47, 51; overt; 3, 16, 24, 114; pervasiveness, 31–32, 42, 45–47
Radicals, 5–6, 66, 121–122
Rationality, 15;
Religious, 36, 58 note 5, 59, 87, 105, 115, 127, 135–137,
Republicans, 93, 95, 97, 101, 104, 106, 108–109, 111, 113, 115–116, 118–121, 123
Revolutionary, 18–19, 25, 36, 42 n6, 119, 121
Roe v. Wade, 105–106

School choice, 117, 120–121
Sexism, 17, 25, 72
Social identity, 51, 61–62, 64, 67–68

Social media, 100, 126
Societal change, 31, 34, 119, 123–124
Survey Monkey, 8, 43, 46

Trump, Donald, 27, 106

Ukraine, 119
Unemployment, 93; fear of, 90

Voting access, 79

Western culture, 16, 25
White Fragility, 1, 35–36, 40; concept, 38, 40; variable, 41–42, 45, 48
White/nonwhite responsibilities, 36–39
Whiteness, 4, 19, 24, 38, 62
"Woke," 5, 50, 113, 128

Youngkin, Glenn, 123

Zionism, 19

George Yancey is Professor of Sociology at Baylor University. He is author of *Who Is White: Latinos, Asians, and the New Black/Nonblack Divide* and coauthor of *Transcending Racial Barriers: Toward a Mutual Obligations Approach.*

Hayoung David Oh, MPH, is the Community Affiliate Research Coordinator at the Woodson Center in Washington, DC.

www.ingramcontent.com/pod-product-compliance
Lightning Source LLC
Chambersburg PA
CBHW032024230426
43671CB00005B/198